TELEVISION IN *SOCIETY*

TELEVISION IN *SOCIETY*

Edited by
ARTHUR ASA BERGER

With an Introduction by the Author

Transaction Books
New Brunswick (U.S.A.) and Oxford (U.K.)

Copyright © 1987 by Transaction, Inc.
New Brunswick, New Jersey 08903

All rights reserved under International and Pan-American Copyright Conventions. No part of this book may be reproduced or transmitted in any form or by any means, electronic or mechanical, including photocopy, recording, or any information storage and retrieval system, without prior permission in writing from the publisher. All inquiries should be addressed to Transaction Books, Rutgers—The State University, New Brunswick, New Jersey 08903.

Library of Congress Catalog Number: 86-4286
ISBN: 0-88738-109-X (cloth); 0-88738-652-0 (paper)
Printed in the United States of America

Library of Congress Cataloging in Publication Data

Television in society

"Collection of articles from Society magazine"—
Introd.
  Bibliography: p.

  1. Television broadcasting—Social aspects. I. Berger, Arthur Asa, 1933-
PN1992.6.T417   1986   302.2'345   86-4286
ISBN 0-88738-109-X
ISBN 0-88738-652-0 (pbk.)

To the memory of Celia Fishman
(who always made two desserts) and
Jack Savel (the self-proclaimed "dictator of taste")

Contents

Introduction   1
   Arthur Asa Berger

Television Commercials
1. Campaign Commercials   17
   L. Patrick Devlin
2. 1984—The Commercial   29
   Arthur Asa Berger

Events and Images
3. Television Ceremonial Events   41
   Daniel Dayan and *Elihu Katz*
4. Huxley on Television   55
   John H. Barnsley
5. Real Police on Television Supercops   63
   Rita J. Simon and *Fred Fejes*

Television Series
6. Cultural Bias in "M*A*S*H"   71
   Roger L. Hofeldt
7. The Politics of "Lou Grant"   79
   Michael Schudson
8. Sagan's Metaphysical Parable   83
   David P. Rabovich
9. Decoding "Dallas": Comparing American and German Viewers   95
   Herta Herzog Massing

Violence and Television
10. Violence and Aggression   105
   David Pearl
11. Researching Television Violence   117
   Alan Wurtzel and *Guy Lometti*

12. Defending the Indefensible 133
    Steven H. Chaffee, George Gerbner, Beatrix A. Hamburg,
    Chester M. Pierce, Eli A. Rubinstein, Alberta E. Siegel,
    and *Jerome L. Singer*
13. Smoking Out the Critics 143
    Alan Wurtzel and *Guy Lometti*
14. Proliferating Violence 153
    George Gerbner
15. Networks Hold the Line 163
    John A. Schneider

Television and Education
16. Assessing Academic Achievement 173
    Bert Briller and *Steven Miller*
17. Facts, Fantasies and Schools 181
    George Gerbner, Larry Gross, Michael Morgan, and
    Nancy Signorielli
18. Reading Performance 189
    Susan B. Neuman
19. Dubious Facts and Real Schools 193
    Lilya Wagner

Values and Social Control
20. Mass Media Values 195
    Gaye Tuchman
21. Television, Mass Communication and Elite Controls 203
    Emile G. McAnany

Industry and Technology
22. Fantasy and Culture on Television 215
    Ben Stein
23. Direct-Broadcast Satellites and Cultural Integrity 229
    Ithiel de Sola Pool

News and Documentation
24. Free Press for a Free People 251
    Eric Sevareid
25. Screening Nuclear War and Vietnam 257
    Marvin Maurer

   Coming to Terms with Television: An Annotated Bibliography   269
    Robert Schmuhl
   About the Contributors 279

Introduction

Arthur Asa Berger

Television and Society

This book comprises a collection of articles from *SOCIETY* magazine dealing with television in broadly sociological terms. That is, it considers how television both reflects and affects society, but it is much more than that. Television is, as has frequently been said, the medium everyone loves to hate. Television has been described as a "cultural wasteland" by some and by others defended as a medium which has brought to the masses more great art, music, dance, and drama than anything before its time.

In recent years scholars in many different fields have begun to consider television seriously and have been doing a great deal of work on the medium and matters related to it. There is a reason for this: statistics indicate that the average television set is on more than six hours in a typical household and the average person in the United States watches television more than three hours per day. Television may be seen as an entertainment medium—but entertainment is by no means an insignificant matter. Our entertainments help socialize us, give us images of one another which can be stereotyped and misleading, and have significant political and economic consequences.

In ever increasing numbers, *SOCIETY* has published material on television—both in its Culture and Society section (where reviews of programs are generally found) and in the body of the magazine itself (where various issues are analyzed, often by scholars with different points of view). What is particularly useful about the material on television in *SOCIETY* is that it is both authoritative and accessible. Many of the most prominent scholars interested in television have written for *SOCIETY* and always in a manner that the intelligent reader will find understandable and thought-provoking.

Television in SOCIETY is divided into two sections. The first focuses on programming and deals with commercials, ceremonial events, important series (such as "M*A*S*H" and "Lou Grant"), significant programs (a production of *Brave New World* on television) and the images of the police on the medium. The second part of the book deals with important issues and topics related to the medium. Here we find discussions of matters such as the impact of television violence, values espoused in television, the impact of television on education, the significance of new technological developments, and the always thorny issue of freedom of the press.

Dealing With Television

There is a great deal of conflicting opinion about television. Here follows a list of some of the issues that are confronted in this book.

First, how do we study and interpret television? Sociologists, psychologists, psychiatrists, anthropologists, literary critics, moralists, theologians, and practically everyone else writes about television. What makes television so difficult to come to grips with is that the medium of television broadcasts various popular art forms (commercials, news shows, situation comedies, action-adventure programs). This raises important aesthetic questions (i.e., how effects are realized, how we judge performance) as well as social and political considerations.

What are the effects of television on individuals and society and how do we determine and measure them? Do we make a distinction between short-term effects and long-term ones? Is it possible to make intelligent inferences about social and psychological effects without empirical data? This is not a trivial matter, by any means; for if we spend so much time watching television, there is good reason to assume that it does have a powerful impact on us. But how do we know this?

What is the role of television in our political and economic life? Is television the crucial factor in our selection of political figures? Is television generating consumer-lust and self-hatred and alienation, as many Marxist critics argue? And what role does new technology play?

Methods of Television Analysis

As we might expect, there are many different ways of analyzing television programs and the various issues and topics connected to the medium. Many of these techniques correspond roughly to academic disciplines, though it is not unusual to find a number of different methods being employed in a given essay.

First of all there are the empiricists—in all the social sciences—who base their conclusions on data usually derived from questionnaires or experiments. Much empirical work is, essentially, audience research and focuses more on the audiences of television programs than on the programs themselves.

Another group of scholars study uses and gratifications—the uses audiences make of television programs and the gratifications they derive from them. From this perspective, watching television is not a simple and mindless process and is, in fact, an activity that is much more complicated than we might imagine. Some typical gratifications television offers include the desire to see heroes and heroines, villains and villainesses in action, the desire to have powerful emotional experiences, and the wish to reaffirm belief that morality is important and good ultimately triumphs over evil. People use television to learn about people and the world, to "kill time," to find out about new products, or to keep informed on political and other areas of life.

So much for the television audience. The second area of interest for television scholars involves television programs themselves or what is sometimes known as *textual analysis*. The focus here is on a program or episode in a series (or an entire series) as a work of art, a text, with certain conventions and formal qualities. The effort here is an interpretative one—using techniques such as semiotics (the science of signs and meaning), psychoanalytic theory, literary critical methods, myth-ritual criticism, etc., to help explain how a given text achieves its effects and generates meaning.

Interpretative efforts are generally humanistic in nature and rely on the force of the argument to convince, rather than data from surveys and questionnaires or experiments. Quantitatively oriented social scientists often have trouble with interpretative essays and label them as "impressionistic" (or other less complimentary terms) but the humanists argue, with some force, that they are interested in meaning which must be elicited from a text and cannot be derived from empirical investigations.

One technique that is basically empirical is content analysis, in which a given set of texts is investigated in terms of some topic (for example, how much violence per hour). This technique yields different results from the interpretative efforts of humanistic scholars. Content analysis has been one of the most used techniques for analyzing television texts since it generates quantitative data. But there is always a nagging question as to whether audiences respond to television programs the way scholars and researchers think they do, so content analysis remains useful but problematical.

The third major method of analysis of television stems from Marxist thinkers who apply Marx's theories to culture in general, and, in our case, to the mass media and television in particular. These critics are interested in concepts such as alienation and hegemonial ideological domination and argue, generally speaking, that television is ultimately a tool used by capitalists to ensure their control of U.S. and other capitalist societies. Marxist scholars see television as a powerful instrument of domination that generates consumer culture (consumer lust for new products to assuage the pains of alienation). It is understandable, then, that many Marxist critics focus their attention on television commercials and the advertising industry in general.

Marxist critics are interested in the relationship that exists between television and society in general. Their focus is a bit broader than those who study audiences, though, of course, audiences, especially class-differentiated ones, are of special interest to Marxist critics. Sociologists and political scientists also often have this societal perspective—a perspective found in many of the articles in this book.

I have suggested that some scholars focus on audiences, some focus on television programs, series, and kinds of programming, and some focus on the relationship between television, its industry, and society in general. In addition, there are some researchers who direct attention on television writers and producers and others connected to the industry. This is, roughly speaking, biographical—though the concern is often with larger matters such as politics, social class, or ethnicity.

There is one last consideration—the medium itself—and the role that technological matters play in the scheme of things. This approach is broadly aesthetic, and concerns itself with the matters such as lighting, use of color, kinds of shots employed, editing techniques, and performance qualities. One of the problems with much sociological analysis of television is that it pays so little attention to aesthetic considerations—perhaps because it doesn't know how to do so.

But much of the power of television is connected to aesthetic matters. Quick cutting, shot framing, sound effects, dialogue, the way characters are dressed and lit—all of these matters play an important role and must have profound effects on viewers, so any analyses of television that neglect this area are missing a great deal. It may be that the next major advance in the scientific study of television (and other visual media as well) will involve the development of some kind of quantitative semiotic content analysis technique, which will enable us to consider aesthetic matters in a nonimpressionistic manner.

I might point out that many scholars and critics of television utilize different methods at the same time, though generally one of these approaches is dominant. There is no reason that a television text cannot be studied from a number of perspectives at the same time, and, in fact, many of the essays in this book do so. Now that we have a general overview of the areas that television researchers are interested in and some of their methods, it is useful to examine some of the more immediate topics that suggest themselves for study.

Focal Points for Television Analysts

In this section I will list and briefly discuss some of the more important and obvious aspects of television which suggest themselves to researchers.

Specific Television Texts

Here we examine a particular program or episode from a series. We are dealing with a text that can range from thirty seconds or so, in the case of specific commercials, to several hours in length, in the case of media events (Olympics, coronations, royal weddings). In *Television in SOCIETY* you will find, for example, a microanalysis of the commercial "1984" and a study of the television production of *Brave New World*.

Television Series

Since series are important in television, it is logical to write about an important and culturally significant series. The series is the dominant format in television and it employs the skills of many writers. This book includes essays on "M*A*S*H," "Lou Grant," and "Cosmos," and other series are also mentioned. In dealing with a series, one problem is in making generalizations which apply to the entire series; it is difficult at times to characterize a collection of programs which might have been shown on television for years. But successful series, which strike some kind of respondent chord in the general public, are obviously important and worth considering, whatever the difficulties.

Television Genres

For our purpose a genre is a kind of program and television is a medium which broadcasts a number of genres such as situation comedies, news shows, game shows, sports programs, talk shows, police dramas, ad infinitem. Some of the articles in this book focus directly on genres. We include material on campaign commercials and media events in which the analysis is direct, while other essays allude to certain genres and deal with them in passing. Discussions of violence on television implicitly concern themselves with action-adventure programs and similar kinds of shows, though violence on television is by no means limited to these genres.

The Television Industry

Programs do not appear out of the blue, as if by magic. They are written, produced, acted, and directed, by people who are members of a huge and extremely powerful industry. The people who own or control this industry and the people who work in it are worth serious attention, for they play an important part in influencing taste and, so many argue, in shaping our culture. The essays on the industry by Ben Stein and, in particular, television writers, and Gaye Tuchman on mass media values, deal with the industry and those who work in it and for it.

Television and Society

This topic is implicit in all sociological analyses of television and the work of serious critics of the medium. I make a distinction between television *critics*, who are interested in the social, political, economic and cultural significance of the medium and its products and television *reviewers*. Television reviewers tend to be journalists who focus, most often, on the entertainment values of a given program or series—though sometimes they cross over the line into television criticism. And criticism, of course, does not mean being negative. Critics, as I use the term, are serious students of television representing all the disciplines, and dealing with many aspects of television.

Topics Related to Television

It is in this rubric that we find discussions of such matters as the image of minorities in television (women, Blacks, old people, Jews, working class people, etc.), and, of great concern to all, television violence. A considerable number of articles in this collection are devoted to that subject. There are debates between academics, who generally argue that there is a strong correlation between television viewing and violence (and certain other antisocial kinds of behavior) and industry representatives, who argue that there is no relationship of any importance that has been demonstrated. I have included two different debates on the subject. One is between George Gerbner, who has conducted research on this subject for many years, and John Schneider, a representative of the television industry and the other, seven years later, is between Gerbner (and some allies) and scholars and others who argue that the evidence is not in yet.

The violence debate as well as the debate about the impact of television on education have to do ultimatley with the impact of television on individuals and society. Television may no longer be seen as a kind of "magic bullet" which is shot into gullible viewers and shapes their behavior automatically, but that does not mean that television is some kind of a "weak sister" that has no significant impact at all. It may not be easy to prove that television has effects in a manner that will satisfy social scientists, but common sense tells us that anything we do for three and a half hours a day must have some impact. These topic essays and symposia deal, then, with controversial subjects and are often argumentative.

New Technology

In this field we consider the impact that new inventions and devices are having in the field of communications in general and television broadcasting in particular. The development of satellites, fiber optics, computers and such are, in many respects, revolutionizing society and their impact has yet to be appraised. The late Ithiel de Sola Pool's essay on satellites is an early and important contribution to this subject.

We may not think of it as such, but television is (or, at least, was, not too long ago) a new technology and its impact has been enormous. There is an interesting debate, of sorts, going on between the "technological determinists," who believe that technological developments are the driving force in societal evolution, and what might be called the "humanistic thinkers" who argue that technology isn't central or determinant, but that values and beliefs are. It may be possible, for example, to automate every job in a factory out of existence, but it may be that we decide not to do so. Or, to take a topic closer to home (literally speaking), it is possible to set up computer networks which allow executives to work at home and hardly ever go into the office. But research seems to indicate that people want to go into their offices and want to get away from home, so even if we can "wire" the nation, we may not wish to do so. Whether one is a technological determinist or not, the new technologies are having important effects on people and society, and it may be that developments in this area will be equal in importance to the programming broadcast on television.

Television is Culture

The programs broadcast on the medium of television are generally described as popular art forms or part of popular culture. But popular culture, we must remember, is a kind of culture and does what culture does—it gives us an understanding of our place in the universe, how to act, eat, dress ourselves, ornament ourselves, and behave in certain situations. The term anthropologists use is *enculturation*, the process by which people are taught the rules, beliefs, codes, and practices of their group (which may actually be a subculture functioning within the framework of the larger culture).

When we watch television we see people who have certain occupations, who dress in certain ways, who use certain kinds of language, who have certain body types, who do certain things, who make certain facial expressions, who pursue various goals, who live in certain kinds of houses, who have certain moral codes, who use certain techniques to solve problems or achieve their goals.

Thus, when we watch television programs we are always learning something—even though we may not realize this is the case. In *Magic, Science and Religion,* Bronislaw Malinowski described the power of myth in nonliterate cultures as follows.

> I propose to show how deeply the sacred tradition, the myth, enters into their pursuits, and how strongly it controls their moral and social behavior. In other words, the thesis of the present work is that an intimate connection exists between the word, the mythos, the sacred tales of a tribe, on the one hand, and the ritual acts, their moral deeds, their social organization, and even their practical activities, on the other.

It is possible to draw clear analogies between the tales and myths of the Melanesians that Malinowski was dealing with and our television programs. Don't our soap operas (modern epics), situation comedies, police dramas, science fiction series, and commercials have the same function? If there is any correspondence at all between human behavior and the myth, the story and the adventure, is there not good reason to consider television, the great collective storyteller, to be a subject worth careful attention?

One of the advantages of a "culturological" perspective is that it frees us from the problems media sociologists get involved with when they start investigating the effects of television on people. There are literally thousands of articles and books on the subject of television; yet, as this book demonstrates, there is still a good deal of controversy about the effects of violence on television and related matters. If we move from a sociological and social psychological perspective to an anthropological one, however, and consider the relationship that exists between television and culture, the situation is different. If we look for the effects of television (and other expressive art forms) on the cultural level rather than on the individual one, we have reason to feel that television is a powerful influence since it is our chief storyteller.

In *Magic, Science and Religion,* Malinowski describes what happens on expeditions when younger tribe members ask older ones about where they are going, what the people are like, and so on. He writes

> The older and more experienced will supply them with information and comment, *and this always takes the form of a concrete narrative.* An old man will perhaps tell his own experiences about fights and expeditions, about famous magic and extraordinary economic achievements. . . . A number of stories about sailors driven out of their course and landing among cannibals and hostile tribes are remembered, some of them set to song, others formed into historic legends. . . . There are tales about distant volcanic islands; about hot springs in which once a party of unwary bathers were boiled to death;

about mysterious countries inhabited by entirely different men or women. [my emphasis]

A glance at the television log in the daily newspaper reveals a strange similarity between some of these tales and what is available on television in various action-adventure stories, science fiction adventures, such as "Dr. Who," "Twilight Zone," "Star Trek," or "Miami Vice." It may be that it is at the cultural level, in terms of affecting people's values and general beliefs, that television is particularly powerful. Television is a narrative medium and narratives play an important role in enculturating people.

Television is a Narrative Medium

Although television offers numerous genres—news, sports, game shows, interviews and talk shows—television is essentially a narrative and thus a *dramatic* medium. Most of the programs on television are dramatic in nature—that is, fictional stories with dialogue, plots, settings, characters in conflict, and resolutions of one sort or another.

In *The Age of Television*, Martin Esslin cites some amazing statistics. He points out that "the time devoted by the average American adult male to watching dramatic material on television . . . amounts to over 12 hours per week, while the average American woman sees almost 16 hours of drama on television each week. That means that the average American adult sees the equivalent of *five to six full-length stage plays a week*!" These dramatic productions, including commercials which often use dramatic techniques, are designed to generate in people an "intended emotional and intellectual response." That is, these dramatic productions are designed to have a powerful impact on people and this impact is often greater than we might imagine. It is also, he suggests, not entirely dependent on the language used, since all the audiovisual phenomena such as vocal expression, facial expression, body language, costuming, props, music, lighting, and setting contribute to the impact of the dramatic presentation—ultimately, Esslin argues, by presenting "personality" to people.

An analysis of a television text that fails to take these matters into consideration is, it is logical to assume, terribly impoverished and simplistic—which is precisely what happens, all too often, in content analyses of mass mediated texts, especially television programs. Television is, above all, a visual medium which presents its fare in terms of powerful visual images which speak directly to viewers. These visual images convey a great deal of information and have enormous power, for they help shape the reality of those who view them. We act—so the sociologists tell us—on the basis of our *perceptions* of reality, not reality itself, and it is television, all too often, which shapes these perceptions. And what isn't a narrative on television tends to be made into one, since it is the story line that captures viewers and holds their attention. This means that experience is transformed and made more dramatic and exciting, packaged so as to be more salesworthy, with little regard for the impact of this phenomenon on the psyches or well-being of viewers.

In the final analysis, as it has often been pointed out, television sells audiences to advertisers. Television programs are created to attract certain kinds of audiences of interest to specific kinds of advertisers. It is the thirty-second, condensed narratives that sell soap and senators that are the most important kind of narrative on television and for which the whole industry exists in the United States.

On Television Genres

There is a great deal of controversy over what a *genre* is or is not. For our purposes I will equate a genre with a kind of television program and not with forms such as comedies or tragedies. An examination of the television listings in any newspaper will reveal a large number of programs which can be subsumed under a relatively limited number of genres. The most important television genres are commercials, news programs, documentaries, situation comedies, soap operas, talk shows, game shows, sports programs (football, baseball, basketball, track), police shows (once it would have been westerns) and other "action-adventure programs," and various kinds of "how-to" programs. This list may be somewhat incomplete but it covers the most important kinds of television programs. It doesn't mention movies but what there is to say about television genres can be applied to them without too much difficulty. Film is a different medium but it, too, relies on some very basic genres such as the science-fiction theme and the musical format (neither of which are in vogue in television anymore).

Are there ways of reducing the various television genres or kinds of programs to something more fundamental, more basic? After considering a number of possibilities, I concluded that, for all practical purposes, there are four important television genres (kinds of programs): *actualities, contests, persuasions, and dramas.*

Let me explain how I'm using each of these terms. By *actualities* I mean any program, such as a news show or documentary, in which the emphasis is on portraying reality, on reflecting what is going on in the world (as opposed to inventing a world of one's own). Although there is an interpretive aspect to news programs and documentaries (this topic is dealt with in the essay on nuclear war and the Vietnam war), they always focus on actual places, events, and individuals.

Persuasions are programs meant to convince people to do something or believe something. *Webster's Collegiate Dictionary* defines persuasion as follows: "to move by argument, entreaty or expostulation to a belief, position or course of action." Commercials are the dominant form of persuasions. Because there are so many different kinds of commercials, many of which employ dramatic sequences, it is difficult to deal with commercials so I have taken their intent as basic.

Contests refers to programs in which there is an element of competition as individuals or teams fight against opponents to attain some goal—winning a prize, a game, etc.. Contests have players, not actresses and actors—at least when the contests are legitimate. The dominant form of contests are sports programs and game shows.

Dramas are one of the most important forms on television and in all media. Soap operas, situation comedies, police shows, science-fiction programs, and hospital programs are dramas. Their common characteristic is that they are all narratives in which there is conflict of either a serious or comedic nature.

These four types of programs can, in turn, be understood in terms of a more basic set of concepts—concepts which help characterize each of the four types of programs to various degrees. Let me explain.

There are, I would suggest, a set of polar opposites that inform or are the most important elements in all program types and genres. I choose to call these polar opposites the *objective* and the *emotive*. By *objective* I mean that which expresses the nature of reality as it is—to the extent, that is, that we can ever know reality. The objective is the world of things that actually happen. The *emotive*, on the other hand, involves the affective aspects of consciousness, personal feelings and emotions.

It is possible to set up a four-celled square which uses the objective-emotive polarity to explicate my four program types which then can be used to give us some insights into the various genres that fall under each program type. This is found below:

	Strong	Contests	Dramas
EMOTIVE			
	Weak	Actualities	Persuasions
		high	low

OBJECTIVE

Let me use this diagram to discuss some important genres. Sports programs are classified as contests and are high under the objective classification (because they are actually taking place in the real world) and strong under emotive, since they are generally emotionally charged for viewers. News programs are high under objective and weak under emotive (that is, they are ideally weak under emotive since the emphasis in news programs should be on presenting facts and not on presenting a point of view—to the extent, of course, that this is possible). Editorials would not be classified as actualities but as persuasions.

Dramas, of course, would be low on the objective scale but high on the emotive one. They are fictions meant to generate strong feelings in viewers. Persuasions, on the other hand, are low on the objective scale and low on the emotive scale as well. This is somewhat problematic, since many commercials are dramatic and exciting. But if we take persuasions at face value, in the most literal sense (and the television editorial would be a good example here), the persuasion is low on affect.

The chart that follows lists some of the more important television genres and shows how they rate in terms of the emotive/objective polarity.

GENRE	EMOTIVE	OBJECTIVE
News	weak	high
Sports	strong	high
SitComs	strong	low
Commercials	weak	low
Documentary	weak	high
Soaps	strong	low
Police	strong	low
Game shows	strong	high
Spectacles	strong	high
Talk shows	weak	high

Using the objective/emotive polarity, it is, I believe, possible to gain a better understanding of the nature of the various genres and of their appeals. A content-analysis of the most popular genres on television would indicate that dramas are exceedingly important and, therefore, that programs which are strong on the emotive side and low on the objective side tend to dominate. Television programming tends to be dramatic, and even genres that are not explicitly dramatic, such as news and commericals, often have a great deal of dramatic content.

In the four-celled square, we find that diagonals are the most distant program types—in theory, at least. Thus actualities and dramas, contests and persuasions, are the furthest removed from one another. This is because the diagonal squares do not share either the objectivity of the horizontal axis or the emotiveness of the vertical axis. Actualities, for instance, are "weak-high" in the emotive-objective scale while dramas are "low-strong" on that scale.

On the other hand, horizontal links are much stronger. Contests and dramas are both "strong" on the emotive scale and have a similar nature: in contests there is competition and in drama there is conflict. In both program types there is suspense. And actualities and persuasions are both weak in the emotive scale, though many television commercials make it hard to classify them that way.

In the same manner, actualities and contests are high on the objective scale and dramas and persuasions are low on this measure. Remember I am using objective in a special way—to deal with real life and real events, as opposed to dramatic recreations of life, or narrative fictions.

What complicates matters is that there are all kinds of overlaps caused by the creation of new genres (the docudrama, for instance) and the fact that at times all the four program types can get mixed together (as in some commercials). What this schema does is enable us to understand what each genre is supposed to be like. If we find, for example, that news programs instead of being strong on the objective are strong on the emotive, we have reason to wonder how useful or valid the news program is. And dramas that fail may do so because they are too high on the objective side and too weak on the emotive.

What I've offered here is a guide to the structure of programs on television and in other media. It may be that the most interesting and artistically successful series on television are the ones that transcend their boundaries (though as I pointed out in my discussion of news, there are dangers involved as well). My schema will, I hope, help us understand something about the nature or structure of television genres and genres found in other media and will be a step in separating out their components and in the direction of a more reasoned and better informed treatment of them.

Attacks on Television

Let me list some of the most common criticisms made about television and explain most of them briefly. This will provide us with a general overview of the subject. I will then offer a list of the defenses which supporters of the medium offer. Most of the controversy about television exists among elite segments of society. Television is certainly unpopular with many of these elements; it is not unpopular with the average American who spends an enormous amount of time with it (though recent figures suggest that some of the appeal of television is waning, as new technological developments offer alternative media and alternative ways of selecting television programs—for instance, videocassette recorders).

1. Television is escapist. It distracts our attention from important matters in the real world—social problems such as poverty, hunger, racism, sexism, and political matters.
2. Television appeals to the lowest common denominator. In an effort to get ever-increasing audiences (and more advertising revenue), television keeps lowering its standards, thus vulgarizing everything it touches and everyone who watches it.
3. Television trivializes everything. It offers stupid, boring programs that simplify issues.
4. Television homogenizes our culture. It destroys regional and local variations on the national culture. That is, by virtue of its immense power, whether it wishes to or not, it obliterates cultural variations on the international level as well as the national and local levels.
5. Television is too formulaic. Because of its voracity for programming it must rely on formulaic (conventionally structured) shows, which are easier to create and understand. The price for this material that, too often, lacks imagination and creativity.
6. Television is a narcotic. People become dependent on it and it takes over their lives—a form of electronic addiction.
7. Television is obsessed with a narrow range of themes. These include sex and violence, death, greed,—which have negative effects on viewers (especially heavy viewers). This focus fails to do justice to human complexity and provides many people with bad role models.
8. Television viewing is essentially a passive experience. Viewers simply sit and watch the "boob tube." Television monopolizes people's leisure hours, and deprives them of the opportunity for social interaction. .
9. Television is commercial-ridden. The fact that television is financed by advertising means that we are subjected to endless commercials, which interrupt the flow of programs and shortens our attention-spans.
10. Television is an instrument of ideological domination. The television industry is owned by capitalists and champions the values of the capitalist social order. It also spreads these values to societies of the third world (cultural imperialism) and thus leads, ultimately, to their continued domination.
11. Television promotes emotional infantilism. Viewers are exposed to dramatic conflicts at an early age which are too difficult for them, emotionally, and so they retreat into emotional infantilism, a quest for sensation, etc.
12. Television uses stereotyped figures. These figures give viewers false ideas about Blacks, women, working class people, ethnic groups, and other minorities and do not provide suitable role models for young people to identify with.
13. Television promotes anxiety—even terror—in people. People who cannot emulate the lifestyle of characters they see on television (characterized by affluence and consumer lust) often feel that they are failures and nobodies whose lives are dull and uninteresting.

Defenses of Television

There are a number of positive aspects to television, which are emphasized by those who defend the medium, the programs it carries and the industry in general. In the material that follows I will briefly discuss some of the more important defenses of television. For most people, I might point out, television needs no defense. If people didn't like television, why would they watch it for more than three hours per day?

1. Television gives people what they want. Often this is considerably different from what elitist critics think people should want (high culture, informative or educational material).
2. Elitists dislike the common man and woman. These elitists use television as a means of criticizing people indirectly, now that it is not acceptable (in an egalitarian society) to criticize them directly.
3. Television is a window on the world. Television shows people what is going on, instead of telling them about it. It gives viewers a much stronger sense of what other peoples and places are like than they had before television.
4. Television aids in communication. It does this by providing people with common experiences to talk about. As such, it is a unifying factor in an increasingly fragmented (by differences in class, race, religion, and ethnicity) society.
5. Attacks on television are without scientific basis. Most of the research that has been done on television is characterized either by armchair theoretizing or poorly designed experiments and studies, which do not lead to reliable conclusions.
6. It inspires people to rise in the world. The characters on television, who tend to be affluent and powerful, give excellent role models which stimulate people to better themselves and rise in the world.
7. Television has transformed politics. It has done this by presenting politicians on television and enabled people to learn about them in a direct manner. The content of a great deal of televized news and talk shows is politics and these programs perform a useful service.
8. Television comforts many people. It is a great aid to the ill and the old—enabling them to keep in touch with things and find inexpensive and continual entertainment.
9. Television can be turned off any time. Individuals make choices which determine what they will see and how long they will watch the medium. There is nothing which says that anyone has to watch television—or any particular programs.
10. Television keeps people up on new products and services. Commercials perform a useful function by informing people and generally entertaining them at the same time. Rather than being nuisances, commercials are appreciated by large numbers of television viewers.

11. Television helps people relax. After a hard day, it is a joy to be able to turn on television and escape from the world of harsh reality.
12. Television educates people. In some cases television educates people literally—as in the case of courses which are broadcast on the medium. But television also educates people *indirectly* by showing them how people solve problems or react to various situations.

With the outline of the great television debate delineated, I believe it is now time to proceed onto the actual essays in this book. They are written by scholars of considerable reputation from a number of disciplines, and should give anyone interested in television and its role in society some very interesting ideas and a good deal to think about.

Bibliography

Berger, Arthur Asa. *The TV-Guided American*. New York: Walker & Co., 1976.
_____. *Television as an Instrument of Terror*. New Brunswick, N.J.: Transaction Books, 1980.
Esslin Martin. *The Age of Television*. San Francisco, C.A.: W.W. Freeman, 1982.
Malinowski, Bronislaw. *Magic, Science and Religion*. Garden City, N.Y.: Anchor Books, 1954.

1

Campaign Commercials

L. Patrick Devlin

Ronald Reagan received almost $30 million in federal funds during the 1980 campaign. He spent $18 million, or 60 percent of it, on advertising. He spent approximately $13 million of that on television advertisements, so that 70 percent of the money that Ronald Reagan spent on advertising in the 1980 campaign was spent on television advertising. In 1976 Jimmy Carter spent 74 percent of his advertising money on television. In 1984 Reagan and Mondale spent approximately $25 million each on advertising. Candidates are spending more on television advertising. Or are they?

An analysis of the money spent on television advertising in the 1952 Eisenhower campaign uncovers some interesting comparisons. In a paper on the 1952 Eisenhower television campaign, Stephen C. Wood estimated that Eisenhower's television spending ranged from $2 million to $6 million when all television time buying—national, state, and local—was factored in. Eisenhower's campaign spent approximately $1.5 million on network television spots. In 1980, Reagan's network spending approximated $6.5 million. If these two network spending figures are analyzed in terms of the 1967 base year for constant dollars, Eisenhower spent $1.9 million on network spots, Reagen spent $2.5 million. If Eisenhower spent a possible total of $6 million while Reagan spent a total of $13 million on television ads, Eisenhower actually outspent Reagan $7.5 million to $5.9 million in terms of 1967 constant dollars.

Well financed presidential candidates always have and always will spend vast sums and a major portion of their budgets on television advertising. Few corporations, aside from Procter and Gamble, McDonalds, or Miller beer, advertise year-round at the volume reached by political advertising during the months of September and October and the first week of November. During a presidential campaign commericals flood the airwaves.

Political commercials come in various time frames. They come in half-hour speeches or biographies. They come in mini programs, or four-minute-and-twenty-second segments that are sandwiched in before Johnny Carson or the evening news. More commonly they come in sixty-second or especially thirty-second segments. Political commercials can also be categorized as to type or format—documentary, talking head, man-in-the-street, cinema verité, and production idea spots.

The advantage of political advertising is that it can be controlled. Candidates may not be able to control what the opposition says or does, or control what the media televises or prints. But candidates, if they are properly financed, can control the message and image conveyed through paid television advertising. There are other advantages of political advertising.

One purpose of political advertising is to make an unknown candidate a better known candidate. Examples of unknowns using television in presidential races to become known is less frequent than in gubernatorial or senatorial campaigns. McGovern in 1972, Carter in 1976, Bush in 1980, and Hart in 1984 used television extensively to become better known during their primary campaigns. Ads are also often aimed at late-deciding or disinterested voters. Ads are unobtrusive and unavoidable invaders into peoples' living rooms. They reach thousands, even millions in large media markets. Many of these uninvolved voters see little else of the campaign except what they may possibly see on the evening news. Lynda Lee Kaid has concluded that "political advertising is more effective when the level of voter involvement is low." Late-deciding or uninvolved voters are the crucial 10 to 20 percent of the electorate. Normally they are reached only through television in the last stages of the campaign.

In 1972, Patterson and McClure researched the effectiveness of political ads and found that only 18 of 100 voters were late deciders. In 1972 many people had made up their minds. The ads of the campaign were found to have influenced about 3 percent of the total electorate, but there was a 23 percent spread between Nixon and McGovern in the final tally. A 3 percent impact along with a 23 percent spread is not much of an impact. In the 1976 campaign there was only a 2 percent disparity between Ford and Carter in the final tally. If the 1976 ads had affected 3 percent of the electorate, there being only a two percent spread, the effectiveness or ineffectiveness of ads might be crucial.

Ads are also used to reinforce supporters and partisans. When partisans saw pictures of Ronald Reagan on the cliffs of Normandy or of Jimmy Carter standing in front of a gigantic American flag at town meetings, these reinforced partisan feelings. For example, partisans watch half-hour programs but few others do. Only one in twenty people—primary partisans—watch half-hour programs. Their partisan feelings are reinforced, and they may give more money to the campaign because of these commercials.

Ads can also be used to attack the opposition. As Reagan's 1980 pollster, Vincent Breglio, maintained, "It has become vital in campaigns today that you not only present all of the reasons why people ought to vote for you but you also have an obligation to present the reasons why they should not vote for the opponent. Hence, the negative campaign, or the attack strategy becomes an essential part of any campaign operation." A mix of positive and negative ads is increasingly used to convince voters why they should vote for one candidate and not vote for the opposition.

Ads can develop and explain issues. Research, by McClure and Patterson has demonstrated that there is more substance and more information on issues in presidential ads than in television news. A sixty-second ad has, on average, five times as much information about the candidate's position on issues than a sixty-second snippet on the evening news. Ads also have a cumulative effect. In presidential campaigns a multiplicity of ads are used and often repeated. Using thirty-second time frames voters see ten or twenty ads during the course of a campaign, with five or six of them repeated. The idea comes across not simply in thirty seconds, but in thirty seconds multiplied by the number of times voters see that thirty-second ad and are attentive to it.

Ads can soften or redefine an image. If a candidate has a reputation for not caring about unemployment or is weak on defense issues, ads can be created to emphasize these postitions and the candidate's commitment to these areas. In 1968 candidate Nixon was redefined through television. In 1976, Jimmy Carter had been accused of not taking strong stands on issues. His advertising man created strong issue-oriented spots to redefine this hazy image through a series of ads in which Carter took strong stands.

Ads are used to target particular demographic groups. In this manner, they go hand in hand with polling. Polling tells where the potential voters are and ad demographics tell how to reach them. For example, women, blacks, males, single mothers, or union members might be targeted voters. Careful buying of airtime is used—for example, the buying of time before, during, or after key programs such as a hockey game to reach more male voters or the Phil Donahue show to reach more female voters. Polling and time buying help to maximize the potential to reach a particular category of voter.

Ads cost money but they can also be used to raise money. Appeals for money often are used at the end of half-hour or five-minute ads. McGovern in 1972 and Anderson in 1980 paid for their television commercials mainly through such appeals. In 1984, Mondale used a special five-minute commercial beamed into house parties to raise money. People did send in money so that future ads went on the air.

Ads are adaptable. They can be made. They can be revised. They can be discarded as the necessities of the campaign change. Multiple generations of spot commercials are extremely common during the presidential campaign. Often several hours of ads, including six or seven distinct generations, are made. Ultimately, ads are used because the competition uses them. Few candidates, aside from Jesse Jackson in 1984, can afford the luxury of forgoing commercials. There is an adage in campaigns stating that half of all advertising money is wasted. Since nobody in a campaign knows which half, all advertising continues.

Primitive Ads

The first advertisements I examine are labeled "primitive ads." These were created in 1952 and 1956. The first Eisenhower campaign used three sixty-second spots and over twenty twenty-second spots with an "ask General Eisenhower" theme. A "Man from Abilene" spot was primitive because it had the announcer's voice screaming at the viewer—"Vote for peace! Vote for Eisenhower!"—in a manner similar to the loud announcers' techniques used in movie theaters during the "March of Time" or "Movietone News." In his spots Eisenhower was ill at ease in front of the camera, and his voice and eyes gave him away as an uneasy communicator. In the twenty-second spots Eisenhower was asked a question by a voter and then answered. Both the unspontaneous and contrived questions and the answers by Eisenhower reading from cue cards demonstrate the primitive nature of these ads.

The Stevenson campaign in 1952 concentrated on half-hour speeches rather than spot commercials. In 1956 "A Man from Libertyville" was created to counteract the "Man from Abilene" approach. Stevenson discussed the high cost of living while holding a bag of groceries. The lesson learned from this spot was, if you want to be elected president don't carry a grocery bag. Eisenhower had been wise enough not to carry grocery bags. Both the Eisenhower and Stevenson ads represent a primitive form of television advertising no longer used in campaigns today.

Talking Heads

The year of the "talking head" spot was 1960. Both John Kennedy and Richard Nixon emphasized ads that had them speaking directly to the viewer in a communicative way. The "talking head" format was as much in use in 1984 as it was in 1960. Within the general format, there are differences. For example, a Nixon spot was formal. Nixon was serious; he had a presidential image. The visual background was blank, while concentrated and complimentary lighting was used on Nixon's face—he was almost angelic. This brightness contrasted with the photogenic darkness that Nixon displayed in the debates. In the debate footage he came across with a five o'clock shadow. The ads—in which he had a dark suit and a light face—were made to compensate for the light suit and dark face of the debates.

A Kennedy "talking head" spot was much more informal. His gestures and his voice were more conversational and he had family pictures in the background. Pictures and plaques were used just as flags or family pictures are used today to give the viewer additional information. Some ad makers want the background to be blank; others want some kind of additional information to be communicated visually. Research by Patterson and McClure found that a candidate can develop a more favorable image through issue-oriented spots like these which seek to convince the voter that the candidate has positions on civil rights or medicare and that he can thus handle the difficult problems of a presidency. These spots convey a better image than "image" spots which try to create directly a favorable feeling about the candidate's personal qualities. Research indicates that the best way to make a positive impression on the voter is to use issues—in this case medicare or civil rights—as a vehicle or a tool to effect a positive image. The purpose of most "talking head" spots is to focus on an issue and use the candidate to convey an impression that he can handle the issue. Most importantly, he should convey the impression that he can handle the job of president.

Negative Ads

The year of the negative ad was 1964. Both Goldwater and Johnson emphasized ads that tried to tear down their opponent rather than build up themselves. Two 1964 commercials are representative of negative commercials made to provoke or bring out negative feelings already within voters. In the "Daisy Girl" spot a little girl is shown in a field of flowers. An atomic bomb explodes with a flash. President Johnson's voice elaborates, "These are the stakes: to make a world in which all God's children can live, or go into the dark." "Daisy Girl" was shown once and then taken off the air because of the outcry and protest it caused, The ad had an afterlife through newspaper articles and radio and television news commentaries about it. The creator of this spot, Tony Schwartz, had a philosophy about making good political ads: commercials attempting to bring something to voters, that is, convey some information and bring something new to them, are inherently not as effective as those that try to appeal to an idea that is already within voters. The goal is not to get something across to people as much as it is to get something out of people. Nowhere in the "Daisy Girl" spot is Goldwater mentioned, but the ad evoked a feeling that Goldwater may indeed use nuclear weapons. The mistrust was not in the spot—the mistrust was in the viewer. Similarly, many voters already had feelings that we were not a very loved people, and that other countries were using us and burning our flag. A Goldwater ad used familiar riot footage with a "Yankee go Home" motif to reinforce the feeling that was already within many Goldwater-prone voters.

The first year in which color was used in presidential commercials was 1968, and color enhances the visual nature of television ads. A Humphrey ad had visual simplicity but little visual variety and excitement. Humphrey simply started small and grew visually as his accomplishments grew and were enumerated by the announcer. Nixon's advertising people took advantage of the first year of color by creating a series of spots giving life and vitality to well chosen still photography to give the effect of visual variety. Photography is important because research has shown that people remember the visuals in spots more than the specifics of the narration. One study found that 80 to 85 percent of the information retained about television commercials is visual. Good presidential commercials have to be visual.

Memorable Ideas

Television is an excellent tool for conveying a memorable idea. In 1972, production spots were created to convey important ideas about candidates. Production spots also allow the use of graphics to make the information more memorable.

In 1972 as other candidates were pictured on the evening news trudging through the snow in the New Hampshire primary, President Nixon was shown on his trip to the Soviet Union. Five-minute travelogues were created to emphasize that Nixon was the first president to visit our former enemies, China and the Soviet Union. These spots stressed that with Nixon we would have a greater chance of having peace with our former enemies. As McGovern became more the issue in 1972, three anti-McGovern spots were shown more frequently. These negative spots were found by Thomas Patterson to reach low- and moderate-interest voters for several reasons. First, they were perceived as entertaining or funny. If people perceive an ad as entertaining or funny that helps them to look at it. Second, committed vote switchers—Democrats who were going to vote for Nixon—had their attitudes reinforced. The idea spots provided reasons for their decision and gave them comfort in knowing that there were many others like them. Similarly, McGovern voters wanted to reduce military spending. When they watched an anti-McGovern commercial about that, it was consistent with and reinforced their perception of the candidate.

In political advertising, selective perception is constantly working. If pro-Nixon voters viewed the defense spot they might say, "I knew that about McGovern. That is terrible. That is why Nixon needs to be reelected to save this country." Undecided voters might look at that defense spot and say, "I didn't know that about McGovern. Is he really going to do that to the air force? Is he really going to do that to the navy?" McGovern voters might look at that defense spot and say, "Right on George! We need to reduce the military." Selective perception allowed different people to take away different ideas from that single commercial.

Nixon's "turn around" spot is also visually important. It is another idea spot, but with additional visual simplicity. McGovern is shown repeatedly rotating—physically and intellectually—from one position in one year to an opposite position in the following year. The announcer ends with, "What about next year?" Voters did not have to remember one specific instance of a McGovern change—not one issue, not one statement from the spot. The impression given was that McGovern had frequently switched his stance. The expectation of future switches was the important idea to get across. That was achieved through a rotating picture.

When the polls showed that literally millions of Democrats were defecting to Nixon, Tony Schwartz, the creator of the Lyndon Johnson "Daisy Girl" commercial, was hired by McGovern. Schwartz created five spots of which "Voting Booth" is representative. This ad was only shown twice—too infrequently to do much good—but the spot represents the best of what Schwartz classified as an "idea" spot. The real problem for McGovern was millions of defecting Democrats. Schwartz tried to reach them in a catchy, stream of consciousness way. He showed an indecisive man in a voting booth thinking out loud, pondering the choices. The speed of the ad made it captivating, yet at times statements could be missed because they were not heard the first time around. Crucial statements were: "This hand voted for Kennedy;" "Me vote for Nixon? My father would roll over in his grave;" "The fellas say they are but maybe they're not;" "My gut feeling, my gut feeling, McGovern." These statements represent the kind of emotional idea that the ad tried to evoke.

Cinema Verité

Filming a candidate in real life settings interacting with people is a technique called "cinema verité." In 1972, McGovern's principal ad creator, Charles Guggenheim, did not believe in the ethics or effectiveness of negative advertising. Guggenheim was an award-winning documentary filmmaker who preferred to film McGovern in real settings interacting with real voters. Guggenheim used the cinema verité technique to show McGovern as a concerned and compassionate candidate. This format allows the ad maker to take footage of a candidate speaking with voters during the course of a day or several days. The footage is then edited down to thirty- and sixty-second snippets in which the candidate concentrates on one issue—in McGovern's case, medicare. The technique can also be used to show the candidate shaking hands, listening, and simply being open and communicative with potential voters in group settings.

Changing Spots

Clearly, 1976 was the year for changing ad campaigns. President Ford used three ad makers and three different advertising campaign techniques. Candidate Carter evolved in his ads from a farmer in a plaid shirt to someone who looked presidential. Therefore 1976 is a good year to examine the changes in presidential campaign advertising.

At first, Ford was portrayed as an effective president who had restored faith in the presidency. Following Watergate and Nixon's resignation, these ads really had Ford running against Nixon and reinforced Ford as an effective president. When Ronald Reagan started doing better in the primaries, pressure for changes in Ford's advertising occurred. In California, Ford agreed to air for the first time in presidential politics "slice-of-life" advertisements. These used paid actors in little theater situations—the tried and true techniques of selling detergents or Preparation H. In one, two women discuss how food prices are no longer going up the way they used to because, "President Ford has cut inflation in half." He is "leading us back to prosperity." When I show the "Two Ladies" ad to an audience, laughter indicates that presidential candidates cannot be sold like soap or Preparation H. The "slice-of-life" technique is too blatantly obvious and has too many product advertising associations.

In Ford's "Feeling Good" ad, featuring happy Americans going about their business, music was used to create an upbeat mood about the country and its people. Music is often an integral part of the mood setting devices of political ads. If a viewer's toe was tapping to the tempo of this ad, the music accomplished what the ad maker wanted.

In 1976, Carter started campaigning by running as a personable outsider. He was the first candidate to run for president wearing a plaid, open collared shirt in his ads. Carter finished the campaign in a suit making a series of "talking head" spots which made him appear to be presidential. In 1976 campaign advertising, the personable candidate became more presidential and the president became more personable. Ford started out using his office as his trump card and finished by using ads that highlighted his personal qualities. Carter started out by using ads that focused on his casual personableness and finished by using ads that made him appear more presidential.

Most candidates in a long campaign use a multiplicity of ads and their ad makers create multiple generations of many different types of ads—often too many different types of ads. Ford's media people created almost two hours of varied television advertising. By making and playing so many different spots, they negated the impact of their more effective spots.

No candidate emphasized documentary ads more than Ronald Reagan in 1980. During the 1980 general election campaign, Reagan ad makers wanted to play down the perception of Reagan as an actor and play up the perception of Reagan as an effective governor. A one minute ad, "The Reagan Record," and a longer four-minute-and-twenty-second version, were the most heavily played ads of the entire campaign. The ad talked about the accomplishments of Reagan as governor and how as a good governor he would make an effective and good president. Partisans did not like the ad because it emphasized things they already knew, but this ad was played over and over again. It was effective in swinging votes of late-deciding voters because its format gave out crucial information.

Man-in-the-street ads have real people saying nice things about one candidate and/or nasty things about the opponent. In 1976, Jerry Rafshoon, Carter's ad creator was on the receiving end of Ford's man-in-the-street ads which characterized Carter as "wishy-washy." Man-in-the-street ads are used to reinforce perceptions of candidates that are revealed in polling. In 1980 Rafshoon wanted to reinforce the perception of Reagan as a scary guy who shot before he thought. Man-in-the-street ads are excellent reinforcing tools but they are seldom persuasive tools. Too often the impression of undecided voters upon seeing these ads is "you can get somebody to say anything about anybody." Because these ads do use real people saying real things, many ad makers use them. They think they have a quality of believability.

Testimonial ads have prominent politicians, movie stars, or television personalities saying things on behalf of candidates. A Ted Kennedy testimonial ad in 1980 used a popular star, Carroll O'Connor, to attack Carter's economic policy and to hopefully convey trust for Kennedy. Testimonials by other personalities or politicians and trust were two things Kennedy did not have in abundance during his campaign. Thus, "Archie Bunker" endorsed Kennedy and said "I trust and believe in him folks."

Independent ads are those financed by individuals or organizations that are separate from the presidential candidates. The real story of the 1980 campaign might be not in the candidates' ads but in those that were independently financed. The ads from the Republican Congressional Committee (RCC) and the National Conservative Political Action Committee (NCPAC) were representative of ads aired by a host of independent organizations. The RCC spent $7 million on television advertising while all of the political action committees spent about an additional $13 million on television advertising. Most of these ads were pro-Reagan and anti-Carter. When added to the Reagan ads, Carter's ad maker concluded that he was actually outspent by 2:1 or 3:1.

Most independent ads are hard-hitting, negative ads. The Republican ads were humorous but the NCPAC ads were deliberately provocative. Terry Dolan, the national director of NCPAC, wanted ads that created reaction, and he was unconcerned about negative reaction. As he said in an interview, "I don't care what Ronald Reagan, Jimmy Carter, or CBS says about our ads. The people we serve are 300,000 throughout the U.S. who could care less about respectability." Independent ads were a potent factor in 1980 and they will continue to be a factor in future presidential campaigns.

In the early years of presidential spots, 1952 through 1968, there was an emphasis on short spots of twenty or sixty seconds. In 1972 and 1976, the four-minute-and-twenty-second spot predominated. In 1980 and 1984, the thirty-second spot did. We have seen an evolution of length preferences dependent on the campaign.

A mix of lengths and types of spots are used in presidential campaigns. An analysis of the 1980 Reagan spots will illustrate this. Between Labor Day and Election Day in 1980, Reagan's "Campaign '80" ran 255 network television commercials. Seventy-four or 29 percent were five-minute spots, 41 or 16 percent were one-minute spots and 140 or 55 percent were thirty-second spots. Of the 74 five-minute spots, 60 were versions of the documentary "The Reagan Record." Of the 41 one-minute spots, 35 were shortened versions of "The Reagan Record." Of the thirty-second spots 10 percent were documentary "Reagan Record" spots, 45 percent were "talking head" spots, and 45 percent were "anti-Carter" spots. Of the total commercial allocation by "Campaign '80," 41 percent were documentary spots, 33 percent were "talking head" spots, and 26 percent were "anti-Carter" spots.

The thirty-second spot has become the dominant time frame for political ads. Research on product commercials has demonstrated that thirty-second spots are just as effective as sixty-second spots in getting the message across. Research has found that five-minute spots are not significantly more successful than sixty-second spots in terms of the quantity of items that can be recalled after seeing a political spot.

Political advertisers have increasingly emphasized the use of the thirty-second spot in relation to the sixty- or four-minute-and-twenty-second spot. For example, in 1972 Patterson and McClure found that only 2 percent of all presidential ads were thirty-second spots while 41 percent of all commercials in 1972 were five minutes in length. In 1980, 55 percent of all Reagan spots were thirty-second spots. From 2 to 55 percent in eight years is a shift reflecting that stations are set up to sell time and viewers are prepared to view commercials in thirty-second units.

Five-minute spots work best as mood pieces, developing feelings through music and emotional appeals, or as spots that give biographic or personal information about the candidate. In 1976, Jerry Rafshoon, creator of the Carter spots, became a champion of longer spots. He later proclaimed, "I'd be very happy if the networks and stations said, 'From now on we'll sell candidates nothing but five minutes.'" In 1976, when Carter was an unknown, five-minute spots were used in abundance by Rafshoon. In 1980 Rafshoon used fewer of them. This happened because as a candidate moves from being unknown to being known there is less need for five-minute spots; however, they are still good as money raisers. In 1984 Walter Mondale raised $1.4 million for his campaign by beaming in a five-minute network commercial to fund raising house parties held around the United States.

In 1984 candidates Mondale, Hart, and Glenn emphasized television commercials in their campaigns. Although Hart's ads were more graphically innovative—using infinity grids, smaller inserted picture frames, and peel-back frames—all candidates used variations of the talking head, cinema verité, documentary, and production idea spots. These types, along with testimonial, man-in-the-street, and negative spots are generic ads that will be seen over and over again in future campaigns. One ad maker may not like or think his candidate could benefit from testimonial or man-in-the-street spots, but four years later another ad maker returns to these basic forms.

More sophisticated cinematography is in use today than was used in the fifties, sixties, or seventies. Carter's ads in 1980 set a standard for beautifully photographed and produced commercials that Reagan surpassed in 1984. In Reagan's initial ads of 1984 the president is neither seen nor heard. Instead we see beautiful pictures of weddings, hugs, churches, boats, flags, and homes. These ads reinforce the traditional values of love, family, church, and community, and renew faith in America. Good feelings have been emphasized in ads since the "I'm Feeling Good About America" series for Gerald Ford in 1976. Pictures of America and its people are really attempts at getting the electorate to vote for an idyllic view of themselves.

Reagan is not unique in his attempts at ads that use this strategy; however, the fine quality of his ads indicate that he has raised the technique to a new art form.

It is difficult to determine the effectiveness of political commercials. Douglass Bailey, who handled the 1976 Ford media stated, "It is extraordinarily difficult to look at a political commercial and judge it. Because any reputable agency . . . can produce pretty commercials . . . but to judge their political effectiveness is very hard to do." Aside from trying to separate a commerical's creative merit from its political impact, there is another reason it is difficult to uncover the effectiveness of political commercials. There is so much happening simultaneously in a campaign that it is difficult to isolate the impact of only the political advertising.

Political ads are but one of the many influences on the outcome of a presidential campaign. Certainly there are other communicative events—debates, speeches, evening news broadcasts—that affect a campaign; yet campaigns have and will continue to spend a massive amount of their available money on political advertising.

Bibliography

Burnham, David. "What You See is Probably What You're Going to Get." *Providence Evening Bulletin* (October 27, 1983).

Kaid, Lynda Lee. "Political Advertising." In Dan D. Nimmo and Keith R. Sanders, eds. *Handbook of Political Communication*. Beverly Hills, Calif.: Sage, 1981.

Patterson, Thomas E. and McClure, Robert D. *The Unseeing Eye*. New York: G.P. Putnam's Sons, 1976.

2
1984—The Commercial

Arthur Asa Berger

There is only one way left to escape the alienation of present-day society: to retreat ahead of it: *every old language is immediately compromised, and every language becomes old once it is repeated. Now, encratic language (the language produced and spread under the protection of power) is statutorily a language of repetition; all official institutions of language are repeating machines: school, sports, advertising, popular songs, news, all continually repeat the same structure, the same meaning, often the same words: the stereotype is a political fact, the major figure of ideology. Confronting it, the New is bliss (Freud: "In the adult, novelty always constitutes the condition of orgasm"). Whence the present configuration of forces: on the one hand, a mass banalization (linked to the repetition of language)—a banalization outside bliss but not necessarily outside pleasure—and on the other, a (marginal, eccentric) impulse toward the New—a desperate impulse that can reach the point of destroying discourse: an attempt to reproduce in historical terms the bliss repressed beneath the stereotype.*

—Roland Barthes
The Pleasure of the Text

Synopsis

The commercial starts with the number 1984 appearing on the screen. We then cut to an extreme longshot of vaguely perceived figures marching through a tunnel joining gigantic structures. We cut then to a longshot of figures marching. They all have had their hair shaven and are wearing dull uniforms. They have no expression on their faces. There is a closeup of their heavy boots. A quick cut shows a blonde woman, with a white jersey and red shorts, running. We see her only for an instant. The next cut shows the figures again and then we cut to a shot of her being pursued by helmet-

---
I would like to express my gratitude to John Minzer of the Media Production Center at the Annenberg School of Communications, The University of Southern California, for his invaluable assistance.

clad storm-trooper figures. There is cutting back and forth in the commercial between the blonde woman and the troopers pursuing her. We see another extreme longshot of the inmates of this institution sitting in a huge room. They are watching a gigantic television set. A figure wearing glasses is addressing the inmates, who sit staring at the television image as if in a hypnotic trance. He is talking about their being free, united, etc. The blonde woman, who is carrying a sledge-hammer, enters the room. She hurls the sledge-hammer at the television screen and there is huge explosion. The explosion creates an image that looks somewhat like that generated by an atomic bomb. The inmates stare, dazed and open-mouthed, at the screen. A message from Apple computers appears on the screen informing viewers that Apple will shortly be introducing a new computer, The Macintosh.

Background

This commercial, directed by Ridley Scott, was shown only once, during the 1984 Superbowl, though it was also aired, as a news item, by a number of news programs. The commercial was created by Apple's advertising agency, Chiat/Day, of Los Angeles. It cost $500,000 to make and $800,000 for air time. Apple was hesitant to use it and only decided to do so at the very last minute. They actually called England to stop production of the commercial, but by the time they called the commercial had already been shot.

It is a remarkable text. The actors in the commercial were skinheads (a subculture whose members distinguish themselves from other groups by shaving their heads) from England, who were recruited to play the roles of the prisoners. The commercial has a much different look from the average commercial and takes a very unique approach to the matter of marketing a product. Ridley Scott, the director (or "auteur") is a distinguished figure in the film world (*Alien, Blade Runner*) and the commercial has his signature—its look, its narrative structure, its message. All suggest an artistically produced film rather than a commercial.

In the remainder of this essay I will examine some of the most important images from the text, discuss how they generate meaning, what that meaning is, and how viewers might be affected by these images, and speculate about the narrative itself. (It is sometimes argued that there is no "minimal" unit in a television text to deal with, unlike film, which has the frame. But this is not a major issue, for one can always isolate important images and scenes for analysis; "shots" or images, therefore, serve the same function as the frame in film.)

Intimations of Orwell

The title of this commercial brings to mind George Orwell's novel, *1984* and the text of the commercial is based on the idea of the dystopia. The world of the commercial is that of a perverted utopian community, a total institution, in which every aspect of people's lives is controlled—especially their minds. We see 1984, the commercial, in terms of *1984*, the book. Here we have an example of what is known in semiotic literature as *intertextuality*. We "read" one text in terms of another. The events in the commercial would have much less significance if we did not know about Orwell's classic novel.

The title also is connected to a great deal of speculation that occurred in the year 1984 about Orwell and his predictions. Thus, merely seeing the title generated ambivalent feelings. Would it be about the year 1984 or about the novel *1984*? (Many social commentators had mentioned that the year 1984 did not bring the kind of society that Orwell imagined.) The title left people in suspense.

The Total Institution

The first shot resolved any questions that might have been generated by the title. We see an extreme longshot of gigantic structures, connected by a tubular tunnel, in which we can dimly perceive figures marching. The scale of the scene is terrifying. The figures are minute and seemingly irrelevant when contrasted with the huge buildings in which they are incarcerated. One almost thinks of blood flowing through veins.

The spatiality of this scene and the image of control and conformity generated by the columns of figures tell us immediately that the commercial is indeed about an Orwellian world. This is reinforced in the next shot, which is a longshot of the prisoners, all with shaven heads and heavy, ill-fitting uniforms, marching sullenly in columns in the tunnel.

The Boots

One important shot occurs when there is a cut to a closeup of the prisoner's boots. The heavy, thick-soled boots, shown moving in unison, reflect the degree to which the inmates are under the control of their masters. (This is an example of *metonomy*, which confers meaning by association, and *synechdoche*, in which the part stands for the whole.) Focusing on the boots intensifies the message. We may even recall the famous shot of the boots in the movie *Potemkin* (1925). Uniforms suggest depersonalization and, in the content of the commercial, dehumanization. The shot of the boots moving in common strengthens this message by emphasizing one part of the human being and isolating it from the image of the whole human being.

The uniformity of the prisoners' feet as they march, the rather sullen and lethargic nature of their marching, all suggest that these inmates have been reduced to the status of automatons. It is the same kind of reductionism that occurs when we refer to young people as "college material" or football players as "horses," though it is much more intensified here.

The Blonde

Into this scene of marching zombies, of dehumanized and depersonalized bodies, there appears, for just an instant, an image of a beautiful blonde woman running down a corridor wearing a white shirt and red shorts. We can see her breasts heaving as she runs. And she runs directly at us, the viewers, on the Z-axis of the screen. The figure appears for perhaps a second or two, and then we return to the marching bodies and scenes of totalitarian control.

Who is she? We do not know. But the fact that she exists tells us that there is resistance in this totalitarian society, that not all are enslaved. We see shortly that she is being pursued by a troop of policemen who look terribly menacing in their helmets with glass facemasks. Her color, her animation, her freedom, even her sexuality, serve to make the situation of the inmates even more obvious and pathetic. Her image functions as a polar opposite to the enslaved men and even though we only see her the first time for a second or two, her existence creates drama and excitement.

The Brainwashing

Here we have a longshot of the inmates, sitting in rows, gazing at a gigantic television screen in the front of the auditorium, where a Big Brother figure is shown speaking to them. They are mute, expressionless, and seem to be almost hypnotized by the figure on the television screen. The message we get from this image is that mind-control is an important element in the operation of this totalitarian society. By implication, of course, control of the media (the gigantic television screen) is vital for control of the minds of the inmates—and perhaps everyone. Is this scene a metaphor for contemporary society, in which we, like the inmates, gaze in a hypnotic stupor at figures whose aim is to brainwash us? Is the distance between the world of the 1984 commercial and U.S. society less than we might imagine? These questions are raised by this image. Are we like these prisoners, are we mind-controlled as they are? We may not wear their uniforms or have shaved heads or be prisoners (or recognize that we are prisoners!) in some kind of a total institution. But that may be because the control is more subtle, the indoctrination less apparent: there may be more control over us than we imagine, and we are called by these images to question this.

Big Brother

We see little of the Big Brother figure—only a few shots in which we see him spouting gobbledygook to the inmates. The choice of the actor to portray this character is significant: he looks like a clerk or minor bureaucrat. He is in his 50s or 60s, wears glasses, and is bland and uncharismatic. He speaks in a low, monotonous voice. Indeed, for all we know, he may only be a minor functionary in whatever vast organization runs this society.

The message we get from a figure like this is that totalitarian institutions are essentially bureaucratic, held together not by charismatic individuals but by drab, conformist, bureaucratic types who do whatever they are told to do in a routine matter. They are not that different from the inmates in many respects, although the control exerted over these figures may be less overt.

The Message

Here is a transcript of the message that the Big Brother figure gives to the inmates. He speaks it, but it is also shown in captions running across the bottom of the screen.

> Today we celebrate the first glorious anniversary of the information purification repentence. We who created from out of this time in all history a garden of pure ideology, where each worker may loom secure, from the test of purveying contradictory thoughts. Our communication is enormous. It is more powerful than any fleet or army on earth. We are one people with one will, one resolve, one cause. Our enemies shall talk themselves to death and we will bury them with their own confusion. We shall prevail. [At this point television screen is shattered.]

This is garbled and confused rhetoric about events we know nothing of, though we can imagine what might have transpired. The language has the ring of indoctrination—there is a "glorious revolution" being "celebrated." The language contrasts, starkly, with the scenario in which it is being used. There is talk in this futuristic, oppressive hyperurban setting of a "garden of pure ideology" and the "security" that the workers should feel from all this.

It is communication that is given the major role here; it is a more powerful force than the military, it unites the workers/inmates/prisoners into a collectivity (or is it a mass society) with "one will, one resolve, one cause." And then there is that wonderfully comic line about the enemies of this society "talking themselves to death." It is the rhetoric of persuasion, and we have the sense that the inmates of this society have been exposed to this kind of talk almost endlessly: they have been brainwashed by doubletalk.

The language, with phrases such as "information purification repentence," is that of mind-control and psychic domination, and the commercial does a wonderful job of imitating it (and perhaps, in a sense, of parodying it). The goal preached is escape from "contradictory thoughts," which leads to "one will." In other words, the essentially human function of considering options and alternatives is to be obliterated—or has been already.

The Explosion

There are several scenes in which we see the blonde woman twirling a sledgehammer as she prepares to throw it at the screen and the police racing toward her. She launches the sledgehammer and it smashes into the gigantic television screen. There is an explosion and we see, briefly, an image vaguely similar to that produced by an atomic bomb.

The explosion, which destroys the image—and by implication the domination by the mass media of the inmates/workers—is the most significant act in the commercial. With this act a great blow is struck for freedom and we are led to imagine, in our own minds, what might follow. We are shown very little. Implicit in this scenario is the notion that once the control of people's minds by a totalitarian regime is broken, the destruction of that regime more or less follows automatically. This does not have to spelled out; it is like lancing a boil—when the system of pressure is punctured, healing can take place. The exploding screen signifies, then, the destruction of the totalitarian order that generates mind-controlling images on that screen.

The Response

After the explosion we cut to a scene in which the inmates are shown open-mouthed, staring in disbelief at what has happened. They are, relatively speaking, emotionless and display no affect other than bewilderment. They have been so brainwashed, we are led to believe, that they are incapable of any kind of response—at least, in the immediate present. We hear a low hissing sound, as if air is escaping from the gigantic television apparatus in the front of the room. The camera pans the inmates as the announcement from Apple rolls onto the screen.

The Announcement

We see the following announcement: "On January 24th, Apple Computers will introduce Macintosh and you will see why 1984 won't be like

'1984.'" The brevity and simplicity of this announcement, which takes but a few seconds, contrasts with the excitement and visual richness of the commercial. In this situation the understatement serves to shout at us and to gain a great deal of interest. Apple Computers tells us that it is introducing a new computer, but also that this new computer has enormous political and social implications—it will save us from ending up as victims of a totalitarian state.

There was a great deal of material about the Macintosh computer in the press and computer fanzines, so those interested in computers already knew about it. When the Macintosh computers went on sale, Apple sold about 17,000 the first day, a figure far beyond what they had anticipated. The Chiat/Day Agency naturally claims that it was its commercial that sold all those computers—a questionable claim.

The Heroine as Mythic Figure

The blonde heroine of this microdrama calls to mind several different heroic figures from our collective consciousness. Here we find how intertextual readings can enrich an event and give an image a great deal of cultural resonance. First, there is something of the "David and Goliath" in this story—a small, seemingly weak, and in this case female character brings down a Goliath figure by hurling a stone (sledgehammer) at it. In the commercial there are some close-ups of the Big Brother/Goliath figure, which simulate the size relationships between David and Goliath. It is a missile to the head that does the job in both cases. And with the destruction of the Golilath, of course, the forces of good can prevail. So the blonde represents a female version of David, and in our collective mythology we might see a replay of the David and Goliath story.

The woman is also an Eve figure. The fact that the Apple symbol is an apple with a bite out of it tells us that. But the blonde heroine also functions like Eve, for ultimately what she does is lead to knowledge of good and evil in a reverse Garden of Eden. Before she shattered the image, the inmates were brainwashed and had but "one will, one resolve, on cause." What information these poor souls had was "purified." Their state is vaguely analogous to that of Adam before he ate of the apple; the tasting of the fruit, which led to Adam and Eve's "eyes being opened" is the beginning of human history.

Thus, the blonde heroine is an Eve who brings knowledge of good and evil, and, by implication, knowledge of reality to the inmates. We do not see their transformation after the destruction of the Big Brother figure— and their immediate reaction of awe and stupefaction—but ultimately we cannot help but assume that something important will happen. It is quite possible that this beautiful blonde figure may also represent, in our psyches, the Apple Corporation. We know that corporations have different images in people's minds often based on symbolic figures in advertisements and commercials. On the basis of this commercial one might guess that the corporate image we have of Apple is that of a beautiful blonde woman who, in our unconscious, liberates men from political and psychological domination and ignorance. In any case, this produces a beneficial image for a computer company since one of the biggest problems computer manufacturers have is fighting anxiety about the difficulties of operating computers. If people see Apple computers as beautiful blondes, so much the better for the corporation.

From a psychoanalytic standpoint, the heroine is an ego figure who mediates between a monstrous and perverted superego figure, Big Brother, and the de-energized and devastated ids of the inmates. We see this in the chart that follows:

ID	EGO	SUPEREGO
inmates	blonde	Big Brother
peverted	normal	perverted
no energy	strong	no heart

As an ego figure, the heroine has to mediate between the inmates, whose ids have been weakened and drained of energy and the brainwasher, whose superego has become monstrous and distorted. One might see elements of an Oedipal conflict, in which a young female and an older, perhaps even fatherly figure have a very difficult relationship.

The Mediator

One function of the mythic hero or heroine is to mediate between opposing forces in an attempt to resolve some basic opposition. The text of this commerical is very binary and the blonde heroine serves to identify and highlight the oppositions found in it. There are, in essence, three characters in this text. First, there are the inmates who function as one character. Then there is the Big Brother character (and the police who are part of him). And there is the blonde heroine. Her function is to resolve the oppositions one way or another, which she does.

In the chart that follows I will contrast the inmates and the Big Brother figure. Here we are eliciting the paradigmatic structure of the text, which according to Lévi-Strauss, tells us its real meaning (as opposed to the surface meaning, which we get with a syntagmatic or linear narrative analysis).

INMATES	BIG BROTHER
obey	commands
uniforms	regular clothes
hairless	hair
listen	speaks
brainwashed	brainwasher
look at	is looked at
mindless	calculating
dehumanized	dehumanizing
alienated	alienating
emotionless	heartless

The blonde heroine, with her gorgeous hair, her vitality, her energy, her force resolves the dialectic by destroying Big Brother and making it possible (we imagine) for the inmates to regain their humanity. She also makes us aware of the depths to which the inmates have sunk, for unlike them she resists, she has a mind of her own, she accepts danger. Thus she is in contrast with both the inmates and with Big Brother, whom she destroys. The inmates and Big Brother are reverse images of one another—both drab, depersonalized and locked into a slave-master relationship that defines each character and on which both may turn out to be dependent.

Alienated Proles

The inmates, workers, automatons—whatever you wish to call them—reflect with terrifying clarity the way modern bureaucratic states can destroy humanity and lead people into a state of radical alienation. We have here a classic case (even if somewhat oversimplified and parodied) of a mindless proletariat being manipulated by a heartless bourgeoisie. This bourgeoisie rules by virtue of its control of the media and the manipulation of the consciousness of the proletariat. The situation in the commercial is one in which the horrors of a capitalist society are shown pushed to their logical conclusion, where workers are now enslaved and the society in which they live has become a totalitarian one.

The blonde heroine's actions symbolizes revolution. She stands for the role of progressive forces (pushed underground in this society) in leading a stupefied proletariat out of its chains. Since this proletariat has been brainwashed, it is incapable of action and is, perhaps, even reactionary. Hence it remains passive while the revolution takes place and can only stare in open-mouthed wonder at the destruction of the power structure that enslaves it.

In this scenario, the power of the media is shown as central and when it is put out of action, the rest is almost automatic. Interestingly enough, this message is not too far removed from the overt message of the Apple corporation—that access to user-friendly computers will prevent a totalitarian society from coming into being. Apple is a "revolutionary" force in the quasi-totalitarian world of hard-to-use computers where power will be held by those who know how to function in the information society. The Macintosh will prevent society from splitting into two groups—those who have access to computers and are part of the information society, and those who know nothing about computers and are condemned to menial or backward jobs forming a class of workers of low status and little economic power.

Apple is the blonde who will prevent a rigid information-based class system from evolving and, by implication, a totalitarian or totalitarian-like society. The Macintosh brings knowledge of good and evil to mankind and womankind, and all it takes is one bite (or is it *byte*, to use computer vernacular).

The Big Blue

It is not too far fetched to suggest that the totalitarian society shown in this commercial is a representation of IBM. Apple sees itself as a small, humanistic, open corporation battling a gigantic, super powerful and highly bureaucratic corporation, IBM. There are two possible readings to this analogy: in the first, the whole story is about IBM. The Big Brother figure is the corporate leadership and the inmates are the white-shirt-and-tie IBM workers who are controlled by IBM. IBM has a reputation for being rather strict about the way its workers and salespeople dress and this commercial may be alluding to the regimentation identified with IBM. The second reading suggests that IBM is the Big Brother and that the U.S. public represents the inmates, duped and controlled by IBM, but about to be liberated by Apple and its Macintosh computer.

The battle, then, is between the beautiful blonde heroine fighting against the monolithic monster bureaucratic corporation full of faceless nobodies mindlessly following rules and regulations, enslaving the multitudes. The Macintosh is the sledgehammer for Apple to throw at IBM—a user-friendly machine which will, democratically, make computing available to all. Apple is now trying to sell the Macintosh to businesspeople, where IBM seems to have a lock on the market. How well it will succeed is questionable since there is not a great deal of business software available yet for the Macintosh and Apple's "blonde" image may, in fact, work against it.

Conclusions

Although the 1984 commercial cost a great deal of money to produce (perhaps three or four times as much as a typical high-budget commercial) and air, due to the notoriety it attracted, it proved to be a worthwhile investment. We must remember that it only aired once—yet it was the subject of a great deal of media attention and it fascinated the huge audience that was watching the Superbowl, when it was shown. As someone in the creative department at Chiat/Day explained to me, "good campaigns end up being relatively inexpensive." A good commercial (and campaign) may cost a great deal to produce and air, but if its impact is sufficiently strong, on attention-per-thousand basis it might work out to be relatively inexpensive.

Chiat/Day (and Apple) took an unusual approach with this commercial. It was in the "un-Cola" genre and focused its attentions not on the benefits to be derived from using a Macintosh but, instead, on the dangers inherent in not using one. The commercial wasn't selling a specific product in a direct manner. Instead, it used indirection and suggestion to build an image for Apple and Macintosh and, at the same time, cast aspersions on its main rival, IBM. In the course of sixty-seconds it created a memorable microdrama (actually a standard commercial format) that worked subtly and indirectly. Like many commercials, it was highly compressed, with neither a beginning nor an ending. (Many commercials don't have a beginning but do feature the proverbial happy ending, with someone using the product or service advertised.)

The ending implied in the 1984 commercial focused on the avoidance of something hateful rather than the gaining of something desirable. In its own way, there is an element of conditioning involved here; we have a condensed form of aversion therapy. The argument, like the commercial, is very binary. If there are only two possibilities, Apple and IBM, and IBM (and all that it and its imitators stand for) is shown to be horrible, one is led to choose Apple. One acts not so much to gain pleasure (though the beautiful blonde attracts us) but to avert pain—Big Brother and the dystopian world (IBM) that he represents.

The 1984 commercial launched the Macintosh brilliantly. Apple continued to attack conformity in the business world in its 1985 commercial, which showed blindfolded businessmen jumping off a cliff, like lemmings. But this ad lacked the polish and aesthetic complexity found in 1984 and it was followed up by rather meagre event, the announcement of a few minor items in Apple's campaign to get businessmen to purchase Macintoshes for their offices.

Some think that Apple is now fighting for its life and that if it doesn't penetrate the business market, it will become a minor player in the computer-sales wars. Others argue that Apple's penetration of the school market and the individual or non-office market is so great that it will remain IBM's major competitor. Whatever the case, its 1984 commercial was successful and a fascinating and extremely rich text.

Bibliography

Barthes, Roland. *Mythologies*. New York: Hill & Wang, 1972.
Berger, Arthur Asa. *The TV-Guided American*. New York: Walker & Co., 1975.
Berger, Arthur Asa. *Television as an Instrument of Terror*. New Brunswick, New Jersey: Transaction Books, 1980.
Berger, Arthur Asa. *Signs in Contemporary Culture: An Introduction to Semiotics*. New York: Longman, Inc., 1984.
Berger, John. *Ways of Seeing*. New York: Penguin Books, 1977.
MuLuhan, Marshall. *The Mechanical Bride*. New York: Vanguard, 1941.

3

Television Ceremonial Events

Daniel Dayan and Elihu Katz

Think of a ritual event of limited scope or even with a pragmatic or technological achievement. An unemployed youth, Prince Charles, marries a kindergarten teacher, Lady Diana. An American missile, Apollo 11, lands on the surface of the moon. This particular event, despite its relative lack of importance, is now endorsed by a state apparatus. It is offered as a symbol. Its actors, its participants, are displayed as representatives of a society's most central values. A given happening is thus transformed into an official ceremony, and proposed as such to the public.

This public includes, first of all, the spectators who gather at the site of the event. London streets swarm with crowds trying to catch a glimpse of the royal procession. Beach life on the Florida seaside in interrupted. Glued to their transistor radios, swimmers peer into the skies in a futile attempt to watch the progress of the missile. By their presence these audiences validate the ceremony, give a first legitimization to the decision of the official bodies that organized it.

The ceremony, combining the original ritual or event, its endorsements by state authorities, and the crowds' response to this endorsement is now adopted by television which transcribes it into a framed text. This framed text, or spectacle, is itself adopted or endorsed by television audiences usually grouped or endorsed into ad hoc viewing communities. The televised text is attracted into a diaspora of home-based ceremonies which include those organized by foreign spectators in their homes. The simultaneous international broadcast which usually characterizes such events constitutes an additional level of endorsement: that of a national event—its public included—by foreign networks.

Major television events can be seen and read as texts, but what is particular about such texts is that they are simultaneously the traces or indexes of a process, the convergence of a whole concert of social gestures or performances. These performances are logically consecutive but temporally simultaneous and, as such, they dialogue with each other, comment upon each other. Each one of the specific performances could be described as an endorsement of the previous one. Each performance is, in a certain way, a response to, and an incorporation of, another performance, This chain of simultaneous adoptions, this multiplicity of endorsements, characterizes events usually associated with the modern forms of civil religion. Such events include England's royal wedding and the moon landing and also the pope's trip to Poland; Anwar El Sadat's visit to Jerusalem; the funerals of John Kennedy, Winston Churchill, and Lord Mountbatten; and the Olympic Games.

One of the effects of this chain of endorsements which is not chronological but simultaneous, is a feeling of spectatorial disorientation in front of a very complex and constantly reorganized architecture; an impossibility to sort out logical levels. We are confronted with a multiplicity of texts of the event, each of which spills out into the others, entertains a metonymic relationship with the others. We are confronted with a multiplicity of texts, each of which takes us further away from the realm of performance, and deeper into the realm of reaction. Instead of the firm, reassuring presence of cinema's enunciative machinery in our back, we are taken into an infinite traveling backward. This traveling backward reveals an interesting dimension of our television events: the space that they allow us to explore, the reality they allow us to experience is not only in front of us on the screen. It is also behind us or beside us. This space is not the space of performance, it is the space of reaction. The focus of the event is largely on its actors. It is also on its viewership. This raises a fundamental question. Are all audiences involved with the same event? Is their experience identical? Is it meant to be identical?

Simultaneous Transmission

We focus on two or three crucial moments in the chain of endorsements we have described: (1) the endorsement of the event by the on-the-spot audience; (2) the endorsements of the event by the national television networks, be they state television, public service television, or commercial networks; and (3) the endorsements of the event by networks representing other countries.

The passage from the on-the-spot audience to the national television audience, or primary television audience, has been described by among others anthropologist John MacAloon in his study of the Olympics as a passage from festival or ritual to pure spectacle. The intervention of television is so essential to the existence of national, statewide rituals that the original ceremony finds itself reduced to not much more than a prop, a structure yearning toward another structure. A structure profoundly influenced by its intermediary status, that of a protelevision show, that of a pretelevised event. The original ceremony is the raw material of a mass ritual performed by television and adequately perceived as such by the public massed on the event grounds, who implicitly recognize this as a fact and consequently behave as self-conscious, improvised actors. What about television audiences, both primary (national) and secondary (international)? For its primary audience, the televised event has a performative nature. It consists of a ceremonially conducted alteration or reinforcement of society's central values; it offers a rearticulation or reaffirmation of the consensus that holds it together. It consists of a symbolic manipulation of what Edward Shils calls its "center." Similar in some way to the discourse of Lévi-Straussian shamans, this symbolic manipulation, by addressing a society's root paradigms affects the audience by reformulating their existence in new ways, by situating it in different frames, or—as in the royal wedding—by refocusing attention on the continued importance of traditional frames.

Entering in a charismatic relationship with the ceremonial actor—with the political leader or with his symbolic representatives ranging from the young royal couple to the astronauts on the moon—a society accepts seeing its reality symbolically reformulated, endows the ceremonial actor with the right of uttering performative statements, gives by its attendance a felicitous character to those statements. The spectators who belong to the concerned society are not only spectators but witnesses, bearers of the experience and, individually, potentially propagators of this experience. This is not the case for secondary television audiences. For them the event is less of a ceremony since they are in some way the voyeurs of the ceremonies of others. For them the event seems much more of a spectacle. Their role as spectators also has to be qualified. In some way they are themselves called upon as witnesses. For the society that produces and originally broadcasts it, the ceremonial event has two functions; the ritual, a double vocation. Internally the event addresses this particular society's symbolic center and rearticulates or reaffirms its values. Externally the same event functions in what we would describe, almost in terms used by Erving Goffman, as a ceremonial self-presentation of a society to other societies in exceptional circumstances.

During the self-presentation the concerned society displays its norms as universal and displays itself as embodying these norms. Ceremonial occasions are used by political systems as instruments of propaganda or of ideological seduction. They are glorifications of states or nations seen during these rare moments when they exemplify the norms that they share with other societies. The spectacle offered is both that of the uniqueness of a given society and that of its conformity with shared standards or ideals.

Israel displays itself as welcoming Sadat in Jerusalem, as overcoming a heritage of violence in the Middle East. Communist Poland offers a triumphal reception to Pope John Paul II. Apollo astronauts plant an American flag on the moon but their conquest, to use their own words, is "a giant step for humanity." This is an American flag but those shapes on the moon are human bodies. The Olympic Games remarkably exemplify this duality in that they are profoundly rooted in the concept of nation—they are always to some extent the celebration of the host nation—but they are also proof of the commitment of this nation to the ethos of internationalism. This display of good will, this self-presentation, has to be acknowledged. Other peoples, other nations, must take notice of it. This is why we cannot see secondary audiences as mere spectators. They are also witnessing a ritual, a ritual formally similar to that watched by television primary audiences but semantically quite different. The British watch royalty. Foreigners watch England.

The fact of simultaneous retransmission leads to a built-in ambiguity, to a fundamental polysemy of the displayed ritual. Internally consensual and externally universalistic in ambition, our events claim at both levels to overcome conflict. This solemn burial of conflict is often rhetorical and many a virtuoso actor of such events uses the multiplicity of audiences to convey in the same breath messages that might be not only different but antagonistic. Thus John Paul II accepts the invitation of the Polish government whose religious policy he legitimizes in the eyes of the world, but once in Poland he dedicates his trip to Saint Stanislaus, whose martyrdom symbolizes to the primary audience the resistance of Polish Christians to repression when it is exercised by temporal rulers. Sadat in Jerusalem invokes for the sake of his primary audience the common heritage of the children of Abraham, but in so doing he uses a rhetoric which places him—to anyone familiar with Moslem Culture—in the paradigmatic position of Mohammed calling for the conversion of the Medina Jews. To the primary audience of the event, Sadat emerges as a new prophet of Israel. To his secondary audiences in the Arab world he reenacts an illustrious precedent: Sadat is not betraying the Arab cause but repeating the gesture of the prophet and warning that the Jews were doomed because of their stubborn refusal to accept the revealed truth.

Experienced actors on the stage of international television multiply gestures that are both theatrical and ambiguous, frame their own roles in simultaneous but distinct scripts, lend their physical existence to alternative and competitive fictions. These fictions are not fictions in the sense that they are unreal. They are not lies. They are constructions that provide actions or gestures with intelligibility. The raw material for these constructions belongs to culture. It is intertextual. The type of intelligibility called upon is narrative. Television ceremonies tend to acquire a narrative form, and the genius of political performers such as Sadat or John Paul II consists in anticipating the narrative fate of their gestures and in imposing both at the primary and at the secondary level their own version of the stories in which they are cast. Role taking on their part leads to an altercasting of their partners and to a distribution of personae, which ultimately results in coopting television networks as vehicles for their versions of the event. Substituting for the Israeli view that his visit to Jerusalem is merely the prelude to a negotiation to be held between closed doors, Sadat enlists the media on this side. His story is by far the best, if not the most conducive to an agreed settlement. Diplomacy in this instance is no longer a technique used to solve crises, but it displays itself as a crisis in progress. Ritual becomes a spectacle without losing its ritual value. Taking full advantage of the role played by television, Sadat translates action into acting, adopts an epic register, enters barehanded in the camp of the enemy.

We should now describe in better detail the specific role played by television in allowing not only mass participation, but mass participation on an international scale to such events. The main characteristic of television coverage seems to impose on ritual events, or on news events endowed with symbolic value, the aesthetics of narrative fiction. Fictionalization is only one of the characteristics we review.

Not Being There

Nobody ever saw a royal wedding or an Easter Mass from a blimp or from a fish-eye lens hanging from the ceiling of a cathedral. These images do not correspond to any previous experience, except possibly that conjured up by visionary writers such as Victor Hugo. Modern television spectators are offered new and unexpected ways of participating in the ritual experience, new aesthetic avenues, which no longer stem from the need of exorcising spectacle but from the decision of fully using its powers. Television provides its events with a narration, with a scenography and with a scenario. It displays in each case an inventiveness, which explains why so often spectators with direct access to the event would rather opt for watching it on their screens.

Television's commitment translates itself in the reverent tone of the narrator's voice. It affects the contents of the narration, leads to the use of elevated or ornamental language. The ordinary concise, terse, matter-of-fact style of the journalists opens itself to cosmic lyricism. It is "a beautiful October night" when Sadat lands in Jerusalem. A "magnificent summer day" enhances the celebration of the royal wedding. The arrival of John Paul II in America brightens the atmosphere, like a "sun coming out of the clouds." The informative prose of the commentators switches to celebratory poetry, but the new poets laureate usually content themselves with short-lived effusions. Narration is not simply an expressive tribute paid by television to the event; it is not simply a conspicuous consumption of lavish metaphors and descriptions. It plays an important part in laying the ground for spectatorial participation.

A public event has a table of contents which we must memorize, and it relies on a cultural repertoire with which we must become acquainted. Spectators are not expected to prepare themselves for the ceremony. Narrators offer them an introduction to its program, a description of its itinerary, a rehearsal of its highlights, a profile of its participants. Once it really starts the event repeats an already known pattern, fulfills a temporal expectation, unravels a melody that the viewers could already sing for themselves. This is also done in visual form. Before broadcasting live the ceremony during which John Paul II closes Saint Peter's monumental doors and thus concludes at Easter time the Holy Year, Italy's state television offers in grainy black and white a flashback on the same ceremony performed in 1975 by Pope Paul VI. This flashback transforms television spectators into instant connoisseurs. Such a connoisseurship allows better participation. In terms of spectacle, it echoes the familiar thriller technique of rehearsing within a give film its decisive suspense sequence in order that spectators anticipate all expected moves and react properly to the unexpected ones. In the domain of rituals, it points to the importance of tradition, to the fact that rituals must be repeated.

When rituals happen too infrequently for their components to be memorized, we need to stress their connection to tradition: to replace, so to speak, ritual experience by last minute initiation and knowledge about the ritual. Spectators are offered access to a dimension which direct audiences might increasingly be expected to feel deprived of: the sense of cultural continuity. Television narrators provide their viewers with a running exegesis, underlining what the event has to say about itself, reinfusing it with a cultural depth. When President Sadat is seen praying in Jerusalem's Al Aqsa mosque, they give us a brief lecture on the Moslem festival of Al Adha. When the pope visits Poland on Saint Stanislaus's day, the life of Saint Stanislaus is submitted to scrutiny. When the same pope leads the Easter Mass in Rome's Saint Peter's square, the Catholic tradition of concluding Holy Years in Rome-bound Easter pilgrimages is traced to its postmedieval origins and associated with such eminent pilgrims as Dante Alighieri or Giotto. Philologically-minded narrations become institutionalized. Files of erudite commentaries concerning various aspects of the ceremony are handed by the BBC services to foreign network narrators of the royal wedding. Television substitutes for tradition by proposing a crash course on the expected protocol, and by offering instant expertise as to the event's components. The pedagogic role means to insure a better participation, and it usually does so in the case of secondary audiences. It may defeat its own purpose when its obtrusive presence succeeds in distancing the event, in interrupting its flow, in holding back its primary spectators. Polish television's spectators of the papal Masses in Warsaw, Krakow, or Yasna-Gora are thus incensed at what they perceive as a deliberate attempt by narrators at breaking the spell of the event. Why—they ask—deliver a course on Catholic ritual to an audience known for its fervent piety? Polish television's exegesis is perceived as an intentional faux pas, as the deliberate projection of a museumlike frame on living faith. It is an ill-paced Brechtian exercise, one which consists in saying that "instead of identifying with the characters, the audience should be educated to be astonished at the circumstances under which they function." Whether justified or not, the anger of Polish spectators stresses an important characteristic of the media event genre. Narration must enhance participation. Pedagogically minded or not, it must remain unobtrusive, self-effacing. It must be heard but not noticed; flow with the event, never obstruct it. In this regard it situates itself at the exact opposite of Brecht's reliance on interruption, picketing onstage, and distancing songs.

The narrator's voice and what it tells are clearly defined as secondary to the event. The voice must be quiet, hushed. The statements are not only reverent, but brief and grammatically simple. They might have to be interrupted at any point. Visual continuity has clear precedence over that of narration. When an event is given media-event treatment, one can expect the editorial function to be performed inside the event and not by the narrator. The narrator provides clarifications, information, but its status is essentially that of a lubricant, its interventions: footnotes or in petto remarks. Most media events, if not all of them, are expressive occasions, forms of discourse. Most media events in both their verbal and nonverbal aspects are intended as acts of communication. Television communicators are expected to avoid superimposing their own message on those which constitute the event. The narrators' performance must frequently step aside in order to leave precedence to the communication acts within the event. When it fails to step aside, the producers' policy often consists in drowning it with the cheers and rumors of the crowd, and this, to the point of depriving the commentary of any intelligibility. The narration has not only to be ancillary to the event's performance, but it has to be so in almost an invisible manner. This invisibility extends to the very nature of the narrator's voice.

The narrator's voice is important by its tone, by its accent, by all in it which refers to a given generation or social group. This last, and apparently secondary feature, was given quite some prominence in what looked to foreigners like a hairsplitting exercise: that of justifying the existence of a double television broadcast of the royal wedding (on BBC and ITV) by pointing to the differences in the respective styles of narrators Alastair Burnett (on ITV) and Tom Fleming (on BBC). Both their narratives were reverent. Both echoed its main values. How, then, did they differ?

It was less, we were told, a question of attitude (slightly more journalistic in one case or slightly more celebrational in the other) than one of vocabulary, cadence, and tone of voice. Youngsters and members of groups less attached to establishment values seemed to find Tom Fleming's voice irritating, comical, or pretentious. They still were quite interested in attending the event on television. Distaste for Tom Fleming's voice was not synonymous with rejection of the royal wedding. Fleming's voice was cumbersome to them, in that by being alien to their own sociocultural values it stood between themselves and the event, prevented them from "flowing with it," making the event their own. It acted as a reminder of distance, preventing them from immersing themselves in the occasion. Alastair Burnett's alternative to Tom Fleming's performance was a means to augment the narrator's invisibility, to heighten audience participation in the ceremony.

Physically contained and culturally inconspicuous, the narrator's attitude actively proclaims a phatic definition of television's role. This attitude is remarkably matched by television's visual treatment of the event, a treatment that actively calls for spectatorial participation and simultaneously tries not to call attention to itself, to remain inconspicuous and unnoticed.

Fictionalizing the Event

The same public event may be treated as a ceremony by national networks or channels, and as news by those of other countries. The same public occasion is thus submitted to two different textual treatments. In one case, an ordinary treatment (news); in the other case an extraordinary treatment (ceremony). Opting for the news treatment flatly rejects the event's aim of being experienced as an occasion. News broadcasts distance the event, offer a cold look at its ideological claims, deny their spectators any possibility of "flowing with" the event. If the event is—as we think—a performative address, it is ironically nullified by being turned into a performative-in-the-third-person, a distant gesticulation. Even when the news broadcast adopts a sympathetic attitude toward the event, the latter's participatory features are lost. Some of these features come very close to those of fiction, especially when one considers the nature of the broadcast's temporal sequence and spatial continuity; the enunciative role imparted to the attendants; the compliance of principals with the implicit rule of never looking at the cameras; the tension established between these principals as symbols and the indexes which point toward their private feelings or emotions.

Temporally, media events treat a given occasion as a happening to be related in continuous manner. The syntagmatic coherence of the broadcast derives from the progression of the event itself, a characteristic of fiction made all the more salient by the fact that the event is broadcast live. This sequential progression is absent in the news where one generally finds what Christian Metz calls "descriptive syntagms." The same event in news is stripped of its temporal dimension; its images withdrawn from their sequences. They become no longer the event's substance but its illustrations or emblems, they are submitted to, and encased into, the continuity of the news speaker's discourse. In news, shots do not really need to entertain any clear spatial relationship to each other. A shot of the pope is followed by a close-up of a pilgrim in prayer. These two shots are enough to conjure up the event, to give us a flavor of what the occasion is about. They do not always tell us where is the pope and where is the pilgrim. Yet, news broadcasts include some of the huge aerial shots that characterize media events. These establishing shots propose a synoptic view of the situation. They convey a sense of grandeur, stressing the event's monumentality, but they have literally a distancing effect. Useful diagrams, maps in motion, they allow a cognitive approach of the event. They do not give access to its experienced space.

Media events allow their spectators to follow the event from within, to explore it, to vicariously become part of it. The event displays a space that the spectators are invited to inhabit through the mediation of the participants, to see through the eyes of those directly involved. What is seen on screen is presented as resulting less from directorial praxis than from the attention of a given character. Images depict the situations perceived by spectators in the text. These spectators may be performers momentarly turned audience. Menachem Begin, Ezer Weissmann, or Moshe Dayan intently listen to Sadat's speech in the Knesset. A composed Queen Elizabeth watches her son pronouncing the vows of marriage. But performers are rarely used as vantage points. Attendants are exactly in the position required to convert the shots selected by the director into expressions of their own attention. Such is the case with crowd members, or, at least, with those whose behavior is not openly incongruous, defiant, or scornful. The interest taken by these attendants in the performance is offered in reverse shots as the subjective justification of the shots that depict it. The attending crowds represent the media event's main enunciators. Renouncing any pretense to a phatic role, television's visual orchestration offers the spectators an indeniably mediated mode of participation. They watch a public event as they would a fiction film.

Television's enunciative team adapts itself to this transformation. It does so by downgrading the role of the studio, with its metacommunicative dramaturgy. It does so by erasing the presence of the main narrator: not only must his voice remain inconspicuous, but he himself is kept disembodied, invisible. It finally does so by reorganizing the visible personnel in function of the event's new status. Typically this personnel is transferred from its usual and assertive discursive position to a new one, imminent to the event. Thus Walter Cronkite, Barbara Walters, and John Chancellor are on Sadat's plane flying to Jerusalem. They have joined the principals, entered the event's prestigious cast, been turned into supporting actors. Thus the networks' special envoys, their reporters on location, more modestly become part of the crowd. Television's enunciative team no longer stands above and outside the event. They have been cast away in a variety of roles, swallowed by the event. They have become part of a story told in the rhetorics of classical cinema. We are only one step removed from a blossoming genre: films about television people, photographers, and journalists.

The transformation imposed on the usual format of television news is by no means total or irreversible. Events progress unevenly, are submitted to stylistic fluctuations, undergo crises during which—as well as in the beginnings and ends of broadcasts—news enunciation takes over. Fiction still serves as a model. The broadcast's intermittent ambition is to offer less a report on an event than the transcription of an experience: that of the attendants, journalists included. As in classical cinema, enunciating the event is not an activity which calls attention to itself. The story seems to tell itself without outside help: therefore, the inconspicuousness, the fluidity of editing; therefore the interdiction made to actors about looking directly toward the camera; the prohibition of a frontal mode of address.

Media-event principals and responding crowds avoid looking at the camera. If they do look at it, their glance is rapidly removed, the shot taken off the air. The pope in his trips, often keeps his eyes closed, absorbed in meditation. When he opens them, he fixes on the ground or the crowds. Similarly the attendant spectators keep their eyes on the principals or focus them on their inner thoughts. Very rarely—almost never in the case of the principals—does anyone's glance meet the camera. While acceptable in the context of the news, looking at the camera is now a misbehavior or a mistake. It must be corrected since it risks breaking the fictional spell by reminding spectators that they are watched but not seen, that the space they fictionally inhabit is out of reach.

The attempt to fictionalize the event also manifests itself through a characteristic inflection of the ceremonial domain. Ceremonies are based on the explicit invocation of myth and on the display of symbols. Media events, though stressing these symbols and providing a gloss on them, switch our attention to cues. Ceremonial performers assume hieratic personae. Television points to the person underneath the persona, to the tension television between one and the other. Sadat visits the Israeli memorial to the holocaust, Yad Vashem. Has he or hasn't he covered his head with a *kippa*, as required by Jewish etiquette? He is seen praying in a Jerusalem mosque. Why the sweat on his brow? Is Lady Diana nervous? Is the stare of John Paul II unusually blunt? Is Richard Nixon sick? Television treatment takes us away from the official gestures and into the feelings of those who perform them. Symbols become almost obtrusive, their lofty inertia an impediment to television's intimate diary of the participants' emotions. Ceremony is what the event is about, but ceremony stands in the way of fiction. There seems to be no recourse when the ceremony is a funeral and its silent hero no longer a person but only a persona; his existence exclusively that of a symbol. In such cases the fictionalization of the broadcast may seem an impossible task. Yet it is achieved. All it takes is a narrative readjustment. Jackie Kennedy is projected as the main figure of her husband's funeral. Her behavior and that of her children allow for affective identification; her struggle with or toward her imposed role points to the young woman underneath the black veils. To take another and striking example, Lord Mountbatten's funeral is narrated by no other than Lord Mountbatten himself. In an eerie effect, his voice hovers over the casket transporting his remains, reinfuses the uncertainties of life, its hesitations and accidents into the rigorous destiny assigned to him as a symbol. "I always wanted to be a sailor . . ." confides the old man's voice and the slow progress of his body toward the grave fades into a childhood dream, evokes the youthful, expectant mood of a *bildungsroman*. Ceremony is there, but respect of admiration for the old soldier are overwhelmed by the discovery of an unexpected intimacy, by feelings of identification and compassion. This fictionalization of public occasions suggests a remarkable affinity between the genre of media events and an earlier film genre, usually devoid of ceremonial ambitions: cinema-verité. Both genres are an attempt to cast within the framework of fiction situations which they have usually not created and over which they have minimal control. As opposed to actual fictional characters who are no more than emanations of the text which proposes them; voices that speak some of its aspect; projections in ventriloquist style of the authorial voice, the protagonists of media events and cinema verité exist outside the fictions which tentatively coopt them. To use Bakhtin's phrase, they are not the product of a "ventriloquation."

They only are made by the text's internal coherence to appear so. Producers endorse them, make them characters. The event rhetorically arranges itself as a fiction centered on them. They, themselves, might betray such fiction, repudiate their part in it and emit from its depths statements that contradict the mood in which they have been encased. This is particularly true of media events since they are broadcast live as opposed to cinema-verité where ulterior editing can easily bring back the rebellious performers within the limits of their assigned personae. This already takes us to another dimension of media events, one which has to do both with the domains of spectacle and praxis: acting.

Ceremony as Fiction

These remarks are based on a comparison between our lofty, highly celebrated television events and a relatively new genre, characteristically situated on the fringes of popular culture. Catering to a largely adolescent or post-adolescent public which it helps to address (in flamboyantly freakish displays) the difficult problem of identity, this genre, cult movies, is totally different from media events by the nature of the registers it invokes. It is characterized by a somewhat similar blur of the distinction between ceremonial performance and fictional text. With their midnight processions of costumed spectators, of look-alikes duplicating the main characters in the film; with the collective singing, dancing, miming by which their audiences greet the corresponding sequences displayed on screen, cult movies start as fictional texts but move toward the realm of performance and are turned into ceremonies. The uncertainty of the status of media events thus seems to be part of a larger and relatively coherent phenomenon. Ceremonies, among other performances, are turning into fictional texts, and these texts are consumed in an increasingly ceremonial fashion. We should stress the relevance of Victor Turner's description of liminality as a laboratory of forms. It is indeed through liminality, either in its subjunctive forms (media events), or in its carnivalesque forms (cult movies) that a new type of public event is entering our lives.

Public events have no fixed forms, and throughout history they have tended to adapt themselves to the dominant forms of publicness. Television, and media events in particular, present us with the discontinuous symptoms of a mutation. What could be called a "theatrical rhetorical order," an actual meeting of performers and public in such places as parliament houses, churches, convention halls—tends to disappear in favor of a new communicative regime based on the potential separation of performers and audiences, and on the seduction of narratives rather than the virtues of contact. This new mode of publicness culminates with television which transfers it to all areas of public life, but it clearly started with cinema, as Walter Benjamin was the first to point out. This is why we propose to call it "cinematographic." This rhetorical order is justifiably distrusted since its dynamics lead to substitute simulation for representation. Our era, as Jean Baudrillard pointed out after Benjamin, might have become that of simulacra, of images without originals, images whose effectiveness is not in the least impoverished by such a lack.

It is important not to condemn this new order globally. The problems raised during the Reagan presidential campaign of 1984 proved it hard for a journalist to engage in a conversation with a recording, or with a recording in process. When more direct channels are available, the cinematographic model of publicness tends to silence not only confrontation, but debate or dialogue as well; to eliminate the maieutic dimension of journalistic probing; to transform political analysts into perplexed semioticians, involuntary film critics. When we move to a much larger scale, media events stop being an impediment to communication. They become its only mean.

Bibliography

Baudrillard, Jean. "La Precession des Simulacres." *Le Simulacre*. Paris: Minuit, 1978.
Dayan, Daniel. "The Tutor Code of Classical Cinema." In Bill Nichols, ed. *Movies and Methods*. Berkeley, Calif.: University of California Press, 1976.
Gibson, William. "Network News: Elements of a Theory." *Social Text 3* (1980).
Metz, Christian, "La Grande Syntagmatique du Film Narratif." *Communications 8* Paris: Le Seuil, 1966.
Todorov, Tsvetan. *Le Principe Dialogigue*. Paris: Le Seuil, 1981.
Turner, Victor. "Process, System, and Symbol: A New Anthropological Synthesis." *Daedalus* (Summer 1977).

4

Huxley on Television

John H. Barnsley

Of the forty novels, essays, and short-story collections he published in his lifetime, only one of Aldous Huxley's (1894-1963) works will certainly be widely read, indeed probably with renewed interest, in the next century—his novel *Brave New World*. It was written between April and August 1931 at Sanary near Toulon and first published in 1932. Despite a mixed critical reception, it has proved to be, along with George Orwell's *1984*, one of the two classic dystopias of the twentieth century, sufficiently popular to be translated to the screen as an NBC "Novel for Television." Indeed, for a novel about the future, most of which fall rapidly into desuetude, the actual future has treated it in the most handsome manner possible: each decade that has passed since its publication has made it seem less fantastic and more plausible and realistic. Due to technical advances, and probably to a change in the *Zeitgeist*, the world of the novel was much more remote when one read it at school than it appears today.

Both Huxley and Orwell wrote their books in an *absit omen* spirit and both tried to depict, as they saw it, possible futures, in each case futures centering upon Britain, though only as an exemplar of a much more general, indeed worldwide, reality. (Indeed this homogenization of the world they imply provides one ground for criticism.) Thus Huxley wrote in his 1946 foreward to the novel: "[A] book about the future can interest us only if its prophecies look as though they might conceivably come true."

Both books are most fruitfully viewed against the times in which they were written. Thus Orwell projects, almost unchanged, the depression years of the 1930s and the wartime 1940s thirty-six years hence. To this he added a fundamental change in the polity, based on the experience of Stalin and Hitler, backed up with a few changes in technology. Huxley similarly, though less obviously, drew upon changes occurring in the 1920s—on which he was a wry and ironic commentator in some of his other novels, such as *Point Counter Point*—and projected them six hundred years into the future. On second thoughts, in his 1946 foreword, he narrowed this down to around a hundred years hence, taking us to about the year 2030. As we shall see, this latter is a realistic estimate, not of the actuality of *Brave New World*'s society, but of its possibility.

The 1920s were in many ways a transitional period for Western industrial societies. It was notably the era in which mass consumption came into its own. This was made possible, as Daniel Bell has commented, by revolutions in technology, particularly the application of electrical energy to household tasks (washing machines, refrigerators, vacuum cleaners, and the like), and by three social revolutions: mass production on an assembly line, pioneered by Henry Ford (and earlier by Eli Whitney), which made the cheap automobile possible; the development of marketing, which rationalized the art of identifying different kinds of buying groups and whetting consumer appetites; and the spread of installment buying, which, more than any other social device, broke down the old Protestant fear of debt and further fueled mass consumption.

These innovations gave people in the 1920s, especially the young, the sense of inhabiting, in Shakespeare's phrase, a "brave new world." There was a new stress, in purchases and behavior, on being "modern." There was a new awareness, which we retain, of the possibilities of technology. A spirit of antinomianism was abroad, as again in the 1960s. Initially this was war-induced, as also in the 1960s, but it was later fueled by the restless dynamics of mass consumption itself.

All these elements of the 1920s find their way into the universe of *Brave New World*, where they are duly extrapolated and satirized. The central spiritual metaphor of the book is the application of Henry Ford's mass-production assembly-line technique to the development of the human fetus, which is raised and chemically conditioned in a bottle (rather implausibly), carried along a laboratory production line and eventually "decanted," where it joins its prechosen caste group, from the élite Alphas to the illiterate Epsilons. The tone is lighter than Orwell's relentlessly grim dystopia, and there are several *jeux d' esprit* at the expense of Henry Ford in particular—such as the renaming of the calendar "A.F.," After Ford, the new age being dated from the introduction of "Our Ford's" Model-T, the communal celebration of "Ford's Day," and such popular adages as "Ford's in his flivver, all's well with the world." There is also some play with characters' names—there is a "Bernard Marx," a "Sarojini Engels," and a "Herbert Bakunin."

The main thrust of the book, however, is a critique, via satirical extrapolation, of modernism, of that constellation of features—economic, social, and technical—that were emergent in the 1920s. There are many aspects to this. There is the previously mentioned application of Ford's assembly-line methods to the fetus. There is the listing of new technologies of instant pleasure: the Feelies, "Vibro-vacuum massage machines." Synthetic Music machines, and the ever-present *soma* ("'Euphoric, narcotic, pleasantly hallucinant'"). There are the consumption-oriented adages taught in sleep—"Ending is better than mending." These sleep-taught maxims—"Everybody's happy now," "Civilisation is sterlization," "Was and will make me ill, I take a gramme [of soma] and only am"—are themselves small satirical cameos of advertising techniques, at once banal and hypnotic. And the point is made that, for instance, new children's games are disallowed unless it can be shown that they require at least as much apparatus as the most complicated of existing games. Further, the characters in the novel generally exhibit an existential, *carpe diem* emphasis, a focus on instant pleasure and novelty, which Huxley, with his practised eye, most probably saw as emergent qualities in the 1920s.

Huxley clearly felt that modernism, particularly as manifested in mass production and consumption, involved a change of values that was both fundamental and dubious. In a central passage Mustapha Mond, one of the ten World Controllers, observes: "Our Ford himself did a great deal to shift the emphasis from truth and beauty to comfort and happiness. Mass production demanded the shift. Universal happiness keeps the wheels turning; truth and beauty can't. . . . One can't have something for nothing. Happiness has got to be paid for."

But modernism as an ethos encompasses more than mass production. Take, for instance, buildings. Lewis Mumford, in particular, has taught us to see buildings, from cathedrals to tower-blocks, as expressions of belief and value, and Lord Clark once commented sensibly: "If I had to say which was telling the truth about society, a speech by the Minister of Housing, or the actual building put up in his time, I should believe the buildings." And here, in contrast to Orwell's decaying, depression-filled streets and apartments, *Brave New World* offers visible testament to the spirit of modernism in the form of pastel-colored skyscrapers. The "Park Lane Hospital for the Dying," for example, is described as "a sixty-story tower of primrose tiles."

The 1920s saw also, at least within the publicized *beau monde*, a loosening of sexual restrictions, which Huxley satirically extrapolates to the near-compulsory promiscuity of *Brave New World*. As he comments in his 1946 foreword: "As political and economic freedom diminishes, sexual freedom tends compensatingly to increase." In *1984* Orwell comes to the opposite conclusion. In that world sexual privation serves two functions: to discourage loyalties outside the Party's control and to transform the resulting frustration into "war-fever and leader-worship." This points to the basic difference between the two books. Huxley creates a world wherein happiness and individual "adjustment" is pursued at the expense of human freedom and the cognate values of creativity and individuality. In Orwell's thoroughgoing dystopia the values of both freedom and happiness are denied: the only goal is the Inner Party élite's pursuit of power for its own sake.

Huxley was also interested in certain then-modern forms of social thought, particularly conditioning theory. Pavlov's experiments with dogs were widely discussed in the 1920s and J.B. Watson published his *Behaviorism* during this period. *Brave New World* is replete with conditioning, pre- as well as post-natal. Oxygen deprivation is used to reduce the intelligence of lower-caste embryos. Embryonic rocket engineers are taught to associate spatial displacement with well-being. After birth, sleep-teaching induces the elementary codes of the society and for khaki-clad Deltas, for example, loud noises and electric shocks are applied at the State Conditioning Centre to give them an "instinctive" hatred of books and flowers—to keep them happy in factories, their future environment. Similarly, television serves, more realistically than Orwell's wholly politicized media, as an umbilicus to the world of consumption and a source of mindless, hypnotic distraction. Its hypnotic influence is such that the perithanatic patients at the Hospital for the Dying remain glued to it to the very end.

We may take Huxley's attention to conditioning as both satiric and admonitory. His world is a Skinnerian one pushed to absurdity. But the widespread efficacy of conditioning, despite the resolute faith of its adherents, is doubtful, and that of hypnopaedia appears to be nil. Interestingly, in his utopian novel *Island* Huxley puts conditioning to the benign use of making the gullible more autonomous; that is, less conditionable.

Even if this stress on conditioning is over-stated, *Brave New World* has still proved a prophetic book. It correctly foresees the arrival of television and contraceptives, though the latter are liable to be replaced in the relatively near future by an injected vaccine which would nullify the effect of a specific hormone (HCG—human chorionic gonadotropin) essential for reproduction. Immunization against pregnancy might then be chosen for up to five years.

Huxley's "test-tube babies"—the most famous feature of the book—still lie in the future, but research continues apace and, aptly enough, Britain is a leader in the field. The first test-tube fertilization occurred in late 1977 in Britain and led to the birth of Louise Brown on July 25, 1978. Other cases have occurred since, though the success rate seems only about ten percent. So far, production of young from oocytes fertilized *in vitro* has been reported for four mammalian species: the rabbit, mouse, rat, and human.

Meanwhile, research is being conducted into *in vitro* gestation, involving experiments with artificial wombs for hamsters, mice, and rabbits. The overriding problem is to supply adequate amounts of oxygenated blood to the growing fetus and to remove wastes from the amniotic bath surrounding it, functions normally handled by a mother's kidneys, liver, and bloodstream. We can, however, expect that this will be achieved, as least for some species, by the early decades of the twenty-first century. Applied to humans, it would of course confront ethical and religious objections. But it might eventually be conceded that such objections have a strong element of the irrational, and such a technique promises a considerable research payoff as well, of course, as establishing full equality of burdens between the sexes. The future will decide these issues, but, as it is, Huxley's once far-fetched vision is beginning to loom on the horizon. *Brave New World*'s "Bokanovsky's Process," a technique for producing identical twins, already has its analogue in the emergent technique of cloning: the first nuclear transplant in frogs' eggs took place in 1952 and the first cloning of mammals, three mice, was reported recently. Producing biologically identical individuals of a species has, again, considerable research potential.

Also futuristic, but subject to present-day research, is *Brave New World*'s prophecy of an end to aging: in the novel people retain their youthful appearance and abilities to around sixty, when they swiftly die. Though it is admitted that "*Soma* may make you lose a few years in time," Huxley's expectation of a life span of only sixty years now appears unnecessarily pessimistic (though it is interesting to speculate if people would trade prolonged youthfulness for a shorter life). As it is, a variety of anti-aging and life-extending chemicals are under active experimentation, and though no firm conclusions have yet emerged, it is quite likely that a successful solution will be announced by the early decades of the next century.

Huxley held the view (expressed in his 1946 foreword) that "It is only by means of the sciences of life that the quality of life can be radically changed." This is a contestable view, though the promise of the life sciences is considerably greater than he anticipated. This is perhaps particularly true of biotechnology, modest current examples of which include brewing, baking, and cheese-making. One of its promises is the introduction of man-made flora and fauna, of entirely new species of life. In fact, the first man-made bacterium—an organism for eating up oil spills—has already been patented, and we can expect new bacteria soon for the commercial production of insulin and, later on, other drugs. The promise here for plant life is considerable. Of the eighty thousand potentially edible plants on the earth, we cultivate only twenty extensively. Careful seed selection and cultivation of hybrids have increased the efficiency (food value, weather and disease resistance, soil adaptability, short growing period, etc.) of these much-consumed plants. This is the basis of the recently vaunted "Green Revolution." But an ultimate "Green Revolution" could be achieved it we could engineer entirely new species of plants directly for human or animal purposes. Again, we are thinking of the early decades of the twenty-first century for realization of this. But still in time for *Brave New World*.

Midway between the date of its writing and the revised date of its setting, *Brave New World* was adapted for television by NBC. Perhaps the most striking feature of this adaptation was that it did not shock. By contrast, Huxley's original work was, in the 1930s and after, considered remarkably *outré* and risqué, with its explicit concern with promiscuity and an end to marriage. The lack of shock value is less a testimony to the blandness of the television production—though there was some unnecessary blandness—than to the way times and our consciousness have changed. Huxley, in this and other works, was partly motivated by a desire *épater les bourgeois*. It takes more to shock them now.

The television version made some alterations and additions to the book. There were physical additions: for example, the fetuses were now raised in plastic bubbles—slightly more realistically than Huxley's decanting bottles—and fusion power and computers—developments outside Huxley's ken—entered the story. There was also a curious linguistic change: sexual relations were referred to exclusively by the euphemism "connecting." The futuristic décor, all in white and seemingly courtesy of NASA, served, in the attention given to it, to give the impression of a body of people living in a single enclosed place rather than a whole new society and to some degree served to deflect attention from the battle of ideas that was the heart of the book.

There were other changes, too: in the book, their energies drained by *soma*, people lived, albeit youthfully, only to around sixty. In the film their lives extended to eighty or ninety and Linda's exceptionally aged presence was glossed over. But in its search for future authenticity, the film surprisingly did not update the Contraceptive Belt in favor of periodic injections.

Silver replicas of the original Model-T occupied a central place on the set and were (though this is not in the book) subject to a diffuse worship by the denizens of *Brave New World*. But Huxley's central point was not clearly made: that the spirit of mass production—extended now to the fetus—involves a fundamental change of values. As Mustapha Mond points out, in a central speech egregiously omitted from the television version, mass production led to an emphasis on material happiness and "adjustment" at the expense of the Shakespearian virtues of truth and beauty and, in this society, of human freedom, itself arguably crucial for the creation and appreciation of truth and beauty.

To which the Savage, raised on Shakespeare, replies: "But I don't want comfort. I want God, I want poetry, I want real danger, I want freedom, I want goodness, I want sin. . . . I'm claiming the right to be unhappy." But the Savage's denunciation was muted on television, in part by his modish portrayal as a kind of latter-day hippie with literary leanings. He was insufficiently uneasy in the Brave New World, remembering that he had been socialized in an Amerindian reservation and had read only two books in his life. Yet his presence is central for the simple reason that, in a society in which everyone is adapted to his or her caste karma, *Brave New World*'s corruptions can only be exposed through an outsider.

Of course the Amerindian culture, with its primitivism and *Penitente* ferocity, is not itself an ideal society and so could not furnish the Savage with a truly constructive critique of *Brave New World*. This is a plot weakness of the book and Huxley decided (in his 1946 foreword) that he should have emerged from a much more utopian community, which, for him (as in *Island*), was a mixture of Eastern mysticism and Western utilitarian progressivism in a decentralized context.

Lacking this, the Savage had only Shakespeare's resonant humanism to rely upon for his denunciations. But by playing down the force of these criticisms—and the key internal critique of Mustapha Mond—the television version shied away from a serious attack on dominant trends—materialism and "adjustment" and the *carpe diem* focus—in American society and, alas, Western civilization generally.

This is a familiar story, with the demands of theatricality superseding the claims of ideas, including critical ideas, to be treated as intrinsically valuable. But although insufficiently incisive, the adaptation did not, like most television, descend into mere highly-colored hokum. It had a sense of integrity. It retained most of the original story and no doubt served the valuable function of leading many on to Huxley's original work.

5

Real Police on Television Supercops

Rita J. Simon and Fred Fejes

Concern about television police shows has been widely expressed. Critics have claimed that illegal and unconstitutional police methods have been presented as legitimate and laudable, with the potential political effect of making such conduct acceptable to the American public. A further question raised by such shows is their impact on the police themselves. Do they undermine the policeman's image of himself, the work he does, his relations with the public? Do the police believe the public to be influenced by the portrayals they see on the television screen? If so, how is that influence likely to manifest itself—in greater fearfulness on the part of the public toward the police, in greater disdain, or in high respect?

Through the cooperation of the Police Training Institute at the University of Illinois, we were able to question two types of respondents. The first were experienced police officers, returned to the Institute for brief refresher courses. The second were police trainees, men (and three women) who had never served on a police force but had passed the initial civil service examination and were deemed qualified for training. Of the 250 respondents, 119 were experienced officers and 131 were trainees. The different statuses of these two groups was a crucial distinguishing factor in their reactions to the manner in which police are portrayed on TV. The experienced officers were consistently more observant, more critical of the portrayals, and more negative about the effects of the portrayals on the public as well as on potential offenders and victims.

The only issue about which the experienced officers and the trainees agreed was that of shows they watch regularly. More of the respondents watch "Police Story" than any other show: 77 percent of the experienced officers and 73 percent of the trainees. It is by far the favorite show. Both groups agreed that "Police Story" offers the most accurate portrayal of the plain-clothesman and the uniformed cop. Respondents were provided with a list of 15 network or locally syndicated police programs shown on TV in the spring of 1977, and asked to indicate which they regularly watched.

Although all but one of these shows ("Barney Miller") have been dropped from network prime-time schedules, most have been syndicated and continue to be shown on local stations. "Barney Miller" was the show watched regularly by the second largest percentage. Three shows—"Starsky and Hutch", "Baretta", and "SWAT"—produced the greatest disagreement. A larger percentage of trainees than experienced officers reported watching these shows, whose common denominator is their portrayal of the police as supercops. More so than in most of the other TV cop shows, the heroes have an entrepreneurial style, a disregard and disdain for the formal hierarchy in which they are expected to operate, and a lot of machismo. When asked which show was their favorite, 48 percent of the entire group said "Police Story": 52 percent were experienced officers and 44 percent, trainees. There was no close second: 17 percent selected "Barney Miller" and 15 percent of the trainees selected "Starsky and Hutch" (as opposed to only 4 percent of the experienced officers). None of the other shows were chosen as the favorite by more than 6 percent of the respondents.

Forty-nine percent of the respondents thought "Police Story" provided the most accurate portrayal of police work. By "accurate" the respondents meant that it described the complexities of police work as well as the boredom, the noncriminal aspects of their job, and the personal sides of their lives. The shows that came closest after "Police Story" were "Barney Miller" and "Adam Twelve". The following quotes illustrate what the respondents mean by accurate and realistic portrayals:

> I especially like "Police Story" because they deal not only with what it's like on the street, but with what it's like about three feet into a cop's gut.
>
> "Barney Miller" is the only show that shows the police making a mistake and that much of our work is not glamorous.
>
> "Adam 12" and "Police Story" portray the officer as a human being suffering from marital, money, and drinking problems and all of the other problems that normal people face in their daily life.

The shows perceived as providing the least accurate portrayals were "Starsky and Hutch" (43 percent—50 percent of the experienced officers and 36 percent of the trainees) and "SWAT" (48 percent of all respondents). The specific characteristics they were referring to were the supercop image, excessive violence, inevitable apprehension of the criminal, and exclusion of the noncriminal aspects of police work. Typical observations from respondents included:

> They never portray the frustrations of developing a good case only to lose it in court.

The shows show too much violence. The facts are that in some high crime areas, the officers working those districts never shoot at anyone during the duration of their employment.

They rarely depict cops finding lost children or helping people. They don't show the calls we get from people to get the dog out of their yard.

More experienced officers than trainees commented on inaccurate TV portrayals. In response to the question, "Do you often notice what the police do on these shows and relate their actions to your own police training?", 57 percent of the experienced officers answered affirmatively compared to 41 percent of the trainees. Seventy-three percent of the officers as opposed to 58 percent of the trainees reported that they observed the police violating the law and police procedures on almost every show. The types of infractions mentioned most often were search and seizure violations (35 percent), excessive use of force in dealing with suspects (33 percent), violations of citizens' rights (29 percent), and procedural violations (20 percent). Of the respondents in both groups who reported regularly noticing violations, about half thought that the portrayals made these violations more acceptable to the public. Most of the other half thought that the public was unaffected by what they saw on the screen.

Trainees were asked if their instructors ever mentioned TV police shows and, if so, to briefly describe the context in which they were disussed. Fifty-five percent answered that the shows were discussed; most often to indicate "that's not the way it is out there and that's not what you are likely to experience." The instructors emphasized that police work is not as glamorous as it is portrayed on the tube. Occasionally parts of shows are rerun to illustrate types of behavior and roles that police officers should avoid. Lack of professionalism and failure to follow proper procedures were emphasized; specific behavior, such as shooting at moving vehicles when people are around, was deplored. The trainees indicated that quite often the discussion was carried out in a humorous vein. Many of the shows were depicted as portraying "the dream world of the policeman," and offering a distorted picture of "the honorable career of a police officer." Professor Christopher Flammang of the Police Training Institute believes the trainees are concerned about the image of the police that the public gains from these shows. He claims that the trainees assume the public cannot appreciate the distortions and stereotypes portrayed on the screen and that they feel their relations with the public will suffer as a result of the public's exposure to the TV cop.

Graduate students in both law and communications were shown the same TV shows about which the police respondents were being surveyed. Twelve shows were observed at least once by two students. These observers were trained to note violations of the following types.

- Issuance of search warrants without probable cause;
- Warrantless searches that are unreasonable;
- Searches that go beyond the scope of the warrant or probable cause;
- Planting of evidence and/or tampering with evidence;
- Illegal electronic eavesdropping;
- Illegal entry to acquire evidence;
- Arrests without probable cause;
- Generalized descriptions that are acted upon and result in arrest;
- Excessive force in effecting arrests;
- Excessive force in dealing with suspects;
- Excessive force in dealing with potential witnesses;
- Excessive force in dealing with informers;
- "No knock" entries, kicking in doors indiscriminately;
- Police circumvention of attorney-client relationship privileges, such as making it difficult for attorneys to locate, or speak privately with, clients;
- Coerced confessions;
- Confessions acquired through deception;
- Perjury by officers;
- Withholding of relevant information by officers;
- Unlawful use of deadly force, such as shooting into a crowd or without warning when chasing a suspect;
- Shooting at a suspect without warning and without identifying oneself as a police officer;
- Negligent driving of police vehicles;
- Failure to obey authoritative commands of superiors;
- Failure to abide by lawful court orders restraining police actions, such as surveillance, decoys;
- Ignoring of other offenses encountered in the course of police activity;
- Harrassment, such as surveillance that infringes upon basic freedoms like life, liberty, and pursuit of happiness;
- Police behavior designed to circumvent formal police procedures or basic constitutional guarantees, such as failure to inform suspects of the right to remain silent.

For each of these categories, the viewer was instructed to place a check mark indicating that the issue had arisen but there had been no violation (e.g., a search warrant had been issued because probable cause had been demonstrated to a judge's satisfaction), the issue had arisen and there had been a clear violation, or the issue had arisen and the observer felt that the behavior was vague or the situation not clearly defined.

The most frequently noted violation was negligent driving of police vehicles: of 55 clearly observed violations, 12 were noted in this category. The next most frequently observed violations were the use of excessive force in effecting arrests, dealing with suspects, and dealing with informers. There were 8 clearly observed violations in each of these categories. The other most frequently observed violations were police behavior designed to circumvent formal police procedures or basic constitutional guarantees—such as failure to inform the suspect of his right to remain silent, warrantless searches that are unreasonable, illegal entry to acquire evidence, "no knock" entries, and ignoring of other offenses encountered in the course of police activity.

A comparison of the number of violations observed for the three shows thought to provide the most accurate portrayals of police work ("Police Story", "Barney Miller", and "Adam 12"—altogether observed 16 times) with the three perceived as among the least accurate ("Starsky and Hutch", "Baretta", and "Delvecchio"—altogether observed 8 times) indicated the most accurate portrayals had 18 violations and the least accurate, 22 violations. The latter group were observed half the number of times. If negligent driving is not considered, the comparisons are 12 violations for the former group and 19 violations for the latter. Thus, the least accurate group of shows had over 50 percent more violations for half the number of observations. Illegal entries, excessive use of force, and police ignoring of other offenses encountered in the course of police activity were the categories most often checked by observers watching "Starsky and Hutch", "Baretta", and "Delvecchio".

Those police respondents who reported always noticing how police are portrayed on television were also more likely to believe that the violations serve to discourage respect for the law (68 percent) than were those who sometimes or rarely took note of police behavior on TV (52 percent).

When asked whether they thought TV portrayals of police interfere with or help the police when they have to deal with a complainant, a suspect, a victim, a witness, or an informer, the percentage who reported that such portrayals interfered with the police broke down as follows: 65 percent thought such portrayals interfered with the police in dealing with a complainant; 61 percent, with a suspect; 62 percent, with a victim; 54 percent, with a witness; and 45 percent, with an informer. In each category the experienced officers were more likely than the trainees to believe that the portrayals hindered the police in their contacts with such persons. To illustrate how they thought the portrayals interfered with the police in their dealing with complainants, they offered such observations as:

> They expect the police to do more than is legally possible.
>
> They expect miracles and we are just human.

Interference with suspects is characterized by such statements as:

> People often assert that they know their rights, but really they don't.
>
> Gets cocky—demands his rights.
>
> The suspect infers from TV certain standards of legal procedure that do not apply.

Interference with victims is described:

> They feel that the only case the police have to work on is theirs.
>
> We must always come up with an arrest.

On TV, witnesses often place themselves in danger. Such portrayals are seen as interfering with police work because:

> People get the idea that they will be rubbed out if they testify against someone.

Informers are often characterized as unsavory types. Such characterizations interfere with police work because:

> Informers on TV are low life who end up getting killed.
>
> The informer is usually the fall guy—it is too risky.

On the other hand, some respondents view the TV portrayals as helpful because:

> The informer thinks he is in the big time. He sees guys like himself getting money and protection.
>
> The snitch always looks good on TV.

To gain a summary reaction, respondents were asked to describe how they felt about the manner in which police are portrayed on TV shows. Seventy-four percent (77 percent of the experienced officers; 70 percent of the trainees) had negative reactions. The most frequent criticisms were that the police are portrayed as supercops, knights in shining armor—or as stumbling idiots subject to brainstorms on how to catch the bad guys; as always arguing with their boss and threatening to quit; as egotistical heroes using unlawful methods to make an arrest.

These findings about police discomfort with the supercop image and concern about the consequences of such an image match the results reported in Alan Arcuri's study of New Jersey police in *Social Action and the*

Law. Arcuri commented that "the great majority of police in the study—67 percent—report that these TV shows lead the public to expect too much from the police." He also cited a study conducted by the Superintendent of the Chicago Police Department, who commented that citizens, perhaps influenced by movies and TV, expect each and every crime to be successfully solved. In conclusion Arcuri noted:

> The crux of police criticism of these shows is that they "lead the public to expect too much." The glamour and excitement shown is too often the rule, when on the "streets," its the rare exception. Catching the crooks is, in like manner, grossly overplayed. In reality suspects may never get caught, and those that are apprehended probably never go to trial. The boredom and daily routine of police work is neglected. Instead, police are often portrayed as miracle workers. Police seem to resent the over-simplification and inaccurate picture of the criminal justice system. More specifically, they appear to recoil at the notion that justice is always done-in a 30 to 60 minute time frame.

It is apparent that the police have a negative view of the image TV projects of them. On the whole, they believe that the glamour, the excitement, and the heroics are detrimental to their work and their relations with the public. They are observant of and sensitive to the substantive and procedural violations they see enacted in the name of police work; they believe such portrayals have more negative than positive effects in their negotiating with suspects, witnesses, or victims. The show that is watched regularly, and is the favorite of most of the respondents, is the one that provides the most realistic—and that means the least glamorous, least heroic—view of their work, "Police Story." Such evaluations by real police suggest that the networks may not have to show the police walking on water or running through fire in order to maintain high audience ratings. It is worth noting that none of the trainees indicated that they were seriously influenced by their viewing of the TV cop shows, certainly not to the point that the shows were likely to deflect them from their plans to become police officers. These data are insufficient for speculation about the influence police shows might have in attracting some people to police work and deflecting others. Such an issue might be well worth future examination.

6

Cultural Bias in "M*A*S*H"

Roger L. Hofeldt

Anyone associated with television is familiar with the diatribes indicting the medium for perpetrating or even creating the ills of modern American society. While not to be taken lightly, such criticisms need to be placed into historical perspective. Newspapers, movies, and radio have all been subjected to the same abuse. Yet, television may be even more vulnerable to such attacks than any of its media forefathers due to the astonishing statistics testifying to its pervasiveness in American life. For example, with over 97 percent of American homes having at least one television set that is on an average of six hours per day, by the time a child reaches the age of 18, he or she will have spent an estimated 18,000 hours in front of the tube, as opposed to 11,000 hours in the classroom. Such numbers as these make television a perfect scapegoat for every pointed finger.

At the same time, the figures make it ludicrous to deny television's socializing powers over both children and adults. David Feldman, in the *Journal of Popular Culture*, even mentions "a dynamic relationship between the changing values of Americans and the content of television." The problem rests in determining the nature of that relationship. This issue has given birth to a still thriving controversy concerning biases in the medium which are being foisted upon the American people. Is television driving public opinion toward new moralities and liberal ideals in a never-ending campaign for change, thereby kindling uneasiness, even violence within its audience; or is it the conservative advocate of the American tradition, responding timidly and sluggishly to change engendered by technology and world affairs?

The argument has proven both dangerous and beneficial to American television. On the one hand, it has made the video airways susceptible to good, old-fashioned demagoguery, with criticisms often degenerating into nothing more than tirades about television's power over the unsuspecting viewer. On the other hand, a relatively new style of research has emerged that examines television in a manner long-reserved for literature, film, and the theater, thereby granting television its long-denied artistic stature and credibility. While the one side dwells on the aforementioned statistics and refers to the "medium" of television, the new critics are busily deciphering the recurrent themes, structures, values, and beliefs revealed by the individual program series.

Detractors of these humanist scholars often bemoan the subjectivity of the "data" supporting their conclusions, and they are quite right. Yet, none of the new critics has ever declared his views "The Final Word" on any program. Arthur Asa Berger, a leader in this field, comments in *The TV-Guided American* that such a shortcoming is due to the nature of the beast itself:

> Dealing with television is Sisyphusian—there is no end to it, for new programs are being born all the time, and just when you have pushed your stone to the top of the mountain, you find there is another one, taller than Everest, staring you in the face.

Obviously, this approach did not evolve to provide the definitive answer, if indeed there is one, to the question of television's biases and their influence on cultural change. Instead, by examining television on its own level—its program material—it is hoped that fresh insights will be born which will stimulate new thinking concerning the medium's relationship with its audience.

The successful CBS comedy series "M*A*S*H" provides excellent material for the study of television as a cultural force. It also proves particularly suited to the new criticism. Inspired by a successful feature film, "M*A*S*H" defies description, falling outside the traditional categories of "situation" and "domestic" comedies. Horace Newcomb, in *TV: The Most Popular Art*, comments that the program "has created a format and attitude of its own," and indeed, no other show has emerged to successfully imitate the "M*A*S*H" style. The formula combines the camaraderie of the acting company with an extremely talented team of writers, blending social comment with an inexhaustible supply of one-liners. With the program now in its sixth season, the formula has proven both flexible and durable.

The setting for "M*A*S*H"—an isolated army hospital in the Korean War—proves a natural for the "comment-comedy" of the program, as *Newsweek* magazine points out:

> The joke—which wasn't a joke to begin with, anyway, but a manifest irony: doctors sent to war to save lives, subversives in fatigues—has steadily gone deeper. Without ever moralizing, "M*A*S*H" is the most moral entertain-

ment on commercial television. It proposes craft against butchery, humor against despair, wit as a defense mechanism against the senseless enormity of the situation.

This surface level antiwar theme may fuel the fire of those who claim that an antiestablishment tone is sweeping the airwaves. For example, inferences run through some scripts that the United States, not North Korea, is the real enemy in the war. Real, old-fashioned patriots are often portrayed as idiots. What's more, infidelity seems to run unchecked throughout the "M*A*S*H" unit. It would, indeed, appear that some basic principles of American citizenship are being ridiculed.

But there is a second level of conflict and commentary actively running through "M*A*S*H". The key to understanding this program lies in apprehending the significance of the characters. Their individual essences and interplay create the "M*A*S*H" message. Not surprisingly, the message comforts rather than threatens the audience.

Unquestionably, Colonel Sherman Potter is the elder statesman of the "M*A*S*H" unit. Surrounded by the artifacts of his long military career and prone to recollection, he is "tradition" personified. As chief arbiter of disputes and counselor for troubled souls, this surrogate father provides the moral leadership for all those around him. Justifiably proud of his accomplishments and worthy of the respect he commands, he is, nevertheless, sensitive to the "changing of the guard," and tips a sympathetic ear to the emerging generation's ideas. He is, in effect, what every Amerian over the age of 50 is "supposed" to be.

Regarded by some to be the "hero" of "M*A*S*H", "Hawkeye" Pierce takes over the counseling responsibilities when Colonel Potter isn't around. His brash, confident manner is an inspiration to the unit, but he cannot adjust to the surroundings. He is a bitter idealist, and his customary cynicism around the camp betrays his frustration. Although he realizes war is a human creation, he cannot turn his back on humanity, as witnessed in an episode where he refused to go home because he was sorely needed at the base. This sense of duty and undying faith in the goodness of man is really Hawkeye's outstanding trait, making him one of television's chief spokesman for American optimism.

However, Hawkeye's idealism is quickly tempered by B.J. Hunnicut's realism. Although he too sees the insanity that surrounds them, B.J. maintains his equilibrium through roots in moral traditions. He is, for example, the devout young family man of the camp. In fact, the one time he does lose his grip on reality is when he falls victim to human weakness and has a one-night affair with a nurse. Predictably, Hawkeye comforts him by suggesting his infidelity was not an "evil" act. Yet, B.J.'s torment is never completely soothed, implying that his "guilt" will forever be with him. Together, B.J. and Hawkeye embody fraternity and teamwork in the face of adversity, as well as the moral conflicts suffered by all during periods of unrest and change.

Major Charles Emerson Winchester III resides in the same tent as B.J. and Hawkeye. Trumpeting his family name and upper-class heritage as though they were keys to respect and special privilege, Winchester is frequently rebuked by the others in the "M*A*S*H" unit, giving this character a historical significance. Americans are told that the early settlers of this country, as well as the immigrants of the following century, fled the aristocracies of the Old World which had grown repressive and insensitive to their needs. America became the great "melting pot," where all men could shape their destinies, supposedly free from the shackles of a rigid social structure. As a member of America's inevitable wealthy stratum, Winchester is a victim of this ideology. Indeed, his first lesson from Colonel Potter, that "neatness don't count in meatball surgery," rings with the same conviction as the Founding Fathers' declaration that "all men are created equal." Although incongruous with the selfless aura surrounding the camp, Major Winchester is expected to contribute like all the others, and contribute he does.

In contrast to the moral and political character of the four surgeons, Radar O'Reilly personifies an institution of American society: Youth and its presumed innocence. Relying on his boyhood teddy bear for security, Radar admires the tradition and authority of Colonel Potter, while bashfully idolizing the irreverence of B.J. and Hawkeye. It's a role-model search common to all adolescents. In addition, his ability to "read minds" is a trait commonly ascribed to youth, as is his stammering shyness around women.

Another institution, religion, is embodied in Father Mulcahey. While some would criticize the "M*A*S*H" treatment of Mulcahey as a timid bumbler, made light of but always respected by the others, there are important reasons for such a characterization. On the one hand, religion and warfare present something of a contradiction. But on a larger level, Americans have always had a difficult time properly placing religion in their lives. They are told to achieve in a materialistic society, but to also worship a Deity that represents love and charity. And recently, the religious institution in America has, indeed, been having its problems. In trying to meet the rapidly changing needs of the population, most denominations have undergone radical secularization. Father Mulcahey's groping for a solid foothold around the hospital base reflects the real-life institution's search for a new identity.

Major Margaret Hoolihan is a natural representative for the American woman. Her struggle to balance haughty assertiveness with an unwillingness to sacrifice her femininity is a common crisis of decision facing modern women. Significantly, she is the "Chief Nurse" and *not* a surgeon. And while the doctors respect her for her expertise, *they* are still the ones who save lives. Occassionally she can be seen comforting the patients, who are usually just homesick boys. What's more, this past year, she even married a strong, masculine lieutenant. The institution of American womanhood remains safe and secure.

Meanwhile, dressed in feminine splendor, Corporal Klinger assumes the role of another American tradition. This nation has long been proud of its reputation for providing a free and open forum for dissent. Klinger's perpetual transvestitism in his quest for a "section eight" discharge salutes the esprit de corps of America's historic crusaders. When organized, their "never-say-die" efforts have brought much progressive change to American society. Individually, however, as in the case of Klinger, they are rarely taken seriously. Instead, their views are simply acknowledged and they are accepted as part of the mainstream of American society—except, of course, by those outsiders who neither accept nor understand this American tradition.

In total, then, what is the "M*A*S*H" message? Newcomb suggests that a "family structure exists," and some elements of that structure do, indeed, appear. But, according to Louis A. Markham, what actually emerges is an entire "community in microcosm,"; of perhaps even more accurately, a microcosm of American society itself. All of the elements are there, embodied by the characters. While there are those who might see Hawkeye's optimism disturbingly "liberal," it must be seen as only one aspect of the whole social structure presented by "M*A*S*H" and not as its chief element. The program does, indeed, offer a good dose of controversy, but its structure does not advocate change. Instead, the society portrayed mirrors America as it is today, or for that matter, America at any point in its history.

War is an unnatural situation. But America's first 200 years have been riddled with equally unsettling events. Two wars for independence, western expansion, the industrial age, the Civil War, two World Wars, the Depression, the Cold War, the atomic age, space exploration, civil rights, computer technology, energy crises, and other far-reaching events have all served to shape America's present by clouding its future. Consequently, America has never had the time to find a solid niche for itself in the cosmos. Instead, it has come to believe it is "God's chosen land," progressive leader of the world. But that "progress" appears to be leading to a dead end—a contradiction as difficult to reconcile as the idea of a hospital in the midst of war.

Yet, the "M*A*S*H" society pushes on, relying on traditional institutions and values. The human compassion of Hawkeye and B.J., the youthful exhuberance of Radar, and the steady hand of Colonel Potter, just to name a few, all carry the "M*A*S*H" team through week after week of crises. Thus, the program suggests that its values and institutions are still viable, even in the face of ugly circumstances, wherever the "American mission" may lead. As such the show is a bulwark against change and social criticism. Although "M*A*S*H" may put America's traditions to a severe test, in the end they ultimately survive. The emphasis is on stability. The tone is one of confidence.

This is certainly nor to suggest that "M*A*S*H" was designed to be a propaganda vehicle, not to recognize it as television par excellence. The dramatic sophistication of "M*A*S*H" may be applauded by those who scorn the current wave of pop comedy ("Happy Days," "Laverne and Shirley," "On Our Own," etc.), but the essence of the two styles is really one and the same. It is the single thread running through all continuing dramatic television series. Every series faces the task of audience reassurance by resolving issues or complications which in some way touch the lives of as many viewers as possible. These problems must be set in a framework familiar to the audience and resolved in a manner consistent with American cultural traditions.

All of the long-running (five years or more) television series have met these requirements. The crises have ranged from the comic predicaments of "Lucy" to the moral questions raised is such programs as "Gunsmoke" and "Ben Casey." Typically, the complications have been couched in some sort of "family" structure, such as Newcomb described for "M*A*S*H". Such a setting appears not only in the domestic comedies of the "Father Knows Best" genre, but also in such violent adventure series as "Hawaii Five-O," where "superfather" Steve McGarrett provides the moral leadership for all Hawaiians. Traditionally the central unit of American society, the "family" format is a common reference point for the audience and a natural arena for problem solving.

Series which fall short of meeting these prerequisites invariably fail to stand the test of time. A good case in point is the CBS comedy "Rhoda." During Rhoda's marriage with Joe Gerrard, the series was a smashing success. The setting was domestic, providing that familiar environment for the audience. But after Rhoda and Joe were divorced, the show became less concerned with "family" matters and concentrated more on the cynical reactions of this single Jewish girl to the eccentricities of living in New York City. With such a framework, the program lost its common denominator with the viewers. The ratings plummeted, and the series would undoubtably have been cancelled had not the CBS network had such a disastrous ratings year.

Meanwhile, "M*A*S*H" has survived through six grueling television seasons, always among the top ten, and seems destined for several more. By using the characters to create a replica of American society, the producers of "M*A*S*H" have discovered another format for examining issues which are relevant to a vast and highly differentiated audience. Indeed, the formula has proven to be even more flexible than the "family" structure. Where one conflict per program used to be the rule, most "M*A*S*H" episodes feature two or more storylines running simultaneously. What's more, the design virtually assures that each question will be resolved in a manner consistent with the audience's cultural heritage. With dissonance avoided, the program becomes very reassuring indeed.

Hopefully, this critical exercise will be typical of a new wave of serious television analysis, carried to as many series of each new TV season, by as many different critics as possible. Richard Adler of the Aspen Institute Program on Communications and Society delineates the challenge:

> If this country has a unifying culture, it is the mass, popular culture; and today, television is the most vital expression of that culture. We need television criticism which will provide both a language for describing what appears on the screen and standards for discriminating excellence from mediocrity.

As stated earlier, such a language has long been a part of the other arts. Why not television as well?

Each year the public clamours for greater government control over television's "excesses" (violence, sex, etc.). But such "watchdog" techniques will only serve to choke-off the cultural artifacts of the television product, removing it from the realm of "art," bringing it closer to that of social control. As Adler suggests, one cannot legislate standards for "excellence" and "mediocrity." Given that television programs are produced for public consumption, those standards will only be realized via an increasingly discriminating public eye.

Bibliography

Berger, Arthur Asa. *The TV-Guided American*, New York: Walker and Co., 1976.
Cater, Douglas, ed. *Television as a Cultural Force*. New York: Praeger Publishers, 1976.
Cater, Douglas, and Adler, Richard, eds. *Television as a Social Force: New Approaches to TV Criticism*. New York: Praeger Publishers, 1975.
Newcomb, Horace. *TV: The Most Popular Art*. New York: Anchor Press, 1974.
Newcomb, Horace, ed. *Television: The Critical View*. New York: Oxford University Press, 1976.

7

The Politics of "Lou Grant"

Michael Schudson

"Lou Grant" began its third season this fall, a third round at providing "quality television." Always a critical success, the program has attained an enviable position in the ratings as well. It is avidly followed not only by the general public but by print journalists themselves, who seem to be pleased with TV's rendering of their world. A small-town editor in South Dakota even insists that that he picks up editorial strategies from the program.

One "Lou Grant" episode drew fire over the summer from the American Health Care Association, a nursing home federation, which attacked the "distortions and lies" in an episode that dealt with nursing homes. While the AHCA persuaded Kellogg's, Oscar Mayer, and Prudential to withdraw their sponsorship of the August 27 rerun of the nursing home segment, the American Association of Retired Persons and the National Retired Teachers Association urged people to tune in, and newspapers editorialized in defense of "Lou Grant".

Such public response raises unusual questions for a television series. What is its political perspective? Does it have one? Or does it, like most television handling political topics, check and balance every strong statement and neutralize any political impact? Is the program, like the character of Lou Grant himself, more nice than strong—or is there a strength in being nice?

"Lou Grant" does take a political stance. A show on Vietnam veterans left no doubt that they have been badly treated by society and by inadequate federal provisions. The nursing home episode left no doubt that nursing home regulation is inadequate, that at least some nursing home operators are heartless, and that American society has badly neglected the elderly. On many issues, "Lou Grant" takes a liberal, reforming stand.

There is a hitch in that stand, however. It has to do with the distinction C. Wright Mills made between "private troubles" and "public issues." Troubles, Mills wrote, have to do with the self and the limited areas of social life of which an individual is directly aware. The resolution of troubles, then, lies "within the individual as a biographical entity and within the scope of his immediate milieu." Issues, in contrast, concern matters transcending local environments and passing beyond the range of an individual's inner life. They concern the "larger structure of social and historical life." The task of what Mills called "the sociological imagination" is to understand the connections of private troubles and public issues, to see personal problems in relationship to social structure.

"Lou Grant" tries to do exactly that, to show how large structural issues impinge on personal troubles. In one program the staff photographer, Animal, takes a number of unnecessary risks on the job. Reporters Billy and Rossi worry about him. With Lou Grant, they discover that Animal is a Vietnam verteran and that the widow of one of his war buddies has been plagueing him recently, accusing him of responsibility for the buddy's death. Meanwhile, in a subplot, Lou meets a young black veteran named Sutton. Sutton wants to, but cannot, find work. Impressed with Sutton, Lou gets him an appointment with the *Tribune*'s personnel manager. The personnel manager turns Sutton down, rather brusquely, because of his "bad paper" (discharge papers). When Lou finds out, he is furious and goes over the personnel manager's head to get Sutton hired. At the same time, Lou is counseling Animal to face up to the widow who keeps calling him and making accusations, while Billy and Rossi pursue a newspaper series on veterans. At the end of the show, Animal makes a reconciliation with the widow, Sutton—who does not know there is now a job waiting for him at the *Tribune*—disappears.

At the end of the program, a personal issue involving a regular on the show, Animal, has been fully resolved. The larger problem of dealing with the difficulties of Vietnam veterans, as represented by Sutton, is unresolved. In both cases, the connection between private troubles and public issues is drawn, and this is the notable advance that "Lou Grant" makes on most other television programs (including some of the news programs).

"Lou Grant" has another message, a much less happy one. The second message is that while private troubles and public issues are related, one has control over the troubles and little leverage with the issues.

An episode concerning illegal immigrants from Mexico highlights this. Rosa Ortega is an illegal immigrant working as a waitress in a restaurant where the *Tribune* staff regularly has lunch. While Lou and Rossi are eating one day, the immigration service raids the restaurant and Rosa is deported. The *Tribune* folks are worried about her two children. When they inquire after them in the Chicano community, they are rebuffed by Rosa's friends, who fear they work for immigration. However, the two children get lost and Rosa's sister comes to Billy for help. In the meantime, the *Tribune* begins work on a series about illegals. The television audience learns a lot about them—from their percentage in the total U.S. population to arguments for and against the notion that they take jobs away from Americans. Rossi goes on border patrol with immigration. With a patrol officer, he finds a woman dead, suffocated when a truck full of illegals was abandoned by smugglers with the illegals locked inside. At first, Rossi thought the woman was Rosa, and he was deeply shaken. Even when, at the end of the episode, Rosa has returned and her boys have been found, Rossi is unmoved by the good news. The image of the dead woman is still with him.

Again, the personal problem has been happily resolved. The larger issue of illegal immigrants is anything but resolved, and its lack of resolution is made abundantly clear to the viewer. Again, luck and the caring concern of the folks in the city room manage a private trouble and, again, their best intentions prove insufficient to control the larger disasters associated with the public issue.

An episode about a dictatorship in the mythical Latin country of "Malagua" follows the same logic. The personal trouble, in this case, is that of managing editor Charlie Hume, who confronts the dictator's wife on her visit to California and makes a scene which embarrasses publisher Mrs. Pynchon. Why did he do this? Because we, learn, Charlie had once been imprisoned and tortured in Malagua for five weeks, but never wrote about it. This private trouble is resolved: Charlie finally writes his story and the *Tribune* prints it, even though it is old news. Charlie and his colleagues are happy that they have stood up for human rights. Meanwhile, the implication is obvious that people continue to be tortured and killed in a Latin American dictatorship while prominent North Americans like Mrs. Pynchon wine and dine the dictators. The program leaves no doubt where it stands on Mrs. Pynchon's behavior. But what can be done about this larger question of dictatorship and torture? The dictator's wife is confronted in Mrs. Pynchon's office by Malaguan students, including her own nephew, who oppose her husband. The ending is ambiguous—we do not know how much she has been affected by this meeting and certainly do not know if she will be able to use her influence even if she wants to when she returns home.

This interpretation of "Lou Grant" is supported by an episode in which the situation seems to be inverted. The show begins with Rossi, his childhood friend Sam, and Sam's fiancée Carol walking through a tourist "Wild West" town. Sam, it turns out, works at a nuclear power plant; though a firm believer in nuclear energy, he is appalled at the poor safety conditions at the plant. He tries to get evidence on the safety violations for the *Tribune*. He is killed in an automobile "accident" on his way to give the materials to Rossi, obviously a fictional translation of the actual case of Karen Silkwood. So here the private trouble appears to end quickly and unhappily—the friend is dead. But by the show's end, a private trouble does get resolved for, in a fashion, the friend returns to life to help resolve it. Rossi needs to get a story to be faithful to Sam and to justify Sam's sacrifice for the *Tribune*. But Rossi keeps striking out until, in the last minute of the show, he is saved by Sam himself. An extra copy of all the materials Sam had gathered appears in Rossi's mail. Rossi's personal trouble is resolved—he will have his story and he will have kept faith with Sam. Indeed, in this last minute we see Sam keeping faith with Rossi. At the same time, while friendship triumphs over death itself, there is no suggestion that the larger issues of nuclear energy will be resolved or even greatly illuminated by Rossi's efforts.

Not every "Lou Grant" episode follows this formula. Many of the episodes focus first of all on an issue of journalism, not a topic covered by journalists. The episode "Murder" does not explore violence in black ghettos but concerns, instead, the strong tendency of the press to ignore murders among minorities. Billy raises one side of the question: why do we fail to report on blacks who are murdered while vain old rich women who defend themselves against burglars with a golf club (the story Rossi was covering) are splashed all over the page? Lou sympathizes but takes the city editor's stand: if you can make interesting the violent death of an anonymous black woman by an unidentified man where we have no clues and no witnesses, then we will run it, and not before. The issue is resolved—Billy humanizes the story, helps catch the murderer in the process, and her story displaces Rossi's follow-up page on the nine-iron-swinging woman. Still, while this episode does tie things up neatly at the end, there is no pretense that the *Tribune's* policy has been altered or that the problems of journalism have been, in the larger sense, resolved.

"The art of writing popular entertainment," critic Robert Sklar has written, "is to create a structure that the casual viewer will accept as serious even while the serious themes are carefully balanced and hedged." He concludes that on "Lou Grant," as on other programs, the result is "an intellectual muddle." But this is not the case. On "Lou Grant," serious themes are frequently well presented. Occasionally the show feels like an adult "Sesame Street," with informative lessons in current events being rescued from documentary dreariness by a modest plotline and a familiar cast of attractive characters. The question is not one of balancing and hedging. The political failure is one that shows well-meaning liberals ultimately helpless to affect large social problems even while they battle effectively with private troubles. I think that is a failure. But the failure of "Lou Grant" is also the failure of American journalism and American liberalism. It is not intellectually muddled but presents our intellectually muddles to us. And that is no small success.

8

Sagan's Metaphysical Parable

David Paul Rebovich

Viewers of public television awaited Carl Sagan's 13-part "Cosmos" with skeptical anticipation. Sagan is another of today's increasingly less anomalous figures—a serious intellectual who finds a need to speak to, or about, the less serious. A Norman Mailer who writes about Marilyn Monroe represents the artistic prerogative turned tedious. A Carl Sagan who kibitzes with Johnny Carson represents the scientist as entertainer, subject to charges of sophistry. Waiting for "Cosmos," one could not help but wonder if Sagan would become the Ed Sullivan of astronomy or, at best, the Jacques Cousteau of the stars.

But "Cosmos" and Sagan did not disappoint viewers' desires for a serious discussion of science and astronomy from a person so qualified to offer one. Indeed, a fair criticism of "Cosmos" is that the scientific material presented—the theory of relativity, the lives of the stars, the conjecture of a fourth dimension—was too difficult for television discussion. Nonetheless, Sagan's skill as a teacher, as someone able to make the complex understandable, was always evident. It is doubtful that viewers could learn more about science in 13 hours than they did from "Cosmos." This is the triumph of the series, and Sagan's performance is far superior to the travelogue narrations of many science-nature shows. Instead, Sagan is reminiscent of the wise and magnanimous "father of Salomon's House" in Bacon's *New Atlantis* who proclaims that the goal of science is "the knowledge of causes and secret motions of things, and the enlarging of the bounds of human empire, to the effecting of all things possible." Like Bacon's scientist, Sagan recognizes the need "to publish it (science) for the good of all nations," for the good of mankind.

While "Cosmos" succeeds where other programs have failed or bored, Sagan's own ambitions exceed those of the conventional teacher of science, the conveyor of facts and method. Sagan seeks to make science not only understandable, but also popular. For the latter task, television is a convenient means, and cynics may see "Cosmos" as a spectacular commercial for

NASA or the "thinking person's" antidote to the banalities of network programming. Indeed, political intention—Sagan laments America's paltry space budget—and a certain intellectual arrogance do underlie the series, but the pervading tone is an optimistic populism. Sagan states that the "Cosmos" project

> is dedicated to the proposition that the public is far more intelligent than it has been given credit for; that the deepest scientific questions on the nature and origins of the world excite the interests and passions of enormous numbers of people . . . that an enormous global interest exists in the exploration of the planets and in many kindred scientific topics—the origins of life on earth, and the cosmos, the search for extraterrestrial intelligence, our connection with the universe. And I was certain that this interest could be excited through the most powerful medium, television.

This populism suggests a public receptivity to discussion of the wonders of the universe and the possibilities of science. But while Sagan's erudition flatters his audience—little did we know we could learn so much—the "Cosmos" series is actually predicated on a pessimistic appraisal of public understanding of the ways of nature and public commitment to modern science. Sagan says

> We have grown distant from the cosmos. . . . But science has found not only that the universe has a reeling grandeur, not only that it is accessible to human understanding, but also that we are, in a very real and profound sense, a part of the cosmos, born from it, our fate deeply connected with it. The most basic human events and the most trivial trace back to the universe and its origins . . . ["Cosmos"] is devoted to the exploration of that cosmic perspective.

More accurately, the series represents Sagan's effort to explain the perspective of the universe provided by modern science. If we have grown distant from the cosmos, it is because we have strayed from science and what it can tell us about nature and man. Sagan is concerned but undaunted. Behind public confusion about what science means and public doubt about what it promises, Sagan sees a potentially receptive audience. He realizes that overcoming public confusion and doubt requires something more than an updated account of what scientists "know" and can "do." To make science popular and an object of public commitment, Sagan sees the need to present the cosmology of science, the way science "understands" the universe and the meaning of that understanding for the human condition.

This judgment assumes an audience reared on, but weary of, the scientific and cultural musings of Jacob Bronowski who, like Loren Eiseley and Arthur Koestler, advocated pursuit of a science which would presumably offer the citizenry both material abundance and substantive excellence. For these spokespersons, a science based on superior reason provides physical liberation and encourages a certain liberality of the mind, a tolerant spirit consistent with principles and ideals like free speech and thought and human progress. But over the last two decades, this optimism about science waned, just as other social beliefs and authorities were questioned. Not only did it appear that science had not realized its intellectual and material promises, it began to lose its identity as an independent cultural activity and was labeled a malevolent tool of big business, the government, and the military. The science of liberation became, instead, the means to control, destroy, and replace man and nature, while breeding a mathematical and bureaucratic cultural conformity.

Even the more recent public concern with ecology did not provide science with dramatically renewed prestige. Ecology and, more specifically, environmentalism appear to be sciences of maintenance rather than progress. They bespeak self-restraint and conservation, prices to pay for an earlier aggressive, truncated, and overly optimistic attempt to conquer nature. Caught in a web of broader anti-establishment trends, scientists abjured their familiar self-confidence about progress and, like the environmentalists, advocated careful reconstructive surgery for a damaged world.

Ironically, this cultural re-evaluation, with its contingent confusion, provided an opening for a progressive science to become once again a topic of popular interest and discussion. In a society confronting a questionable present, seemingly unamenable to conventional political and ideological solutions, the nostalgic escapism of an optimistic science-fiction provided a modicum of relief. Americans were entertained by prognoses of mysterious and exciting futures, of new challenges of the universe and, most of all, projected technological solutions. Oddly, the public flirtation with the occult served a similar end. Occult studies, while indicating public dissatisfaction with contemporary culture and values, possess an optimistic component and were, in a curious way, the repository for an idealism often associated with science. Popular occultists seemed to be saying that if man could only obtain those "secret truths," things would be better. Self-proclaimed promoters of the scientific enterprise saw this fascination with space exploration and the secret mysteries of nature as providing an opportunity for them to make their claims for science, albeit in more flamboyant, less serious, terms than before.

Erich Von Daniken, less a scientist and more a propagandist for space exploration, made his immensely popular argument that earth's civilizations were founded by extraterrestrial beings. This "fact," according to Von Daniken, suggests that earthlings have misunderstood their identity and destiny and have overemphasized the significance of traditional terrestrial achievement, institutions, and belief. Man's extraterrestrial roots, in scientifically superior beings, entail for him a determined pursuit of science, particularly space exploration, and a diminution of concern for traditional civilization, its intellectual debilitations and conflicts. Science is king; religion, philosophy, and politics are products of our foolishness.

Scientists were humored. Von Daniken's "data" were the product of a crazed exegesis of archeological artifacts; but people read his books, most notably *Chariots of the Gods*, and watched the endless television documentaries. Although scientists enjoyed the publicity for science and astronomy, Von Daniken was making a mockery of the substance of science and the scientific method itself. Just as damaging, he was coopting one of real science's most compelling claims—that knowledge would be advanced and human progress assured by space exploration. Von Daniken's popular and unserious argument required a serious response. However, the serious promoter of the scientific enterprise would have to do more than debunk or clarify the claims of scientific speculators; to be both significant and successful, he would have to respond to the frequently expressed criticisms of science and technology previously ignored by science's supporters.

Sagan seeks to make these responses in "Cosmos." A substantial portion of the series is devoted to distinguishing the methodology and findings of real science from magic, religion, and other forms of speculation. Sagan skillfully presents the mysteries of the universe and shows science's ability to explain them. But presentation of scientific insight into the workings of nature does not necessarily convey a "cosmic perspective"; and neither necessarily qualifies as a philosophical and social justification of the scientific enterprise. But justifying modern science, which is Sagan's paramount purpose in "Cosmos," is the most efficacious means of popularizing it. The series as a whole thus possesses a purpose and grandeur greater than any one of its segments. But, to the viewer, the uniqueness of Sagan's view—his conclusion that science provides the means to transcend the human condition—and the specifics of his argument are initially difficult to ascertain.

On the surface, "Cosmos" seems to be an eclectic collection of 13 scientific and historical vignettes addressing themes and forwarding positions associated with Bronowski, Koestler, Eiseley, and Von Daniken. While extricating himself from Von Daniken's more outrageous fancies, Sagan is captivated by the possibility of extraterrestrial life and its revolutionary implications for our science and philosophy. Less romantic, if not less prosaic, than Eiseley and Koestler, Sagan speaks about the universe with their same reverence and implies that science is the key to the kingdom of true knowledge. More specific than Bronowski on science's cultural ramifications, Sagan shares his optimism for a society which vigorously pursues the scientific enterprise. Regarding contemporary society, Sagan echoes the sentiments of a host of commentators who bemoan the existence of oppression, warfare, famine, the sterility of contemporary culture, and the persistence of unenlightened opinion. But Sagan's claim that science, rather than religion, traditional philosophy, or politics, is the path to redemption seems, like those of many would-be reformers, an overly simplistic and unsubstantiated solution to the ills of the day.

Teaching the lesson that science will enable man to transcend the human condition is the primary goal of the series. From a scientist of Sagan's stature, it is not too much to expect an argument with clearly articulated assumptions and carefully justified conclusions. "Cosmos" suffers in this regard, illuminating the difficulties of making a philosophic argument in a long television series, where viewers exercise selective perception and possess varied levels of understanding. The elusivenesss of specifics in Sagan's argument also reflects the structure and organization of the series itself, in particular Sagan's decision to dramatize not only how real science works but what science means for man. To confuse matters further, Sagan is not averse to resorting to simplistic negative arguments at the expense of detailing his own position. A variety of thinkers, from Plato to the medieval scholastics to contemporary theologians, are portrayed as intellectual impediments to enlightenment and progress.

Sagan's dramatizations, his use of stunning visuals ("to engage the heart as well as the mind") and historical skits, are not without substantive components. But they tend to accentuate his conclusion rather than highlight his assumptions. To the extent that the viewer gets caught up in the drama, he finds himself tempted to accept Sagan's conclusion without being precisely certain why. For example, the segments on comets and the lives of the stars reveal some of the wonders of the universe and how modern science has demystified some of the more perplexing questions about nature. These discussions are masterpieces of science education, but Sagan is not content simply to demonstrate science's considerable ability to explain natural phenomena. A subtheme, never clearly stated, is fear: man ought to fear a universe in which comets collide with planets and suns burn out. The scientific impulse emanates, Sagan hints, from man's fear of a universe which he does not totally understand or control. Man ought to pursue a science which protects him.

The tone and emphasis of the argument shift in the discussions of Mars and Venus. Here, Sagan shows that science has succeeded in repudiating the irrational, erroneous, and arrogant assertions of religion and traditional philosophy. Science offers intellectual progress; and in terms of explaining the atmosphere of Venus and the "canals" of Mars, it surely does. But Sagan seems to force the viewer into making a distinct choice between a progressive science and non-progressive philosphy or religion as ways for understanding reality. The argument to reject religion or philosophy because of their scientific shortcomings is as old as it is naive and does not enlighten us about science's meaning for man.

Sagan devotes a considerable amount of time to intellectual and biographical sketches of some of the key figures in the history of science. In these segments, we see how scientists have labored, against all odds, to advance man's knowledge of the universe. If the viewer forgets that Kepler was as much an occultist as a physicist, that Newton refused to extricate the Deity from his own cosmology, that Einstein's scientific brilliance was matched by his confusion about the technological implications of his discoveries, one does remember Sagan's more general point. Scientists have always been forward-looking intellectuals who dared conventional belief, even in the face of public derision and persecution. Historically, scientists are the "good guys" in the progress of Western civilization. But Sagan tells us less about the history of science and more about historical figures who ought to be canonized by a people committed to human excellence and progress.

This overly simple historical interpretation is carried to an embarrassing extreme when Sagan projects our future contact with advanced extraterrestrial beings. Since these beings will be superior scientists, we have nothing to fear. As long as mankind demonstrates its respect for knowledge, our contact with extraterrestrials will be marked by mutual respect and entail an interplanetary cultural vibrancy. Man's history teaches us that scientists respect intellectual change and one another. Despite Sagan's interesting discussion of different biologies and life forms, he falls victim to the anthropomorphism he otherwise critiques by assuming that extraterrestrial scientists will be like their human counterparts. This assertion is, however, quite consistent with, and reinforces, his conclusion in the last segment of the series. The answer to the question "Who Speaks for Earth?" is the scientist. The scientist is the exalted pursuer of knowledge and the witness for the paramount values and aspirations of mankind and, for that matter, any rational species. If Sagan himself cannot convince us of science's overwhelming virtue and cosmological significance, he implies that the existence of superior extraterrestrials will. He invokes Pascal's wager with a modern twist.

The dramatic, self-fulfilling quality of "Cosmos" does not mean that there is not a serious argument presented in the series. In fact, each segment is part of Sagan's larger, more direct analysis of the meaning of science for man. For viewers familiar with Sagan's bestselling books—*The*

Dragons of Eden, The Cosmic Connection, Broca's Brain—and sympathetic to his cause, the dramatics of "Cosmos" appear to be a stroke of genius. For those less familiar and less convinced, "Cosmos" seems propagandistic, if for no other reason than that Sagan's argument is disorganized. But there is a logical argument here, more readily understood when one realizes that the 13 segments of "Cosmos" deal with four basic topics: the powers and mysteries of nature; man and nature; science's cultural and social benefits; and projections of man's scientific future.

Sagan's universe is at once beautiful and infinite but changing and mysterious, a challenge to those who would know it and a potentially revengeful enemy to those who arrogantly claim they already do. "Cosmos" explores some of the fundamental and historically perplexing questions about the universe—its creation, the origins of life, the geology and environment of the planets, the lives of the stars. Sagan's purpose in these discussions is twofold: to inform man of the vastness and complexity of the universe and to demonstrate how modern science has begun to unravel some of nature's mysteries.

But science teaches us more than facts about the cosmos. Science teaches us rules, laws by which the universe operates and changes. The fact that man can determine laws of nature is a reflection of the interconnectedness of the universe's component parts. Sagan wants to explain how man is ultimately connected to the universe, and it is science that teaches man this special knowledge. The most important natural law for understanding the origins of mankind and its relationship to the universe, Sagan says, is evolution predicated on adaptation. Progressive adaptation explains man's origins, the survival of the species, and man's identity as earth's most intelligent creature. Given the perpetuity and universality of natural laws, adaptation is also the key to man's future, his destiny as a creature of nature. In a universe that changes, man must seek to understand the rules of change so that he can survive and flourish by perpetually adapting to the conditions of change.

Science "is by far the best tool we have for the purpose of adaptation. In fact, modern science is the apogee of man's historical adaptation to the environment, an accomplishment and never-ending task which is the sine qua non of the species. Since man's ultimate identity lies in the very structure of the universe, there is also a philosophical imperative to understand the deepest mysteries of the cosmos. This scientific and philosophical quest, Sagan suggests, points to an undeniable biological reward, the further adaptation and evolution of the species to a more advanced stage.

In the meantime, the pursuit of the scientific enterprise is, in Sagan's terms, culturally and socially beneficial. As a philosophy linked with the practical, science offers obvious material rewards. As an activity of intellectual exploration, science advances knowledge by liberating the mind, encouraging an openness to hypotheses and experiment. This scientific spirit transferred to society discourages provincialism and religious, ethnic, and nationalist fanaticism. A society which accepts and proceeds according to the scientific method is more likely to employ rational, rather than ideological, solutions to its problems. Such a society will be secular, tolerant of new ideas, and unified around the common quest to advance knowledge for collective well-being.

The most obvious and important way, concludes Sagan, to improve the substance of scientific knowledge and to infuse society with the scientific spirit is to pursue space exploration and meet the intellectual and technological challenges it offers. The projected future of a society which vigorously pursues scientific research and space exploration is a tremendous technological advance, a more rational and humane society—given man's newly-acquired cosmic perspective—and a likely encounter with extraterrestrial intelligence. The latter event, claims Sagan, would vindicate the social meaning of science and probably result in earth's joining a "community of intergalactic civilizations" whose common bond would be the language of the universe, science.

For the faithful and attentive viewer who seeks to understand Sagan's "cosmic perspective," the series is a disappointment. The viewer is required to piece together Sagan's comprehensive justification of the scientific enterprise by weeding through the visuals and dramatizations and rearranging the essentials of Sagan's argument. This organizational problem of the series may be the result of Sagan's overambition, his desire to make science understandable and popular, interesting and entertaining, as well as justifiable in a profound philosophical sense. If this is the case, some of the confusion and disorganization of "Cosmos" is excusable. But "Cosmos" then fails at its most serious and, according to Sagan, important level. It fails because Sagan does not overcome the difficulties of interfacing an argument of the utmost seriousness with the attempt to respond and appeal to popular values, expectations, and fancies about the future. The specifics of Sagan's argument to justify the scientific enterprise compete with the other dimensions of the series—Sagan's desire to raise viewers' curiosity about nature and how science works, his own cooptation of popular themes of science fiction and speculation for his purposes, and the use of drama and dramatic generalizations as a teaching device.

"Cosmos" disappoints for reasons less excusable than overambition and disorganization. Sagan's explication of the "cosmic perspective" offered by modern science sounds terribly familiar. It ought to; essentially, it is an updated version of natural Darwinism extended, as it was a century ago, to society. What saves, or ought to save, "Cosmos" from triviality is its updated quality. But here, too, it disappoints, because Sagan decided not to highlight and detail two of the most important elements of his argument, the concept of artificial selection and the notion of the triune brain. And, most inexcusably, Sagan neither mentions any of the traditional criticisms of science as a philosophical and social activity nor addresses his argument specifically to these criticisms.

While Sagan explains how science is progressive, based on hypotheses which may later prove to be incomplete or false, he does not discuss the ultimate philosophical status of this potentially false knowledge. Sagan puts himself in the unenviable position of making an argument from scientific authority while implying that today's science may be overturned by tomorrow's advances. He praises science's ability to control nature and offer material advance; yet he extricates science from its contributions to the debasement of nature and its encouragement, directly or indirectly, of a materialist social ethic. Science offers man the comforts of a technologically advanced society; Sagan does not care to state that technological societies are industrialized societies, organized along bureaucratic lines. Although lamenting the "bureaucratic mentality" and claiming that religion and politics reenforce this stifling, potentially destructive mind-set, Sagan admits no connection between science, technology, and bureaucracy. Science, we are told, helps man overcome the debilitations of followership. How this works in practice, for society as a whole, is apparently a yet to be explored mystery.

Above all, science enables man to adapt to his environment, and this capability is the most compelling aspect of Sagan's argument. Through science, man can practice artificial selection to transform nature and the environment to meet his needs and attain his goals. The ultimate example of artificial selection is the science of adaptation applied to the human species itself. Genetic engineering, a logical extrapolation of the scientific impulse, poses serious problems for man, admits Sagan. But he does not explain how either science or his "cosmic perspective" helps resolve moral problems other than through experience and experiment. This is particularly disturbing because Sagan suggests frequently that science is superior to any other existing philosophy or value system. However, when faced with answering the question, what ought to guide man's pursuit of science or, more properly, progressive adaptation, Sagan is silent.

This dilemma is presumably resolved if one understands the "cosmic perspective" and the substance of science. The study of the development and structure of the human brain reveals, says Sagan, the fact that science emanates from the brain's most evolutionary advanced component, the neocortex. The neocortex developed as the species dealt with the challenges of the environment to the extent that "reason" replaced biological impulse as the most efficacious means of survival. Instinct and impulse still exist in man, and irrationality marks much of human activity. This behavior, the product of the primordial parts of the brain, the R-complex and the limbic system, manifests itself in political conflicts, social strife, and psychological confusion. Science, according to Sagan, is dissociated from human foible. Moreover, if man continues to pursue an understanding of nature—to exercise his rational faculties—through space exploration, it follows that the debilitating elements of his physiology will become extraneous. The human practice of science results in an improved adaptation of the species and biological development to a more advanced life form. The problems of humanity, the tensions and conflicts in humans and between them, will be left behind. In biological terms, science is our cosmic destiny and the means to transcend the human condition.

Sagan's interpretation of the notion of the triune brain has been criticized as simplistic. Nonetheless, it is the key to Sagan's most important and probably best argument. What is disturbing is that he really does not elaborate on it in "Cosmos" and prefers to talk more about the stars and the exciting future of space exploration. One may assume that Sagan wants to avoid simply repeating his more detailed discussion of the triune brain in *The Dragons of Eden*. This is unlikely since, in substantive terms, "Cosmos" is not much more than a summary of his popular writings. Sagan does not highlight his argument about evolution in "Cosmos," one suspects, because the viewer would thus be moved to ask, what about the meantime? How does man conduct himself today, pursuing science and technology but still under the influence of the problematic aspects of the brain?

Sagan says that he has an answer—the scientific method applied by and on society. Yet, his failure to detail what this means and inability to focus on crucial aspects of his justification for the scientific enterprise indicate an uncharacteristic uncertainty and ultimate honesty in Sagan the spokesman for science. It is reasonable to assume that Sagan knows that as a philosophical treatise on the meaning of science for the human condition, "Cosmos" is trivial. As a blueprint for a society which would vigorously pursue the scientific enterprise, "Cosmos" is embarrassingly incomplete. Sagan, then, is either frighteningly naive—indeed, "Cosmos" does resemble a piece of "social science fiction'—or guilty of duplicity—"Cosmos" does not, as Sagan claims it would, explain the cosmic perspective of science.

Such criticism may be too harsh and cynical. As a television series, "Cosmos" is refreshing, stimulating, entertaining, and educational. It is not a typical philosophic exhortation. Perhaps "Cosmos" is meant to be understood not as a treatise on science but as a parable about science, man, and the human condition. Sagan and "Cosmos" teach the lesson that, all things considered in this difficult world, science is a praiseworthy pursuit and deserves our affection and commitment. The viewer has the prerogative of examining the meaning and depth of this teaching, of joining Sagan in the quest to understand the universe and science's relevance for man. The problem with teaching through parables, however, is that most people take them at face value and do not understand, or soon forget, their meaning. This is a lesson Sagan may soon learn.

9

Decoding "Dallas": Comparing American and German Viewers

Herta Herzog Massing

The relatively new and highly successful television development of the prime time serials started off by "Dallas" has been the subject of interest for various theoretical and disciplinary orientations. Several focused on the text and the hypothesized spectator-text relation. In the tradition of literary analysis and of film theory "Dallas" has been studied as melodrama in its serial form and non-closure structure which also characterizes daytime "soaps".[1] Soap opera analysis has stressed the gender differences and implications for the day and evening versions.[2]

Another major focus has been the reading of the text in the context of and as a symptom of popular culture.[3] Critics of popular culture, and of things American in particular, have concerned themselves with the question whether the worldwide diffusion of programs such as "Dallas" made possible by the growth of the new media technologies may eventually result in worldwide cultural assimilation at the expense of indigenous diversity.[4]

Until recently, however, little was known empirically about the qualities of audience response to "Dallas" or any other of the prime time soaps, in the U.S. or abroad. This pilot study was a first attempt to examine the meaning of "Dallas" for German television viewers.[5]

Audience analysis today still lacks a broad theoretical framework. Considerable discussion, notably on the concept of audience gratification, has mainly served to highlight the complexities of viewer response.[6] As pointed out recently, however, progress is being made in a convergence of content-oriented analysis.[7] The "reading" of the import "Dallas" on the part of German television viewers has been one task of this study. The second concerns selected aspects of the multifaceted meaning of the program, particularly the possibilities for the projection of various socio-psychological interests and needs in their cultural-ideological context.

The German field work for "Dallas" was carried out in November 1982. It consisted of intensive qualitative interviews, supplemented by a brief projective personality test[8] with a small sample of fifty-one viewers of the middle and lower middle class, divided equally by sex and age group (16-25 and 45-60 years of age), living in large and small towns in various sections of Germany. It consisted both of people who had watched the program from the very beginning and other less regular viewers. In the spring of 1985 a comparable group of control interviews was carried out with 51 "Dallas" viewers living in various sections and cities of the United States. The main findings follow.

The Importance of the Setting

As postulated by our theoretical stance, the milieu of "Dallas" turned out indeed to be a very important element of its appeal for German viewers. While interestingly foreign, it still conforms to what they think of or are willing to accept as typically American. Viewers are impressed with the physical environment such as the Southfork ranch, the big highways, the city traffic and skyscrapers of "Dallas" as well as the lifestyle of the Ewings for whom "money does not matter." The Ewings display some strange habits, it is noted, such as wearing a cowboy hat to the office, the "eternal drink in their hands" or the dining out "at every occasion." But life is generally easier in America, one has heard, money there is made easier and therefore probably also spent more easily. And rich people anywhere, it is reasoned, do not lead ordinary lives. Germany has its rich people too, although "they do not show their wealth" like the Ewings, a point noted with some condescension as well as appreciation for the "insights" afforded. The plot is not altogether far-fetched, German viewers concluded; the story could happen in Germany, at least in relation to the kinds of problems faced by the Ewings.

Family Structure as a Bridge

The three-generation Ewing clan is a bridging element, tying the story together for German audiences. Fitting with the hierarchical concept of the traditional German family structure, it helps the viewer to relate to the characters of "Dallas".

Jock (the character had not yet died at the time of the interview) is a very important person for the German viewer. In the spontaneous listing of the characters of "Dallas," Jock was nearly as often mentioned in first place as his son J.R.. Jock is perceived as the patriarch of the family, founder of a business which he built through hard work. He is judged tough in his business dealings but never shooting from the hip, determined to defend his business interests even against his wife whom he dearly loves. Miss Ellie fits the stereotype of the good mother: she is always working for peace, trying to hold the family together. Some of the older viewers are impressed that she dares to show independence even against her husband when her moral principles are involved.

To the younger viewers, Bobby is the "kid brother of J.R.," while the older viewers see him as the "younger son of Jock." Generation differences also show in the perception of Sue Ellen, wife of J.R.. The older viewers see in her the woman ruined by her husband. The younger ones tend to see her as a somewhat unstable person (she has some extra-marital affairs and a drinking problem), badly treated by her husband but unwilling to pass up the Ewing riches. Sue Ellen is her own problem, they say.

J.R. the Television Scoundrel

J.R. is the one truly melodramatic character of "Dallas" who does not fit cultural mores. He is perceived as "a scoundrel the like of which has never before been shown on German television." In his unscrupulous mad quest for more wealth and more power for and through Ewing Oil, he establishes an "interconnection between business and family life" which intrigued some of the male viewers. J.R. does not stand for the threats of business as an institution as has been surmised from an American point of view.[9] German viewers see in him an individual scoundrel of excessive dimension, responsible for problems that can happen in every family. He is the unpredictable devil ex machina; without him there would be no story. His laugh always "signals the next outrageous incident."

Identification with a Macho Ideal

A remarkable facet of this scoundrel is his success: J.R. never fails. He is masterful in his plots (a *Koenner*), successful with women he merely uses and with his dirty business machinations. He always finds a way out (*Hintertuerchen*) in contrast to his counterpart Cliff Barnes who is unanimously seen as the "eternal loser." For some viewers in the group—not nearly as many as suspected by the German press—J.R. is indeed the reason for their enjoyment of "Dallas." He sparks their admiration for a macho ideal. They would like to dare being as unscrupulously cunning and aggressive and get away with it as he does. They are not like him but wish they were.

Other Forms of Need Projection

A sizeable number of viewers in this case study recognize in the story and its characters other aspects of their own often barely understood or accepted longings and problems. In a variety of ways "Dallas" provides them with a temporary release through projection. Here are a few examples, as indicated by the verbal statement of the viewer and supported and further illuminated by the test material:

> A 16-year-old high school student struggling to reconcile his childhood dependency needs with his strivings for masculine maturity is quite outspoken in his negative assessment of Miss Ellie (very rare in the total group): She is a "grandma-type", he says, and he does not like her. He admires, however, Dusty, the friend of Sue Ellen. Although a cripple physically, he says, he is able to give her the manly support she does not get from her husband.
>
> A young dental assistant from a very modest background identifies with Pam, wife of Bobby Ewing. "She is not a *real* Ewing yet she made it," being loved by her husband and successful in her independent business activities.
>
> An older housewife sees in the "disparity between the splendid facade of the Ewings and their inner turmoil" a replica of her own situation. As shown also in the test data, she is troubled to maintain a social front despite inner feelings of inadequacy and insecurity.
>
> For viewers having a hard time to maintain control of themselves "Dallas" provides a chance to let go emotionally. A retired government employee with marked sadomasochistic tendencies he controls with great difficulty says: "I am looking forward to this weekly sprinkler." It is of course "mindless night entertainment," he stresses yet he furnished unusually detailed descriptions of many of its incidents, mostly the catastrophic ones. The process of watching is for him the opportunity to experience feelings, to emote, something he ordinarily does not permit himself.

The patterns of projection were varied. Obviously they would depend on and be limited by the possibilities inherent in the story.

In the case of "Dallas" the multitude of projections of more or less accepted feelings is facilitated through the person of Miss Ellie. It helps that she (the actress Barbara Bel Geddes) "looks German." The main reason, however, is her role in the story. As matriarch of the family and her continuing efforts for a peaceful family life, she asserts and reaffirms the superego and so reassigns the viewer's projection to its properly disengaged, denied or suppressed stage.

Daydreams with Dallas

This second major type of viewing satisfaction is quite readily recognized and articulated. Daydreaming is a type of enjoyment quite typical for soap operas generally. Yet the daydreams of German "Dallas" viewers have a unique feature. The viewers love to participate in the exciting life of the Ewings who can afford every luxury. But, it is noted, the Ewings also have enormous problems. Theirs is not a safe or sane or happy world (*keine heile Welt*):

> Of course you dream with them about having that much money . . . but you also see that money alone does not make you happy. [F, 24 years old, social worker]

Thus the viewer does not feel so badly off after all, being less burdened with comparatively lesser problems than those the Ewings have to face all the time:

> I'd love to have their money, have a big car like every one of them has. I would have a horse and ride over my ranch! And my husband is really not as considerate as Jock—but he is not as mean as J.R. either. And I do not know anyone like him among my friends or neighbors. I really would not want to be in their shoes. [F, 46, wife of a business man]

For the German viewer the daydreaming escape into the life of the Ewings contains the return ticket to reality. It is doubly rewarding, being experienced as a dream and as confirmation of the viewer's everyday life.

Dallas the Available Spectacle

Finally some viewers, mostly in the young age group, seemed to watch "Dallas" without much personal involvement. It is available on a free night in their weekly schedule, and program choices are quite limited as the German viewer has as a rule only one other national and one regional channel to choose from. They rate "Dallas" a "superb spectacle." With its multiple plot structure they can "count on something to happen every time." They are curious about what new ideas will come up. "Dallas" is always good for a mild arousal that is not upsetting because its incidents occur in a familiar structure.

German Compared to American Response

The U.S. interviews were conducted a couple years after the German ones. Interestingly, the story development does play a role in viewer response. Certain observations of difference, however, can be made quite reliably.

Differences in Perception

For the U.S. viewer, the mise-en-scène of "Dallas" concerns a rich or very rich Texan oil family in its business involvements and private lives, both interrelated and short on morals. As in the German interviews, the emphasis on these points varies some from one viewer to the other. The U.S. interviews, however, generally show a broader emphasis on the business setting compared with the German emphasis on the geographic setting and way of life. It is "big business after-the-dollar without scruples" for U.S. viewers, a situation they do not consider unfamiliar or particularly unrealistic. The threat of the big corporation, however, which they decode to show that money can buy anyone's silence or service is softened because the unscrupulous greed and power strivings are shown as infights within the family. Thus the average person—the viewer—does not feel threatened. Moreover, the presentation of socio-ideological conflict in terms of familial conflict is considered typical of the soap opera. "Dallas" is perceived to be the evening version of this familiar genre with its many story lines. (It must be more extreme, of course, because it is aiming for millions of viewers and high ratings.) Soap opera style also emphasizes lust and immorality which is how the U.S. respondents tended to characterize the various conflicts, problems and intrigues detailed by the German viewers in their description of the show.

Technical Interest

A second major difference relevant for program impact concerns the U.S. viewer's tendency to constantly switch between an objective stance of technical interest and the subjective viewing experience, their emotional relating to the program. The U.S. viewers, for example, referred to the story characters frequently in terms of the actor's name and specialty, such as "Howard Keel, he is Farlow, Miss Ellie's second husband, but he does not sing." They keep abreast of the business contracts of the show's stars and consider the resulting implications for plot development. Mark, for example, might not really be dead (he crashed into the ocean but his body was never found) but will be "kept in" for Pam for when Bobby's character leaves the show. Thus, the stance concerning presumed production needs influences the U.S. viewer's response to the various characters as well as the program's personal meaning for the viewer.

J.R. and Cliff Barnes

J.R. is for the U.S. audience clearly the key character of the show. Responsible for all the tricks, he is not so much the macho ideal as he is the rat, sneaky, cunning, the underhanded guy necessary to keep the show going. He is "mean but he plays his part very well," one viewer explained. Cliff Barnes, on the other hand, is not the eternal loser that he is to the German viewers, but the really bad guy who tries to steal everything the Ewings have.

The Family

The Ewings are not perceived as members in a hierarchical family structure by U.S. audiences, as they are by German viewers, for whom the hierachical structure reflects their own cultural tradition. Rather, they are seen by U.S. viewers as individual agents, brought in or taken out and replaced as needed. The family serves as a construct, a frame of reference for all soap operas. The Ewings "stick together," it is said, which gives the story its frame and is perhaps also a reading reflecting the looser family structure seemingly characteristic of American society.

The Viewer as Script-Writer

The "script-writer" stance of the viewer also has a bearing on the nature of the personal meaning of "Dallas" for the U.S. viewer. For the German viewer the projection and temporary release of subjective psychological needs is a major reason for program enjoyment. This type of response seems to be far less important among U.S. viewers. They either tended to share the German viewers' day-dreaming reaction (albeit in a somewhat different form), or they indulged in "kicking the plot around," exercising their own predilections in competition with the producer of the show. Such musing over possible story development, often with other family members or friends watching the show, was mentioned by German viewers as a by-product of viewing activity, but is a main form of relating to the program for the U.S. viewers.

Fantasizing or "Daydreaming"

The fantasizing of the U.S. viewer appears to be more realistic and lacking the pronounced masochistic aspects of German "daydreams" surrounding "Dallas". U.S. viewers find it fascinating to watch the glamour, the beautiful women, the handsome men. The women in particular stress enjoying the gorgeous clothes. Said one, "these women wear things to take a shower which are nicer than we see worn to the nicest restaurants in Iowa." Male viewers enjoy playing around with the idea of having that much money available or having those million dollar tax problems, or going to bed with one of the sexy women. The program offers an escape from their ordinary situations. They fantasize about winning the lottery, one respondent noted. They talk about being envious: "sometimes I think why can't I have all these gorgeous clothes" or "I wish I had that money and a good figure." They do not tend, however, to draw the typical German response that all these riches are not worth having after all because of myriad problems accompanying them.

Emotional Reactions and Values

Part of U.S. viewing satisfaction is a participatory response to the incidents in which the characters are involved. A sizeable number of viewers described their main satisfaction in terms of trying to outguess what is going to happen in the show "after the commercial" as they watch it, or what might happen the next time, and how they feel about it. They try to see how close they come in their guesses. They laugh and joke and enjoy feeling superior ("how stupid can she [Lucy] be!"). They follow with concern about the cruelties shown to characters they like.[10] They hope that J.R. will be taken down a peg or two—not too much, of course, because, J.R. obviously "makes the show." U.S. viewers are pleased when their predictions are right *and* when they correspond with their own values and prejudices. "Dallas" demonstrates and proves some viewers' negative concepts of the "wheeling and dealing of high finance," their opinion that "being rich is bad because you can do anything if you are rich." And it also shows positively, particularly in the person of Miss Ellie, that a family should be fiercely loyal. For the American viewer, Bobby is a "nice All-American boy" and Pamela "the independent woman of today who can handle a responsible job."

Conclusion

U.S. viewers decode "Dallas" as a "seamy soap opera" which permits them to fantasize and to exercise their creative ingenuity and attitudinal predilections. Their response seems to lack the cathartic element found among German viewers, a difference which in part is due to the greater experience with the soap opera genre among U.S. television viewers.

The answer to my initial question—do viewers in different countries read popular culture differently?—must be answered affirmatively.

Notes

1. Jane Feuer, "Melodrama, Serial Form and Television Today," *Screen*, vol. 25, no. 1 (Jan-Feb. 1984).
2. Muriel Cantor and Suzanne Pingree, *Soap Opera* (Beverly Hills: Sage, 1983).
3. Mary S. Mander, "Dallas: The Mythologie of Crime and the Occult," *Journal of Popular Culture*, vol. 17, no. 2 (1983).
4. Comments at an international Forum on "The relationship of Art and Economics" convened in Paris by the French Minister of Culture (*New York Times* and *International Herald Tribune*, Feb. 21 and 25, 1983).
5. Elihu Katz started at about the same time a large-scale study of "Dallas," comparing primarily the readings of its message among U.S. viewers and several ethnic groups in Israel.

6. Jay G. Blumler and Elihu Katz, eds., "The Uses of Mass Communication, Current Perspectives of Gratifications Research," *Sage Annual Review of Communications*, 1972, vol 2.
7. From a report, "The Export of Meaning: Cross Cultural Readings of American TV," Elihu Katz and Tamar Liebes, delivered at the Manchester Symposium of Broadcasting, March 5, 1985.
8. Karen Machover, *Personality Projection in the Drawing of the Human Figure*, American Lecture Series, (Springfield, Ill: Charles C. Thomas Publisher, tenth printing 1978). (The test, developed in conjunction with clinical data and other tests, such as the Rorschach, postulates that in content and formal features the drawing of a human figure, male and female, will reflect the body image of the test person and that such self-projection is symptomatic of his adjustment level, his conflicts, stability and sexual maturity. The "Dallas" test drawings were analyzed by clinical psychologist Harriett Moore.)
9. Mandler, "Dallas: The Mythologie of Crime and the Occult."
10. Adolf Zillman, "Anatomy of Suspense," *The Entertainment Function of Television*, Percy H. Tannenbaum, ed., (Hillsdale, N.J.: Lawrence Earlbaum Associates, Publishers, 1980).

10

Violence and Aggression

David Pearl

Public interest and concern have long focused on the issue of violence on television. Attention to that issue began in the 1950s and has remained ever since. Although the field of television and human behavior has gone far beyond the study of violence, many researchers are still committed to finding an answer to the question about the effects of televised violence on the viewer.

One reason for this continued commitment is that, despite all the research that has been done both for the report of the surgeon general's advisory committee and since then, the conclusions are not completely unequivocal. While much of the research shows a causal relationship, proponents of the "no effects" position, while in diminished number, continue to argue their case.

Violence in Television Content

The first congressional hearing on television programming took place in 1952, when the House Committee on Interstate and Foreign Commerce investigated television entertainment to ascertain if it was excessively violent and sexually provocative and if it had pernicious effects. Over the next twelve years, the Senate Committee on the Judiciary held many more hearings; because data were so scarce and sparse, the hearings were lengthy, acrimonious, and widely publicized. Television as a cause of delinquent behavior became the focus of inquiry. The congressmen were critical of the industry, and the broadcasters were defensive.

During the period from 1952 to 1967, analyses of programs found a great deal of violence on them. One analysis in 1954 reported an average of eleven threats or acts of violence per hour. Later analysis confirmed that violence on television was increasing and that it was increasing more rapidly on programs with large numbers of children in the audience.

Two governmental commissions looked into the problem of television violence in the late 1960s. One was the National Commission on the Causes and Prevention of Violence, which issued a report in 1969 summarizing available information about the prevalence of violence on television and the evidence for its effects. Data from laboratory experiments, it concluded, demonstrated that viewing violent programs increases the likelihood of a viewer to behave violently. The other commission was the Surgeon General's Scientific Advisory Committee on Television and Social Behavior. In 1972, the committee issued a report stating that the convergence of evidence from both laboratory and field studies suggested that viewing violent television programs contributes to aggressive behavior.

Content analyses by Gerbner in 1967, 1968, and 1969 showed that the frequency of violent acts remained about the same as in previous years except for a decrease in fatalities; cartoons were more violent than primetime programs; the networks differed somewhat in the amount of violence they broadcast; two-thirds of the leading characters were violent; retribution by violence was common; and most of the male roles were violent.

These years of intensive scrutiny not only saw the beginnings of an annual content analysis of television programs, but many other studies of television violence and other kinds of research were started. The events of the period also led to a series of arguments and controversies that are not yet resolved.

The two major governmental inquires made the problem of television violence more visible to both scientists and the public. They also increased acceptance of the notion that violence on television leads to aggressive behavior by viewers. The most important aftermath of the two commission reports was the controversy among scientists, on the one hand, and the unexpected apathy of the public, on the other.

Much of the controversy among the scientists revolved around the cautious conclusions of the surgeon general's committee. This caution seemed to lead to different interpretations of the research results, with some readers—including newspaper writers and television critics—reporting that television had no effect on aggressive behavior and others that it did have an effect. In general, behavioral scientists felt that the committee had been too cautious and conservative. Some people blamed the tentative and somewhat ambiguous phraseology of the report on the makeup of the committee; the television industry had been asked to name members to the committee, and the industry had veto power over those who were being considered for appointment. The other scientific controversy has centered on the usefulness, legitimacy, and pertinence of monitoring television violence. During this period, the public was not much interested in television violence for reasons not discernible, although a few citizens' groups, such as Action for Children's Television, were beginning to gather strength.

The year 1975 brought several new developments. Congress again became concerned with violence on television and also with obscenity and sexual provocativeness and prevailed upon the Federal Communications Commission (FCC) to do something. The FCC commissioners worked with the networks to establish the "family viewing hours" in the early evening. This arrangement was challenged in the courts by writers and producers who argued that it violated the First Amendment and infringed upon their right of trade. The judge ruled in their favor, but the networks continued the family hour on an informal basis.

During this time also, a number of citizen groups raised protests against various broadcasting practices. The American Medical Association adopted a resolution asking broadcasters to reduce the amount of violence because it was a threat to the social health of the country; the National Parent-Teachers Association held public forums throughout the country and began monitoring television content; and the National Citizens Committee for Broadcasting linked advertisers with violent content. A subcommittee of the House Committee on Interstate and Foreign Commerce held several hearings in cities throughout the country. Their report, published in 1977, indicated dissatisfaction with the situation, but it did not place blame on the broadcasters nor ask for any action.

Information on trends in violence depends on the definitions of violence and on the analytic procedures used. Nonetheless, all analyses agree that the evening hours after 9 p.m. contain more violence than other hours on television. Beginning with the 1975-76 season there was some increase in the early evening hours and some decrease in the later hours, although the later hours remained the most violent. There was a slight overall increase in violence between 1976 and 1977 and a slight decrease between 1977 and 1978. In 1979, it was about the same as in 1978. Over the past ten years, there has also been more violence on children's weekend programs than on prime-time television. It appears that the violence on television that began back in the 1950s has continued. There have been a few changes and fluctuations, but, in general, television, despite the concerns of congressmen and citizens' groups, remains a violent form of entertainment.

Effects of Televised Violence

Discussion about the effects of televised violence needs to be evaluated not only in the light of existing evidence but also in terms of how that evidence is to be assessed. Most of the researchers look at the totality of evidence and conclude, as did the surgeon general's advisory committee, that the convergence of findings supports the conclusion of a causal relationship between television violence and later aggressive behavior. The evidence now is drawn from a large body of literature. Adherents to this convergence approach agree that the conclusions reached in the surgeon general's program have been significantly strengthened by more recent research. Not only has the evidence been augmented, but the processes by which the aggressive behavior is produced have been further examined.

In the past ten years, several important field studies have found that televised violence results in aggressive behavior. A study funded by the Columbia Broadcasting System reported that teenage boys in London, according to their own accounts of their activities, were more likely to engage in "serious violence" after being exposed to television violence. Two independent studies by the same investigators followed three- and four-year-old children over a year's time and correlated their television viewing at home with the various types of behavior they showed during free-play periods at day-care centers. In each study there were consistent associations between heavy television viewing of violent programs and unwarranted aggressive behavior in their free play. It was concluded that, for these preschool children, watching violence on television was a cause of heightened aggressiveness.

In a five year study of 732 children, several kinds of aggression—conflict with parents, fighting, and delinquency—were all positively correlated with the total amount of television viewing, not just viewing of violent programs. Two additional studies were able to compare aggressiveness in children before and after their communities had television. In one study there was a significant increase in both verbal and physical aggression following the introduction of television. In the other study, after the introduction of television, aggressiveness increased in those children who looked at it a great deal.

A long-term study currently has been collecting extensive data on children in several countries. Results are available for grade-school children in the United States, Finland, and Poland. In all three countries, a positive relationship was found between television violence and aggression in both boys and girls. In previous studies by these investigators, the relationship was found only for boys. The sheer amount of television viewing, regardless of the kind of program, was the best predictor of aggression. Two other field studies reported similar results with different groups of children. One on teenagers found that those who perceived a program as violent or who thought that violence is an acceptable way to achieve a goal were more violent than the others. The other reported that the positive correlations between violence and aggression in English school children were about the same as for American school children.

In contrast, in a large-scale study sponsored by the National Broadcasting Company a group of researchers reached a different conclusion. In this technically sophisticated panel study, data were collected on several hundred elementary school boys and girls and teenage high school boys. For the elementary school children, measurements of aggression were taken six times during a three-year period, and for the high school boys the measurements were taken five times. The elementary school children gave "peer nominations" of aggression, and the teenagers gave "self reports." Both the elementary school children and the teenagers reported on which television programs they watched, and, for purposes of the analyses, the investigators picked those programs that could be classified as violent. The results showed that for the measure of violence on television and aggressive behavior taken at the same time, there were small but positive correlations. This is consistent with other cross-sectional survey results. When the measurements taken at different times were compared, no relationship was found. These investigators wanted to learn whether the short-term effects of television would accumulate over time and produce stable patterns of aggressive behavior in the real world. They found: the study did not provide evidence that television violence was causally implicated in the development of aggressive behavior patterns in children and adolescents over the time periods studied.

According to many researchers the evidence accumulated in the 1970s suggests overwhelmingly that televised violence and aggression are positively correlated in children. The issue now is what processes produce the relation. Four such processes have been suggested; observational learning, attitude changes, physiological arousal, and justification processes.

Observational Learning

Proponents of the observational learning theory hold that children learn to behave aggressively from the violence they see on television in the same way they learn cognitive and social skills from watching their parents, siblings, peers, teachers, and others. Laboratory studies have demonstrated many times that children imitate aggressive behavior immediately after they have seen it on film or television, but there are still questions about the role of observational learning in field studies. A longitudinal study published in 1977 gave the first substantial evidence that observational learning is the most plausible explanation for the positive relation between televised violence and aggressive behaviors. Several other observational and field studies agree with these results. Although these studies can be criticized on methodological grounds—the "clean" outcomes of laboratory experiments are rarely found in field studies—they nevertheless are important supports for the learning of behaviors from the observations of models.

Researchers have also analyzed specific issues related to observational learning. In the first place, if children see someone rewarded for doing certain things, more likely they also will perform these acts. Thus, if children see a television character rewarded for aggressive behavior, they will probably imitate that behavior. If the actor is punished, the children are less apt to imitate the aggressive behavior. These vicarious reinforcements—either reward or punishment—can influence the behavior's occurrence. The persistence of the behavior seems to be related to the children's own reinforcement, in other words, if the children themselves are rewarded or punished.

Observational learning may be related to age. Some investigators say that, by the time children reach their teens, behavior may no longer be affected significantly by observational learning. Young children, who do not see the relation between the aggression and the motives for it, may be more prone to imitate the aggressive behavior. Children start to imitate what they see on television when they are very young, some as early as two-years-old.

Identification with the actor or actress whose behavior is being imitated is also thought to be important, but the evidence is not clear-cut. For example, it has been shown that both boys and girls are more likely to imitate male than female characters, and the males are the more aggressive. Girls who are aggressive may identify more with the men characters. When children were asked to try to think in the same way as an aggressive character, they become more aggressive. It appears that there are no simple relations between observational learning and identification.

Another approach had been to tie the observational learning to specific cues on the programs, even apparently irrelevant cues. A tragic case from real life is the incident of a gang who burned a woman to death after a similar event occurred on a television show. In both the show and the real incident, the person was carrying a red gasoline can.

If these ideas about observational learning are analyzed in cognitive-processing terms, it can be hypothesized that children encode what they see and hear and then store it in their memories. To be encoded, the behavior must be salient or noticeable, and, to be retrieved in future behavior, it must be rehearsed with the same cues as those in the first observation present. If a child rehearses aggressive acts by daydreaming about them or uses them in make-believe play, the probability is increased that these acts will occur. There is some evidence that aggressive fantasies are related to aggressive acts.

These hypotheses are relevant to another theory, namely disinhibition. In disinhibition theory, it is assumed that children and others are inhibited by training and experience from being aggressive. If they see a lot of violence on television, they lose their inhibitions—they are disinhibited. This is an interesting idea, but some theorists say that cognitive-processing theory does not need to call upon disinhibition functions to explain observtional learning, even though disinhibition probably occurs. Rather, if children see a great deal of aggressive behavior on television, they will store and retrieve that behavior for future action.

Attitude Changes

Watching television influences people's attitudes. The more television children watch, the more accepting they are of aggressive behavior. It has been shown that persons who often watch television tend to be more suspicious and distrustful of others, and they also think there is more violence in the world than do those who do not watch much television.

Attitudes in psychological theory are "attributions, rules, and explanations" that people gradually learn from observations of behavior. It can be assumed that, if someone watches a lot of television, attitudes will be built up on the basis of what is seen, and the attitudes will, in turn, have an effect on behavior. A clever experiment showed how the television movie "Roots" changed attitudes and subsequent behavior. Unruly behavior of white and black high school students was recorded before, during, and after the show was broadcast. During the week that "Roots" was shown, the black students were more unruly, as measured by after-school detentions. This change was interpreted to mean that the black students had a change in attitudes toward obedience after watching "Roots."

Looking at violent scenes for even a very brief time makes young children more willing to accept aggressive behavior of other children. This acceptance of aggression makes it likely that the children will themselves be more aggressive. Other studies have shown that children's attitudes are changed if adults discuss the program. In an experimental study, one group of children who regularly watched violent programs were shown excerpts from violent shows and then took part in sessions about the unreality of television violence and wrote essays about it. The other group who also watched many violent programs were shown nonviolent excerpts, followed by a discussion of the content. The group who saw the violent television and then took part in the sessions on unreality were much less aggressive than the other group.

Processes involving physiological arousal are thought to have three possible consequences. One is desensitization. For example boys who regularly looked at violent programs showed less physiological arousal when they looked at new violent programs. Another possibility is that merely the increase of general arousal level will boost aggressiveness. A third alternative suggests that people seek an optimal level of arousal; aggressive behavior is arousing, and the persons who are desensitized may act aggressively to raise their levels of arousal. Then, once the desired level is reached, aggression will continue, because the behavior most likely to be continued is the behavior readily retrievable from memory. All these theories need more empirical verification.

In the justification theory, it is assumed that people who are already aggressive like to look at violent television programs because they can then justify their own behavior, even if only to themselves. They can believe that they are acting like a favorite television hero. In this theory, watching televised violence is a result, rather than a cause, of aggressive behavior. So little research has been done on this theory that it cannot be evaluated.

Contrary to these four theories is the catharsis theory, which predicts that aggression will be reduced after watching violence on television. Supposedly through catharsis, the need or desire to be aggressive is dissipated by looking at violence on television. Since practically all the evidence points to an increase in aggressive behavior, rather than a decrease, the theory is contradicted by the data. In general, it appears that observational learning and attitude changes are the most likely explanations of television's effects on aggressive behavior.

Another aspect of the entire question about violence and aggression must be examined: What is meant by "violence" on television? Objective and reliable measure of violence are necessary before inferences can be made about its relationship to aggressive behavior. How these measures have been made and what has been revealed are to be found in an examination of the content analyses of televised violence. Such measurements have been the source of considerable controversy.

Violence is assessed primarily by use of two procedures: content analysis and ratings. In a content analysis, the first step is to design the recording instrument. The trained coders observe the television programs and code them in accordance with predetermined criteria, with the aim of measuring violence as precisely and consistently as possible. In the rating procedures, the raters are given lists of television programs and asked to rate them in terms of violence. The raters may be television critics, television researchers, or ordinary people; children have sometimes been used as raters. Sometimes definitions of violence are given to the raters, but many investigators believe that definitions are not necessary.

The longest and most extensive analysis of television programs is the Cultural Indicators Project at the University of Pennsylvania's Annenberg School of Communications. The project consists of two parts: One part is the "message system analysis," which is an annual content analysis of one week of prime-time and weekend daytime dramatic programs. The second part is "cultivation analysis," which is a means of determining conceptions of social reality that television viewing may cultivate in various groups of viewers.

Violence seems to be something everybody feels they can recognize when they see it, yet it is difficult to define unambiguously. Many different definitions are now in use, and there is much disagreement about them. The Cultural Indicators Project defines violence as:

> the overt expression of physical force (with or without a weapon, against self or other) compelling action against one's will on pain of being hurt or killed, or actually hurting or killing.

The Columbia Broadcasting System's monitoring project defines violence as:

> the use of physical force against persons or animals, or the articulated, explicit threat of physical force to compel particular behavior on the part of that person.

The Parent-Teachers Association is concerned with gratuitous violence, which they define as "violence to maintain interest, violence not necessary for plot development, glorified violence."

Other definitions are: "Physical acts or the threat of physical acts by humans designed to inflict physical injury to persons or damage to property"; "acts involving the use of force, threats of force, or intent of force against others"; and "how much fighting, shouting, yelling, or killing there is in a show."

Most of the definitions involve physical force, including hurting or killing. Some definitions include psychological violence and violence against property; others do not. Some include comic violence, accidents, and acts of nature, such as floods and earthquakes. The rationale for including "acts of nature" is, according to those who include them, that they are analyzing entertainment and dramatic programs in which the writers and producers have deliberately put in violent "natural" events. Obviously, the reported amount of violence in a program will depend on the definition.

Another problem is found in deciding how to isolate specific acts of violence. In other words, if one wishes to count the number of violent actions, it is necessary to know when a violent action starts and stops. The Cultural Indicators Project states a violent action is a scene confined to the same participants. Any change in the characters is a new action. The CBS monitoring project defines a single violent action as:

> One sustained dramatically continuous event involving violence, with essentially the same group of participants and with no major interruption in continuity.

As with the definitions of violence, the different unitizations produce different results. For example, CBS finds less violence in programs than does the Cultural Indicators Project.

Index of Violence

The Cultural Indicators Project has developed an Index of Violence that combines several violence-related measures into a single score. The index is composed of three sets of data: the prevalence, rate, and role of violence. "Prevalence" is the percentage of programs in a particular sample containing any violence at all. "Rate" is the frequency of violent action. "Role" is the portrayal of characters as "violents" (committing violence) or as victims (subjected to violence). These three measures are combined into a formula that yields the Index of Violence. There has been controversy about this index, but its users maintain that although it is arbitrary—as is true of all indices—it is useful to illustrate trends and to facilitate comparisons.

The interesting characteristics of violence on television are its overall stability and regularity despite fluctuations by networks, genre, and time. The percentage of programs containing violence has remained about the same since 1967, although the number of violent acts per program has increased. Children's shows are violent in a cyclical way, up one year and down the next.

The amount of violence on television, according to some researchers, will almost certainly remain about the same as it has been, and they do not call for its total elimination. The concern is more with the kinds of violence, who commits violence, and who is victimized, because these portrayals may be critical mechanisms of social control.

The cultivation analysis aspects of the Cultural Indicators Project has a basic thesis that the more time viewers spend watching television, the more they will conceive the world to be similar to television portrayals. Thus people who view a great deal of television—and who consequently see a great deal of violence—are more likely to view the world as a mean and scary place. These heavy viewers also exhibit more fear, mistrust, and apprehension than do light viewers. Because there are more victims than there are aggressors, this finding may ultimately be of more significance than the direct relationship between televised violence and aggression.

11

Researching Television Violence

Alan Wurtzel and Guy Lometti

The subject of television violence and its impact on viewers is a complex question for which there are no simple answers. After more than thirty years of scientific investigation, the issue of television violence remains open to debate. Although the body of literature on television and violence continues to expand, results have been largely inconclusive, and there are still few definitive answers.

Recently, the National Institute of Mental Health (NIMH) released a report entitled *Television and Behavior: Ten Years of Scientific Progress and Implications for the Eighties*. Among many of its findings was the conclusion that a causal relationship exists between television violence and aggressive behavior. However, a careful examination of the research which was used to support the NIMH position indicates that the evidence does not warrant such a conclusion. ABC feels, therefore, a responsibilty to place the NIMH report—and other research regarding television's effects—into perspective.

This research perspective on television and violence was written to provide broader insight and understanding of the primary issues involving research on television and violence. The information is presented in a straightforward manner so that we can reach beyond the scientific and academic community and communicate with the general public. Included is a summary of ABC broadcast standards and practices policies and procedures which are the guidelines employed by the network to ensure that when violence is depicted in entertainment programming it is handled responsibly.

Science vs. Values

The issue of television violence can be addressed on two different levels: as an objective *scientific* question and as a subjective *values* issue. In dealing with subjective values, divergent opinions and viewpoints are unavoidable because conclusions are based upon reasoning which is both rational and emotional. Despite the ability to develop strong positions on either side of an issue, there is no definitive way to prove that any one position is absolutely and unequivocally correct. By contrast, scientific study requires rigor, objectivity, and the adherence to a predetermined set of rules and procedures. Conclusions must be based solely on empirical evidence and must be judged by analyzing the assumptions which underlay the study and the methods which are employed in the research.

The NIMH conclusions are based entirely upon scientific evidence. Therefore, they must withstand the rigor of scientific analysis and review. Our careful examination of the research indicates that the conclusions which the NIMH reaches are unsubstantiated when subjected to scientific analysis.

In May of 1982, the National Institute of Mental Health released the first of a two-volume report entitled *Television and Behavior*. The first volume is essentially a summary report detailing the advisory panel's conclusions on a broad range of research topics relating to television and its effects. The publication of this research summary stimulated controversy and debate despite the fact that Volume 2, which contains all relevant technical information and background reports, was not released until the following October.

During the five-month interim between the publication of Volumes 1 and 2, the national press reported and reviewed the findings of the NIMH panel—focusing in particular upon the conclusions which addressed the issue of television and violence. Without the benefit of any supporting research material it was impossible to evaluate the NIMH position on this subject. With the release of the technical volume, however, it is now possible to assess their conclusions.

Background of the NIMH Report

The 1982 NIMH report, *Television and Behavior*, is a follow-up to the 1972 *Surgeon General's Report on Television and Violence*, a study which was initiated after a series of congressional hearings on the impact of television violence on behavior. This government inquiry resulted in one of the most ambitious social science undertakings in recent history. Over $1 million was allocated to sponsor original research directly addressing the relationship between viewing television violence and subsequent behavioral violence. The result of this elaborate investigation, documented in the surgeon general's report was inconclusive with no direct causal relationship established between television and violent behavior.

Ten years after the publication of the surgeon general's report a follow-up review was initiated. This update was conducted under the auspices of the NIMH by establishing a seven-member advisory board; of the seven participants, four had contributed to the surgeon general's original study. The NIMH Advisory Board commissioned researchers to review and evaluate all of the research to date concerning television and behavior. Included in the review was some of the same research which had been sponsored by the surgeon general in 1972. Despite the impression that the 1982 NIMH report contains new research, in fact, only one new violence study is actually reported.

The NIMH report, *Television and Behavior*, is essentially a review of existing research which has already appeared in the literature and which has been previously assessed and evaluated. Thus, the NIMH is *not* a new addition to social science literature; it is simply a reiteration of information which has already been made available. Nevertheless, the NIMH Advisory Panel arrived at four major conclusions concerning the relationship between television violence and aggressive behavior and social attitudes.

- NIMH conclusion no. 1: the research findings support the conclusion of a causal relationship between television violence and aggressive behavior.
  ABC response: the research does not support the conclusion of a causal relationship.
- NIMH conclusion no. 2: there is a clear consensus among most researchers that television violence leads to aggressive behavior.
  ABC response: there exists a significant debate within the research community over the relationship between television violence and aggressive behavior.
- NIMH conclusion no. 3: despite slight variations over the past decade, the amount of violence on television has remained at consistently high levels.
  ABC response: there has been a decrease in the overall amount of violence in recent years.
- NIMH conclusion no. 4: television has been shown to cultivate television-influenced attitudes among viewers. Heavy viewers are more likely to be more fearful and less trusting of other people than are light viewers as a result of their exposure to television.
  ABC response: the research does not support the conclusion that television significantly cultivates viewer attitudes and perceptions of social reality.

Following are detailed analyses and evaluations of each of the four NIMH conclusions.

In the technical report chapter on television and violence, the author cites and evaluates 14 studies which lead him to the conclusion that "overwhelming evidence" exists to establish a positive relationship between viewing television violence and subsequent violent behavior. Despite the NIMH panel's assertion that some 2500 studies were conducted on the subject of television and behavior, only 14 are used to substantiate the claim of direct cause and effect. Before we analyze these studies in detail, we must discuss three key aspects regarding all television violence research: (1) the definition and measurement of violence and aggression; (2) the use of correlation to imply causation; and (3) the use of "convergence theory" to reach a conclusion.

Central to the issue of the impact of television viewing on violent behavior is the very definition of the term violence. When we talk about the need for a definition, we must consider two separate issues: (1) the definition of violent actions or depictions within television programs, and (2) the definition and measurement of violence and/or aggressive behavior.

The problems involved with arriving at a definition of violence are many because violence is not always obvious and clearcut. The circumstances under which an action occurs, the acceptability of the action by a culture's norms and mores, and the use of an action as self-protection are all examples which can radically alter whether or not an action is considered violent.

Nevertheless, we can arrive at a useful practical definition from Krattenmaker and Powe: "Violence is the purposeful, antisocial infliction of pain for personal gain or gratification that is intended to harm the victim and is accomplished in spite of societal sanctions against it." Obvious as this definition might be, there are a number of researchers who would strongly disagree. Some, for example would insist upon calling any action in which pain is inflicted, even in self-defense, violent. Others would want to expand the definition to include unintentional violence such as accidents, slapstick comedy, or even acts of nature like a hurricane or tornado.

Scientists have been arguing over definitions for years and we will not resolve the disagreement here. The point, however, is that the way in which violence is defined will play a large part in determining the amount of violence which is found in program content. So it is important to keep in mind the specific definition of violence employed in any particular study. It is also important to recognize that when different studies use different definitions of violence, we cannot compare their findings.

Controversy over the definition of violent content is only one aspect of the debate. (It should be noted that there is no universally acknowledged definition of the terms "violent" and "aggressive" as they are applied to behavior. Since most researchers use the terms interchangeably, we will consider them synonymous.) Of equal importance—and equally controversial—is the way in which scientists attempt to *measure* violent or aggressive behavior. In order to address the question of television's impact on behavior, we must first be able to define, identify, and measure violent behavior. Otherwise how can we know that there has been any effect at all?

The crucial question, of course, is whether or not exposure to television violence causes its occurrence in real life. The concern which everyone has is over *real* violence: the purposeful, antisocial infliction of pain which is intended to harm a victim or destroy property. Of course, it is simply impossible to observe this kind of behavior in research subjects on a systematic basis. Consequently, researchers have substituted other measures which can be observed and analyzed. But these measures are not violent behaviors as we commonly define the term. For example, research studies have measured violence with paper and pencil tests; by asking children to rate their classmates as to who is most aggressive during play; by observing children playing in a schoolyard; and during laboratory experiments by requesting a subject to ostensibly inflict electric shocks on others.

We might assume that the violence which the studies refer to is antisocial, harmful violence but in reality it is not. The research does not address the crucial question with which we are all concerned: "Does exposure to television violence cause people to commit actual violence?" As two critics of the current violence research, Krattenmaker and Powe, have stated, "The social science research to date simply has not left this question unanswered; it has left it unasked."

Correlation to Imply Causation

The NIMH report concludes that a cause-effect relationship between television viewing and aggressive behavior has been clearly established. This assumption is based on a variety of studies which utilize "correlational" techniques. Few research techniques create as much confusion and are subject to as much misinterpretation as correlation. A correlation is simply a statistical measure of the interrelationship or association between two different variables. The problem with a correlation is that while it can tell us the degree to which two things are related, it can not tell us which came first nor whether one caused the other. In fact, it is often the case that despite a high correlation between two things, the association is actually being caused by a third condition which affects the other two.

For example, consider the fact that there is a high correlation between sales of bathing suits and sales of ice cream. Thus, it would appear that the sale of bathing suits and the sale of ice cream are related since as one goes up, so does the other. However, we can never say that bathing suit sales "causes" ice cream consumption to rise, nor can we say that the increase in ice cream sales "causes" people to buy more bathing suits. It is more than likely that neither really has much to do with the other despite the fact that they are highly correlated. Rather, it is because both bathing suit sales and ice cream sales are affected by a third condition: hot weather during the summer months. It is this external third condition which actually causes both the sale of bathing suits and the sale of ice cream to rise.

The point is, correlation can never tell us anything about causation. Thus, when we talk about correlation between television viewing and aggressive behavior, all we are really saying is that there seems to be some relationship between the two. And when a causal relationship does exist (determined by other methods) a correlation does not necessarily indicate which of the two variables is the cause and which is the effect.

A correlation between viewing television violence and aggressive behavior could be produced by any of the following: (1) viewing violence leads to aggression; (2) aggressive tendencies lead to viewing violence; (3) both viewing violence and aggressive behavior are the products of a third condition or set of conditions such as age, sex, income, or family socioeconomic level. In those correlational field studies which do control for these third factors, the extremely small levels of association between television and behavior virtually disappear. This indicates that the "relationship" between television viewing and subsequent behavior is more likely the result of a variety of external conditions which have absolutely nothing to do with television itself. Some of these third variables include the level of aggressivity among peers, parental behavior (aggressivity, anger, etc.), parent-child interaction (ways children are punished, nurtured, etc.), demographic factors, and intelligence.

Another important point to remember about correlation is the strength of the association and the amount of behavior which it can "explain." Correlations of 1.0 are "perfect" in that they indicate that there is a direct relationship between two variables. A correlation of zero indicates absolutely no relationship. Correlations which run from zero to .20 indicate very weak relationships; those which run from .20 to .60 indicate moderate relationships and those running from .60 to 1.0 indicate strong relationships. Virtually every study cited by the NIMH report found correlations of less than .20 in associating television viewing with behavior. This weak correlation combined with the inability of correlation to determine causality indicates that the NIMH's conclusion is unwarranted.

Use of Convergence Theory

The NIMH report acknowledges that no single study conclusively links viewing television with violent behavior. However, the advisory panel insists that because there is a "convergence" of scientific evidence their conclusion is justified. In social science, convergence—the analysis of many different studies which point in the same basic direction—is sometimes used when no definitive evidence can be found to clearly support a position. The problem, however, is that the use of convergence can perpetuate unintended biases, flaws, or illogical assumptions which may exist within even a large body of research literature. It was the application of the convergence approach which led to the widespread belief among the scientific community of the time that the world was flat, and that the sun revolved around the earth. By relying on a similar approach and by refusing to challenge basic assumptions, a variety of scientists made the same mistake despite the fact that convergence theory would suggest that they were all correct.

NIMH Studies

The NIMH technical chapter on violence and aggression in Volume 2 cites fourteen studies which the author suggests proves a positive relationship between television and violence and which the NIMH report relies upon to reach its conclusion of a cause-effect relationship. Of these fourteen studies, half were conducted in foreign countries with cultures, norms, and programming much different than those found in the United States. Approximately one-third of the studies were unpublished and consequently were never subjected to scientific peer review and evaluation. Two studies were not even cited as research investigations but were reported as "personal communication" between the researcher and the NIMH author. The lack of scientific documentation in a number of cited studies makes a thorough analysis and evaluation of the work impossible. Further, a number of significant studies which the author uses to substantiate his case for causality were, in fact, either written by the author himself or by his colleagues.

Despite the assertion of a distinct cause-effect relationship between television and aggression, only four field experiments (which contain the only type of research methods that can support such a causal claim) were reviewed. Of the four, one found no relationship between television viewing and aggressive behavior; one found no long-term effects; one found no differences in the level of aggressive behavior between viewers and nonviewers; the one which did find an effect used delinquent Belgian adolescents who were exposed to unedited theatrical motion pictures and not television programming. Further, elements in the design of the latter study preclude a valid causal interpretation.

The remaining studies are not able to adequately address the question of causality. In these field surveys, the relationship between television and aggression was quite small. Few, if any, statistical controls were employed to take into account third variables which could affect the relationship. However, when statistical controls were used, the relationship between television and aggression was reduced to insignificance. For example, in one study, the results showed a small, positive relationship between television and aggressive behavior. Further analysis revealed that this relationship was spurious once third variables such as sex and grades in school were taken into account. The TV and aggression relationship was reduced to zero. The technical report chapter only cites the first part of this analysis, however, and it fails to mention that the relationship between television and aggression was not established in subsequent analyses.

There are two other studies cited by the NIMH which merit a brief mention. The first was conducted by Belson and investigated the relationship between television and aggressive behavior among adolescent boys in London. Although the NIMH report states that Belson found a relationship between television and aggression, in fact, the relationship was not straightforward. Those boys who viewed a great deal of television and those who viewed little television tended to behave *less* aggressively than did moderate viewers. This finding—not reported by the NIMH—runs counter to the report's conclusion that there is a positive and direct relationship between the amount of television viewed and subsequent aggressive behavior.

The only new research report on television and violence in the NIMH report is a study by Milavsky et al. conducted by NBC. The study was conducted in two United States cities over a three-year period and employed a number of highly sophisticated research techniques designed to eliminate many of the technical criticisms which have invalidated previous research efforts. The NBC findings do not support the NIMH conclusion of a causal relationship between television and aggressive behavior. Although the study appears in its own chapter in the NIMH report, it is not discussed in the chapter on violence which the advisory panel relied on in drawing its conclusion.

In sum, a review of the studies and their findings strongly indicates that the NIMH Advisory Panel's conclusion of a causal relationship between television and violence is ill-founded and unsupported by any of the research data which is currently available.

The NIMH panel arrives at this conclusion based upon two points: first, that a majority of academic researchers believe that a causal relationship exists between television and aggressive behavior; and second, that the sheer number of scientific studies in the literature supports the contention as opposed to the number of studies which do not.

Opinion of Researchers

In fact, there is no consensus among researchers regarding the relationship between television and aggression, and a spirited debate continues within the scientific community. In a recent study by Bybee, 486 academic researchers were asked their professional opinion of the influence of television on aggressive behavior. Only 1 percent reported that television was "the cause" of aggressive behavior. Further, the majority did not feel that television was an important contributory cause of aggressive behavior. Clearly this is not a consensus.

While it is true that there are more studies published in the literature which have found some effect between television viewing and aggressive behavior, this says more about the academic research process and the criteria employed for publication in scientific journals than it does about the television violence issue. It is an acknowledged fact that research studies that report an effect are far more likely to be accepted for publication than those studies which do not find an effect. Since editors naturally prefer to report results, publication policies can result in a distortion of the scientific evidence which actually exists. In the academic research field, where an individual's professional standing is based largely on published work, there is a real incentive for researchers to produce studies that do demonstrate an effect.

The research literature on television and violence has been reviewed and evaluated by other academic scientists than those who participated in the NIMH study. Although many have concluded that the research evidence does not support the conclusion that television violence causes aggressive behavior, their work was ignored by the NIMH panel.

The only way to address the question of how much violence is on television is to systematically analyze a representative sample of television programming by conducting a "content analysis." To accurately identify content trends, these analyses must be performed over a period of years. Only two such content analyses were included in the NIMH report. Of these two analyses only one—by Dr. George Gerbner and his colleagues at the University of Pennsylvania—is used by the NIMH to support its view that violent content has remained at a consistently high level.

Since 1967, Gerbner and his associates have produced the yearly Violence Profile—an analysis of the violent content of network television programming—research that has been supported by NIMH funding. An additional conflict is the fact that Dr. Gerbner is a member of the NIMH Advisory Panel which is responsible for the report and for its conclusions.

The other major content analysis study included in the NIMH report is conducted annually by the CBS Office of Social Research. The CBS study and the Gerbner study utilize radically different definitions of violence and consequently arrive at very different conclusions. While Gerbner maintains that violence is at a consistently high level, the CBS data indicate that the level of violence has decreased over the past decade. Since the NIMH relies so heavily upon the work of Dr. Gerbner and his colleagues, we will first analyze their content analysis and then compare it with the CBS study.

Gerbner Content Analyses

The Gerbner content analyses have generated a great deal of controversy within the research community, including Newcomb, Coffin and Tuchman, and Blank. Criticisms focus on three major issues: (1) the definition of violence which Gerbner uses; (2) the index which Gerbner constructs and uses to report the amounts of violence in programming; and (3) the sample which is analyzed and used to generalize to a full-year season.

The way in which violence in program content is defined is crucial because more than anything else, it affects the study's findings and conclusions. Earlier we discussed the difficulty in arriving at a commonly agreed upon definition of violence. Gerbner defines violence as: "the overt expression of physical force against self or other, compelling action against one's will on pain of being hurt or killed, or actually hurting or killing." What makes the Gerbner definition unique is that this definition is applied not only to serious and realistic depictions of violence, but is expanded to *include* comedy and slapstick, accidents, and acts of nature such as floods, earthquakes, and hurricanes. By employing such a definition, the Gerbner analyses arrive at violence figures which distort the amount of realistic violence actually on television. For example, in a number of Gerbner content studies, over one-third of all the violence counted did *not* result from human action but was caused by accidents or acts of nature. Without an understanding of the violence definition, we would incorrectly attribute far more violence to programming than actually exists.

Gerbner uses a Violence Index to measure the amount of violence on network television. A number of researchers have concluded that the Violence Index is an arbitrary and idiosyncratic measure which does not accurately reflect program content. Rather than simply count the number of violent incidents per program, Gerbner combines various numerical scores, some of which are weighted to reflect his own theories and controversial assumptions. For example, the Violence Index arbitrarily *doubles* the "rate of violent episodes per program," *doubles* the "rate of violent episodes per hour of programs," and combines together percentages with straightforward numerical sums. In response to this overwhelming criticism of the index, Gerbner replies, "The rates are doubled in order to raise their relatively low numerical values to the importance that the concepts . . . deserve."

By adding together the research equivalent of "apples and oranges," the index provides a biased and inaccurate picture of television content. As one noted researcher, B.M. Owen, commented, "One is always free to add apples and oranges if one wishes, but it isn't at all clear what the result means, and some people may take it seriously."

Gerbner and his colleagues utilize a one-week sample of prime-time network programming to generalize about the entire yearly television season. The use of one week's worth of programming to represent the total content of a fifty-two-week season is clearly inadequate.

CBS Content Analysis

The CBS study uses a thirteen-week sample of prime-time network programming to represent a full year, clearly a more adequate, representative sample than Gerbner's. CBS also employs a more reasonable definition of violence: "The use of physical force against persons or animals, or the articulated, explicit threat of physical force to compel particular behavior on the part of a person." This definition attempts to analyze only realistic violence and consequently excludes from the analysis accidents, acts of nature, and comedy or slapstick.

The CBS findings have shown a measured downward trend in the amount of violent program content among the three networks from 1973 through 1981, the last year for which data are available. Although the CBS study offers a much different picture of violent content than does the Gerbner study, the NIMH report dismisses their findings without comment.

Only the Gerbner and CBS studies measure television content over a long enough period of time to permit any sort of trends to be identified and measured. The NIMH report does mention a number of one-time content analysis studies but they are of little value in addressing the primary question. For example, one study cited by the NIMH utilize the capsule program descriptions in *TV Guide* as the method of analyzing the violence that appeared in programming.

The cultivation theory suggests that viewers absorb a unique and biased "social reality" from watching television. According to the theory, which has been put forth by Dr. George Gerbner, television presents a distorted reflection of the world which does not accurately represent what exists in real life. Consequently, people who watch television will perceive the world from a "television perspective" and not as it really is. Although the NIMH Advisory Panel indicates that the case for this cultivation theory has been clearly established, Hawkins and Pingree, the authors of the technical report chapter reach a different conclusion. They state, "the evidence concerning the causal direction of television's impact on social reality is not sufficient for strong conclusions."

As in the case of the content issue, the NIMH relies almost exclusively on the research of Dr. Gerbner and his associates to substantiate their claim that the cultivation theory is true. Although a number of other researchers have conducted work in this area, over half of all the studies reviewed by the NIMH were either conducted by Gerbner himself or by his associates. Thus, his methods and conclusions are clearly central to the issue of cultivation.

A number of independent researchers have been strongly critical of the cultivation hypothesis and of the research that supports it. Their criticisms address three key issues: (1) the use of correlation to imply causation; (2) the methods by which attitudes are measured; and (3) the application of certain research techniques in attempting to answer the research question.

The cultivation hypothesis states that television viewing causes distorted social attitudes and perceptions. Although the cultivation research utilizes correlational techniques, the theory's proponents interpret the findings to suggest causality. As we have demonstrated earlier, correlation can not indicate cause and effect. Further, in every cultivation study reported by the NIMH report, the correlation between television viewing and an individual's attitudes are extremely small, when they are found at all. In most cases, only 3 percent of a person's social attitudes are related to television viewing. In other words, 97 percent of a person's attitudes and perceptions are related to factors *other* than exposure to television.

What is especially significant is that television's miniscule relationship to social perceptions decreases even further when we consider such important external conditions as the individual's age, sex, race, and place of residence. Once these variables are taken into account, the cultivation effect of television on social attitudes and behaviors is virtually nonexistent.

The second area of criticism regarding cultivation research concerns the way in which viewer's attitudes and perceptions are measured. Individuals are asked a series of questions: one possible answer being the "TV answer," which the researchers say reflects how the world is shown on television, and the other response, a "real world" answer, which the researchers say reflects how the world really is. For example, a respondent might be asked to estimate how likely they are to be a victim of crime. Overestimating their chances of victimization is considered the "TV answer" since the researchers believe that exposure to violence on television cultivates fear and mistrust. Critics of the cultivation theory suggest the questions that are asked are highly selective, and items which do not support the cultivation theory are simply omitted. In addition, the "TV answer" is often arbitrarily determined by the researchers. Further, it has been found that on occasion, of the two responses from which an individual must choose, *both* were incorrect. Thus, the respondent is placed in the situation of having to select an answer when the only alternatives available are both wrong.

Research Techniques

One of the major criticisms of the cultivation theory involves the various procedures that are used to investigate the hypothesis. A number of researchers have attempted to replicate the findings of Gerbner and his colleagues and were unable to find the effects which were predicted by the cultivation theory.

Other researchers have been highly critical of specific methods. For example, a number of studies used a sliding baseline in segmenting individuals into the crucial "heavy" and "light" viewing categories which, according to the theory, determines how they will perceive the world. Instead of establishing a strict definition of "heavy" and "light" viewers, these categories are frequently determined by the idiosyncracies of each sample. Further, although the categories are not consistent from study to study, findings are compared as though they were identical. For example, in one study school children who watched three hours of television were classified as "heavy" viewers; in another, children who watched three hours were classified as "light" viewers.

Another point of criticism is that cultivation researchers group together viewers who fall into differing categories. When these groups are analyzed separately, the findings do not support the cultivation theory. For example, cultivation researchers group "nonviewers" who do not watch television with "light" viewers who watch less than average. When nonviewers are analyzed independently of light viewers, their fear and mistrust scores are actually *higher* than light viewers. Similarly, "extremely heavy viewers" are grouped with "heavy viewers." When extremely heavy viewers—who view eight or more hours of television daily—are analyzed independently, they are found to be *less* fearful and mistrusting than heavy viewers. In both of these instances, when unlike groups were analyzed separately, the findings were in direct opposition to what the cultivation theory predicts.

Overall, when the cultivation theory is examined closely, it is found to be far less compelling than the NIMH report indicates. Consequently, there is no justification for the strong conclusions which the advisory panel reached.

Conflict is a legitimate aspect of literature and drama yet we also recognize the sensitivity and care we must exercise when considering its use. ABC Television has established policies and procedures which enable us to handle violence and other controversial themes responsibly and tastefully. We make every effort to maintain the integrity of the story line but we do not accept the gratuitous use of violence nor do we tolerate stories that glorify violence or suggest that violence is without consequences to those who use it. The care and concern with which we approach violence is indicated by the various procedures and resources which we utilize in the evaluation of dramatic material and is outlined as follows.

Broadcast Standards and Practices

All entertainment series and specials are produced under the scrutiny of the Broadcast Standards and Practices Department (BSAP). Each program script is carefully reviewed by Broadcast Standards and Practices Department editors and every violent action within the script is carefully evaluated. Each violent action must have a thematic justification and the depiction should portray only the minimum necessary to maintain the integrity of the story line. Gratuitous or excessive violence is eliminated and unique and detailed depictions of violent actions which might be copied or emulated are either modified or eliminated. In addition to reviewing all scripts, every program is screened and approved in a rough-cut and final form by the Broadcast Standards and Practices Department editing staff before the program is considered acceptable for broadcast on ABC.

One of the tools which the BSAP editors use in evaluating program content is the Incident Classification and Analysis Form (ICAF) system. The ICAF was developed by the BSAP Department in conjunction with social scientists from the ABC Social Research Unit. The ICAF enables every editor to systematically categorize, quantify, and weigh every violent incident within a program and provides editors with a qualitative and quantitative measure of a given program's violent content.

The ICAF system is especially useful because it not only counts incidents of violence but differentiates the severity of the violence and considers the overall context within which the violence is portrayed. The ICAF system enables the BSAP editor to identify those elements within a program that may be excessive and gratuitous and is an important aspect in the overall evaluation of program content.

The ICAF system is continuously monitored and reviewed by the ABC Social Research Unit. This procedure maintains its high levels of reliability and validity and ensures that the ICAF remains a sensitive and accurate instrument for the identification and categorization of violent program content. Used in conjunction with the editor's professional judgment, the ICAF is a highly effective tool for maintaining ABC's standards of acceptability and appropriateness.

ABC Social Research Unit

The Social Research Unit is a part of the ABC Marketing and Research Services Department. One of its functions is to provide support services to the Broadcast Standards and Practices Department. In addition to the administration of the ICAF System, the Social Research Unit provides BSAP with relevant research information to ensure that all policies and guidelines reflect the most current data available. Contemporary social science research is reviewed on a continuing basis and plays an important role in maintaining appropriate standards for the portrayal of violence in programming. In addition to reviewing research which appears in the scientific literature, the Social Research Unit conducts a number of proprietary studies which are designed to assess the impact of our programming on viewers and to survey audience attitudes toward depictions of sensitive program material.

Another related activity of the Social Research Unit is to conduct workshops and seminars for the broadcast standards editing staff. Training workshops are an important element in professional growth and are held on a regular basis. This service ensures that established policy guidelines are consistently and accurately applied to the evaluation of all ABC programming. At a typical training workshop, representatives from the Social Research Unit, as well as outside expert consultants, discuss and evaluate editing policies and procedures. The case study approach is frequently used and has proven to be an excellent method in increasing and refining the abilities of the broadcast standards editors. In addition, ICAF procedures are regularly reviewed to retain the high reliability levels of the coding and to refine and improve the overall ICAF system.

The goal of these workshops and seminars is to increase the capability of the BSAP editors by improving their editing skills and by broadening their perspective and understanding of the viewing audience.

At the very beginning of this article we indicated the complexity of the television violence issue. Our review of the scientific literature demonstrates how true that statement is. Research is clearly a valuable means by which we can understand more about the medium of television and its social impact. But research is only useful after we have assessed each study's strengths and weaknesses and placed it in its proper perspective. Our analysis of the research which the NIMH has used to substantiate their conclusions regarding television and violence indicates that there are more unanswered questions than there are definitively settled issues.

At the same time we recognize our responsibility to ensure that when violence is presented in the context of a dramatic program, there exists a legitimate and thematic justification for its inclusion. Further, it is our practice to limit the portrayal of violence to that which is reasonably related to plot development and character delineation. The excessive depiction of violence is rarely necessary and gratuitous portrayals are considered inappropriate for the television medium.

We believe that ABC's policies and procedures have proven to be an excellent method of exercising our responsibility. We will continue to demonstrate care and concern in the future by providing our viewers with programming which meets the highest standards of appropriateness and social responsibility.

Bibliography

Belson, W. *Television Violence and the Adolescent Boy.* London: Saxon House, 1978.
Blank, D.M. "The Gerbner Violence Profile." *Journal of Broadcasting* 21 (1977):273-79.
Coffin, T.E. and Tuchman, S. "Rating Television Programs for Violence: A Comparison of Five Surveys." *Journal of Broadcasting* 17 (1972):3-20.
Krattenmaker, T.G. and Powe, L.A., Jr. "Televised Violence: First Amendment Principles and Social Science Theory." *Virginia Law Review* 64 (1978):1123-70.
Newcomb, H. "Assessing the Violence Profile Studies of Gerbner and Gross: A Humanistic Critique and Suggestion." *Communication Research* 5 (1978):264-82.
Owen, B.M. *Measuring Violence on Television: The Gerbner Index.* Springfield, Va.: National Technical Information Service, 1972.

12
Defending the Indefensible

Steven H. Chaffee, George Gerbner, Beatrix A. Hamburg, Chester M. Pierce, Eli A. Rubinstein, Alberta E. Siegel, and Jerome L. Singer

The National Institute of Mental Health (NIMH) project for which we were senior scientific advisers resulted in the publication of *Television and Behavior: Ten Years of Scientific Progress and Implications for the Eighties.* The two volume report was prepared as an update to a 1972 report to the surgeon general. The new NIMH report has recently come under public attack by some members of the television industry. The substance of that criticism, which we believe to be unfounded, calls for an informed response.

This article is specifically intended as an open reply to a statement written by Alan Wurtzel and Guy Lometti for the American Broadcasting Companies, Inc., the text of which precedes us in this issue of *Society*. The ABC statement purports to be a rigorous and objective refutation of the NIMH report; however, it is neither rigorous nor objective. It is a shallow attempt, ostensibly for public consumption, to focus on only one portion of the NIMH review, rehash industry attacks on independent research of the past ten years, ignore or distort both the evidence presented in the NIMH report and the consensus of the field, and present conclusions that obscure the issue and deceive the readers. It would be no exaggeration to compare this attempt by the television industry to the stubborn public position taken by the tobacco industry on the scientific evidence about smoking and health.

A telling indictment of the ABC position is inherent in findings on the effects of television that are ignored in their statement. Research has long since gone beyond the issue of violence. The summary (Volume 1) of the NIMH report devotes only 9 out of 91 pages to that topic. Similarly, only 72 out of 362 pages of technical reports in Volume 2 deal with violence and aggression. Some other topics include: health-promoting possibilities;

effects on cognitive and emotional functioning; effects on imagination, creativity, and prosocial behavior; and effects on education and learning. These are all parts of related body of data that only confirms the obvious conclusion: television is an influential teacher of children and adults. Ironically, the networks have pursued and used the concept of positive programming in defense of some of their children's productions. The research on positive effects is no better or worse than that on violence and aggression. Yet the industry, by some convenient logic, accepts the former and disputes the latter.

What is especially distressing about ABC's effort to discredit a carefully developed assessment of research is that it only serves to confuse and deter the considerable opportunity for constructive change. It is now more than a decade since the original surgeon general's report. In testimony before Senator Pastore in March 1972, all three network presidents acknowledged, with some qualification, the findings on televised violence and pledged to improve television for children. (The most forthright and responsive statement was made by Elton Rule, president of ABC.) Surely the creativity, talent, and considerable resources of the television industry could have been put to better use than the renewed campaign of obfuscation and evasion after ten years of significant scientific progress. Instead of a positive response to that evidence, quality programming for children on commercial television has become increasingly rare.

The ABC argument is scientifically indefensible. By the very manner in which it was constructed, it is only the latest example of unwarranted resistance to the clear policy implications of overwhelming scientific evidence. The renewed attempt to evade, undermine, and discredit the work of hundreds of scientists summarized in the NIMH volumes and to shape the course of public discussion by selective attention and misrepresentation, is unworthy of an industry that professes—and is licensed—to serve the public interest.

The ABC response reads like a slick brief for the defense replete with carefully worded misinterpretations, omission of large bodies of relevant evidence, and sheer misstatements of facts. It begins by calling into question the entire body of research reviewed in the NIMH report as "simply a reiteration of information which has already been made available." ABC sees this as a fatal flaw, despite the fact that the foreword to the NIMH report and most of the press coverage made clear that the report was not based on new research, but was a comprehensive and integrative review of existing research, The ABC interpretation suggests that once published, research findings quickly go stale and lose their validity or relevance. On the contrary, findings accumulate with later studies, testing, confirming, and extending those published earlier.

What is especially lacking in rigor or objectivity is the premise by ABC that research on violence stands in isolation from the larger body of research reviewed by the NIMH report. Perhaps the most telling confirmatory evidence on the effects of televised violence is that it is now only one part of a massive body of research. A pattern of effects has emerged for all this evidence. It would be anomalous if the findings on violence and aggression did not fit into this larger pattern.

Ignoring that crucial issue, ABC isolates four specific conclusions from what is actually a minor part of the NIMH report. We address only some of the many violations of the principles to which the ABC statement claims to be dedicated. We begin by discussing the ABC summary of and response to each of the four NIMH conclusions that are addressed. First, to the conclusion, "The research findings support the conclusion of a causal relationship between television violence and aggressive behavior"; ABC responds, "The research does not support the conclusion of causal relationship."

The attribution of causality is a complex way of defining relationships, even in the physical sciences. The question is not how irrefutable the causal conclusion may be, especially in the social sciences, but can it be invoked at all. In 1972, the Surgeon General's Scientific Advisory Committee, of which two distinguished members were full-time scientists for NBC and CBS respectively, and of which three other members had been part-time consultants to the industry, came to the unanimous conclusion that there is "some preliminary indication of a causal relationship, but a good deal of research remains to be done before one can have confidence in these conclusions." The update provided much additional research to add confidence to the conclusions.

Most research in the field has concerned itself with the linkage between "televised violence" and "aggressive behavior." Rarely have scientists attempted to observe, let alone induce, "violent behavior." The ABC statement uses a subterfuge in equating aggressive behavior with violent behavior and then asking if televised violence causes violent behavior. While few studies, for obvious reasons, can legitimately explore that connection, one notable instance does exist. The study by Belson did find such a causal connection between televised violence and actual antisocial behavior. Despite the fact that the study was funded by CBS, when it was independently published in book form, it was dismissed by the industry as merely "correlational." That charge is now leveled by ABC against the NIMH report's conclusions.

Although even the stimulation of harmful tendencies in millions of children is of no small consequence, ABC obfuscates the issue. It states baldly that "the point is, correlation can never tell us anything about causation."

Even theoretically, let alone in a practical way, this is not true. Correlation is a necessary but not sufficient condition in a causal relationship. To argue that a study is "correlational" as the industry did with the Belson study, is not legitimately to dismiss its significance. If there had been no correlation, the question of causation would have been settled long ago. Study after study by independent investigators found significant correlations.

Wurtzel and Lometti develop something called "convergence theory" to argue that scientists can be led to accept any "widespread belief" on which many different studies seem to converge. If there is any substance to that curious criticism, it must be in the basic assumption behind the operation of the television industry itself. Ten billion dollars annually are expended on the "widespread belief" that advertising induces people to buy products. There is no more definitive causal relationship between advertising on television and subsequent buying behavior than there is between televised violence and later aggressive behavior.

No researcher cited by NIMH argues that television violence is the only or even necessarily the main factor in aggression. The conclusion on which there is a significant "convergence" is that it is a contributing factor. Having set up a straw-man relationship between causation, correlation, and convergence, ABC argues that only a handful of studies support the NIMH conclusions.

The ABC statement begins: "The NIMH technical chapter on violence and aggression in Volume 2 cites fourteen studies which the author suggests proves a positive relationship between television and violence and which the NIMH report relies upon to reach its conclusion of a cause-effect relationship." The chapter referred to is a comprehensive review not just of fourteen studies but of the larger penumbra of research on televised violence which further illuminates this body of findings. Ninety-five publications are referenced in this chapter, most of which support the major argument.

Wurtzel and Lometti point out that this chapter does not discuss a study by NBC researcher Milavsky, one that dismissed television's effect on aggression as negligible, "although the NBC study appears in its own chapter in the NIMH report." Precisely because another chapter was devoted to the NBC study would it have been superfluous to incorporate its findings in the chapter under discussion. It was NIMH and our committee that invited the NBC researchers and requested the inclusion of the NBC study as a separate chapter of Volume 2. What ABC implies was an omission is the result of a conscientious effort on the part of NIMH and our committee to include all relevant research. The conclusions of the NBC study were carefully considered in the final evaluation and summary published in Volume 1.

ABC has not refuted the NIMH conclusion of a causal relationship between television violence and aggression, and has misstated both the convergence and weight of evidence bearing on the issue. To the second summarized conclusion, "There is a clear consensus among most researchers that television violence leads to aggressive behavior"; ABC responds, "There exists a significant debate within the research community over the relationship between television and aggressive behavior."

ABC found one (unpublished) study, by Bybee et al., that it could construe as suggesting there is no consensus among academic researchers. ABC misrepresented that study. The sample polled was not all "academic researchers," as ABC states but members of professional societies in speech and journalism, an unknown proportion of which are researchers. More importantly, researchers in the field of television include many social scientists who were absent from the sample.

Even more deceptive is ABC's interpretation of the results of that survey. The issue is not whether television is *the* cause of aggression. No responsible researcher makes that claim. All complex behavior has many causes. What the research results showed is that television is a significant contributor to such behavior. On that point, the Bybee study cited by ABC actually showed a clear consensus. About two-thirds of those polled agreed that television increased children's aggressive behavior. Had more scientists from other fields been included, that consensus would probably have been even higher. The authors of the Bybee study are themselves distressed at ABC's misrepresentation of their findings.

Attempting to neutralize the findings in the great preponderance of published studies, ABC claims that studies that find an effect are more likely to be published than studies with no findings. That seeming anomaly would have disappeared if ABC had correctly stated that well designed studies, with clearly developed hypotheses, and careful statistical analyses, leading to scientifically defensible conclusions, are more likely to be published in reputable scientific journals than poor studies with inconclusive results. It is insulting to the research community to state as ABC does—badly and without qualifications—that "since editors naturally prefer to report results, publication policies can result in a distortion of the scientific evidence which actually exists." In that sentence, the ABC statement attempts to discredit the entire formal process of scientific publication.

ABC cites seven references to claim that many academic scientists have concluded that the research evidence does not support the causal linkage. That list of seven all but exhausts the list of "many." ABC has not refuted the NIMH conclusion that there is a clear consensus among research scientists on this issue. To the third summarized conclusion, "Despite slight variations over the past decade, the amount of violence on television has remained at consistently high levels"; ABC responds, "There has been a decrease in the overall amount of violence in recent years." ABC's contention about a decrease in the overall amount of violence is based on an in-house CBS report and is not supported by independent studies. It also does not necessarily contradict the NIMH conclusion.

Singled out for special attention by ABC is an extensive and long-standing research project called Cultural Indicators, conducted at the University of Pennsylvania's Annenberg School of Communications since the late 1960s. The project began as a study for the National Commission on the Causes and Prevention of Violence (the "Eisenhower Commission") and continued under various foundation and medical auspices to investigate many aspects of television content and viewer conception of social reality.

Ignoring its proper name, broad scope, many publications and assessment by NIMH and others, ABC reaches back six years to claim that "the Gerbner content analyses have generated a great deal of controversy within the research community." Of the authors cited as being responsible for the "controversy," Coffin, Tuchman, and Blank were network employees and Newcomb a humanistic scholar whose dialogue with the Cultural Indicators team was as supportive as critical of the effort. All complex research relevant to social policy does and should be debated. ABC conceals the actual debate from the readers of its statement; it does not mention the rebuttals published in the same journals—and usually in the very same issues—as the works cited. The ABC authors repeat perennial network objections as if they had never been addressed and dealt with both in the literature and in the NIMH report. At least three chapters of Volume 2 of the NIMH report provide critical overviews and assessments of all aspects of the content analyses ABC insists are "controversial." One of these, an overview of measures of violence in television content, compares several measures including those of Cultural Indicators and the CBS study. It finds "no detectable trend," and observes: "Regardless of measure, changes that within the scope of 2 or 3 years would appear to constitute an upward or downward shift become, in the long run, oscillations." That and other similar reviews of the research evidence by independent scholars led NIMH and our committee to conclude that despite variations over the years, violence on television, "remained at consistently high levels."

The ABC statement supports its contention of a decrease in the amount of violence by reference to a CBS study not subject to peer review or other scientific scrutiny and not regularly published. It was introduced into the 1981 congressional hearings on "Social/Behavioral Effects of Violence on Television" as the industry's attempt to counter evidence presented by researchers at the hearing. An examination of the 1981 hearing record shows that CBS succeeded in "reducing" the amount of violence reported by excluding a significant (and unreported) amount of violent representations. The violence monitoring effort announced by ABC itself with much fanfare a few years ago did not seem to yield results suitable for its own statement.

ABC argues, "the CBS study and the Gerbner study utilize radically different definitions of violence and consequently arrive at very different conclusions." The CBS study definition of violence, not cited by ABC, is: "The use of physical force against persons or animals or the articulated, explicit threat of physical force to compel particular behavior on the part of a person." Wurtzel and Lometti state that "Gerbner defines violence as: 'The overt expression of physical force against self or other compelling action against one's will on pain of being hurt or killed, or actually hurting or killing.'" The two definitions are in practice virtually identical. ABC argues, "What makes the Gerbner definition unique is that this definition is applied not only to serious and realistic depictions of violence, but is expanded to include comedy and slapstick, accidents and acts of nature such as floods, earthquakes, and hurricanes." Both definitions include the use of physical force in any context. The difference is not in definition, as ABC claims; it is in what CBS chose not to include in its report.

The counts CBS excluded from its report were those it claimed, without evidence, to be "harmless" acts of "accidental" and "humorous" violence. The evidence reviewed by NIMH indicates that violence in any context may teach powerful lessons and can be harmful in its effects. Even with such manipulation, the CBS study was only able to reduce its violence score from 138 incidents a week in 1972-73 to 105 a week in 1980-81. That is still more violence in one week of prime-time watching alone than most people experience otherwise in a lifetime. It can hardly be seen as contradicting the NIMH finding that "violence on television remained at consistently high levels."

How much of all that mayhem is "accidental" and "humorous" violence that the networks claim is "harmless"? Here again, ABC is wide of the mark. They claim that "in a number of Gerbner studies, over one-third of all the violence counted did *not* result from human action but was caused by accidents or acts of nature." (Emphasis in the original.) ABC deals with prime-time programs alone. The source of ABC's observation on "human action" is the original report to the surgeon general, *Television and Social Behavior Volume 1, Media Content and Control.* Those figures refer not to prime time but to the combined results of prime-time and weekend daytime children's (mostly cartoon) programs. In cartoons, humanized animals rather than humans, strictly defined, commit most violence. Therefore, the "over one-third of all the violence counted" was not "caused by accidents or acts of nature" but mostly by cartoon "animals" committing anthropomorphic mayhem. ABC uses cartoon violence only to obfuscate the facts, not to express concern over the most violent and exploitive part of programming, what the trade calls the "kidvid ghetto." A careful look at table 67 in the original report would have revealed that when only regular programs (rather than cartoons) are considered, as in prime time, nine out of ten acts of violence are perpetrated by human agents. Table 69 in the same series also shows that of these acts of hurting and killing people only one-fifth appear in a "light" or "humorous" context, with consequences that, according to available evidence, cannot be blithely dismissed.

Where does that muddle leave those real "acts of nature such as floods, earthquakes, aand hurricanes" that according to ABC "distort" the amount of violence reported? In light of the facts they also shrink into insignificance. An analysis of Cultural Indicators data for fifteen sample periods since 1969 shows a grand total of only thirteen fictional "acts of nature" hurting and killing. The viewer bombarded with violence every hour of prime time has to watch an average of three and a half weeks to encounter one act of "accidental" violence. The social pattern of such victimization (i.e., what types of characters tend to get hurt or killed "accidentally") may be far from inconsequential. The rarity of the occurrence makes the ABC claim groundless. The argument that an "expanded" definition "distorts" even one set of violence figures used in the NIMH report is both deceptive and trivial.

One of the oldest claims of network publicists, renewed here despite ample clarification through the years, is that the Violence Index "is an arbitrary and idiosyncratic measure which does not accurately reflect program content." ABC maintains that rather than counting the number of violent incidents per program, "Gerbner combines various numerical scores, some of which are weighted to reflect his own theoretical and controversial assumptions." This ignores responses published since 1972 and the annual publication of the Violence Index in which the "simple count of the number of violent incidents per program" is separately tabulated for the convenience of those who prefer that simple measure to also considering the pervasiveness of violence in all programming and lethal vs. nonlethal consequences. An extensive review of tests in Volume 2 of the NIMH report found that the Violence Index "meets the critical statistical and empirical requirements of an index: unidimensionality and internal homogeneity."

ABC's quibble with the sample employed in the Violence Index is similarly misdirected. Without citing any support, the ABC authors state that "the use of one week's worth of programming to represent the total content of a fifty-two-week season is clearly inadequate." As explained many times,

Defending the Indefensible 141

and reviewed in at least two technical chapters of the NIMH Report, but ignored by ABC, experiments with up to seven weeks of programming have not produced notably different results. The NIMH review concluded:

> These studies thus indicate that while a larger sample might increase precision, given the operational definitions and multidimensional measures that are sensitive to a variety of significant aspects of television violence, the 1-week sample yields stable results with high cost efficiency.

The consistency of violence and other measures of fictional demography and power from year to year would be hard to explain with a sample that is inadequate to the task for which it was designed.

The extensive research evidence supporting the definition of violence and its measurement in samples of television content has not been examined by ABC; it has been ignored. The ABC claims appear to be designed for the uninitiated, repeating contentions network publicists have been propagating for over a decade. The ABC statement did not refute the NIMH conclusion that violence on television remains at consistently high levels. To the fourth summarized conclusion, "Television has been shown to cultivate television-influenced attitudes among viewers. Heavy viewers are more likely to be more fearful and less trusting of other people than are light viewers as a result of their exposure to television"; ABC responds, "The research does not support the conclusion that television significantly cultivates viewer attitudes and perceptions of social reality."

ABC challenges the extensive body of research findings on television's cultivation of viewer attitudes and conceptions of reality. The ABC statement claims that even though the NIMH report accepted many of the findings of the cultivation analysis, "the authors of the technical report chapter reach a different conclusion." Those authors stated, "the evidence concerning the causal direction of television's impact on social reality is not sufficient for strong conclusions." The technical report chapter by Hawkins and Pingree supports the cultivation theory and confirms findings cited by NIMH. "Causal direction" is not an issue in cultivation theory which holds that the pervasive and repetitive patterns of television cultivate, rather than only create, attitudes and perceptions. After the passage cited by ABC, Hawkins and Pingree observe that "the relationship between viewing and social reality may be reciprocal." In their view of many studies, including their own, Hawkins and Pingree conclude:

> Is there a relationship between television viewing and social reality? Most studies show evidence for a link, regardless of the kind of social reality stud-

ied. These studies cover a diverse range of areas including prevalence of violence, family structures, interpersonal mistrust, fear of victimization, traditional sex roles, family values, images of older people, attitudes about doctors, and concern about racial problems.... Relationships between viewing and demographic measures of social reality closely linked to television content appear to hold despite controls.

Another example of the criticisms cited by ABC is the assertion that cultivation researchers group nonviewers with light viewers. When nonviewers are analyzed independently, ABC states "their fear and mistrust scores are actually *higher* than light viewers." Similarly, it is said that extremely heavy viewers are grouped with heavy viewers, but when extremely heavy viewers are analyzed independently, "they are found to be *less* fearful and mistrusting than heavy viewers." The facts were reported in an article in the same journal from which ABC selected its information, but they were omitted from the ABC statement. Nonviewers and "extremely heavy viewers" are very small and atypical groups (about 5 percent of the population each). Their deviant responses are trivial in size and not significant statistically. The inclusion of these deviant groups means that the NIMH conclusions about cultivation are underestimated; when they are excluded, the resulting patterns are even stronger for the remaining 90 percent of the population.

A series of additional repetitions of criticisms already dealt with in the research literature and reviewed in the NIMH report further strains the credibility of the ABC "critique." Clearly its authors are aware of the scholarly exchanges that have taken place; they seem not to have missed a single negative comment, no matter how far-fetched. Yet they seem to be oblivious to the more numerous extensions and confirmations of findings by independent scholars in the United States and abroad.

The ABC statement deceives the reader not familiar with the research literature. It is thus the ABC statement and not the NIMH report that distorts, in its general design as well as its details, the evidence on television and violence that it purports to place in perspective.

13

Smoking Out the Critics

Alan Wurtzel and Guy Lometti

Our review of the NIMH Advisory Panel's critique of our preceding statement indicates that its conclusion is without merit. Not only is it unsuccessful in challenging our fundamental criticisms regarding the NIMH report, but it fails to address many of the most salient issues included in our statement regarding the research on television and its relationship to subsequent violent behavior.

Critiques have tried to compare our critique of the scientific research on television violence and its impact to the reaction of the tobacco industry, which attempted to refute the scientific evidence regarding the hazards of smoking. Such an analogy is completely without merit. In 1964 there were 6,000 studies regarding smoking and its impact; by 1979 there were a total of 30,000 studies in the literature. A comparison of these figures with the 100 or so studies dealing specifically with the impact of television violence on subsequent behavior, or the 14 studies specifically cited by the NIMH in support of their cause-effect contention, will place the smoking research vs. television research argument into perspective.

In the smoking research, the independent variable was the number of cigarettes smoked—a clearly defined and quantifiable measure. In the case of television, it is the ill-defined menu of violent programs an individual views, using a criterion that changes from one study to the next. Consider the dependent measure of the effect we wish to study. In the case of smoking, it is the incidence of cancer, heart disease, emphysema, and death. When it comes to television, researchers *never* measure violent or criminal behavior but substitutes for these behaviors (using paper and pencil tests, for example, or observations of children making faces), many of which are not validated and are clearly unrelated to our real-world concern over actual violence. There are no statistics regarding the impact of television violence similar to those concerning the impact of smoking, and no single responsible researcher has ever claimed such an impact.

The ABC statement was not prepared as a response to the entire NIMH report. Its stated intention was to address the issue of television and violence since this had received the greatest amount of press coverage and comment. We addressed not only the NIMH report regarding its evaluation of the research on violence, but a substantial amount of material regarding the research techniques that have been used to study the question of television violence and its possible impact on behavior and attitudes. This material was ignored by the NIMH critique.

The reference by the critique to a "slick brief" is inappropriate. Our document was designed to address a number of significant social science issues from a research perspective. While the ABC statement was written to be understood by the general public, it deals with the issues on a strictly social research basis. Most of the salient points in the original text are referenced to a scholarly article that has appeared within the scientific literature. The statement is a social science evaluation of the issues regarding television and violent behavior.

We have demonstrated that the NIMH report on violence was not a "comprehensive and integrative review of existing research." A number of significant studies that did not support the NIMH panel's conclusions were ignored. Other studies were cited but never considered in the overall evaluation of the research. We did not suggest that old research is necessarily "stale" or loses validity. Newton's laws of motion in physics are as valid today as they were when they were first postulated. We suggested that research that is significantly flawed in methodology or analysis, regardless of how old or new, is simply bad research. That it has appeared in the literature for a long period of time does not necessarily guarantee its validity. Frequently, science accepts initial premises only to revise them once new evidence becomes available or once peer review indicates significant flaws in the methods or conclusions. This approach is fundamental to the scientific method.

The NIMH critique accuses ABC of ignoring television's potential as a "teacher." They contend that a massive body of research points to the fact that television entertainment is a teacher. They ask, how do we contend that violence has no effect? Our response revolves around three points.

First, the research literature examining television's ability to teach does not report large and consistent effects. Studies assessing the impact of "Sesame Street" and "The Electric Company" (two programs specifically designed to teach) indicate that any educational gains found among the children sampled were most likely due to the interaction these youngsters had with parents and teachers about the programs. Second, television has the capability to present viewers with ideas and behavioral models, but this is a very complex capability which depends upon a multitude of variables regarding the characteristics of the individual, the way in which the information is presented, and the reinforcement (or lack of reinforcement) in the "real world." For example, "prosocial" behavior such as Fonzie in "Happy Days" registering for a library card is an action which is likely to be reinforced by parents and teachers in real life. Conversely, aggressive behavior in which a child may engage is likely to be discouraged by parents and teachers. Third, the analogy raised between the impact of television commercials on consumer behavior and the ability of the medium to instigate violent behavior is completely invalid. Commercials are socially sanctioned, and the sponsor uses recognized (and regulated) techniques to present a product in an attractive and desirable manner. In the case of violence, network guidelines prohibit the glorification of violence or its depictions in any way to suggest that it is an activity that should be emulated or copied. Violence is not socially sanctioned, and television does not operate within a social vacuum.

The fundamental point is that violence and the way it is depicted on network television bears no resemblance to the way in which prosocial, positive, and socially sanctioned activities are presented. The attempt to link the two is a comparison that cannot be made logically.

The critique's citation of the conclusion of the 1972 surgeon general's report is misleading. The original source acknowledges that insufficient evidence exists for a cause-effect relationship to be determined reliably. Our careful review and evaluation of the literature leads us to accept that conclusion. We make the point that a complete reevaluation of the research and its validity is in order. It is not our intention to reproduce the content of our argument in this rejoinder. We questioned, in detail, some of the fundamental research methods and techniques that have been used to substantiate the NIMH conclusions about causality. These include the samples utilized, the way violence is defined in program content, the measurement of violent behaviors, and the statistical methods that have been employed in the research. The conclusions some researchers have reached based upon this faulty methodology are unwarranted. The preceding NIMH critique is simply a reiteration of the entire argument that was carefully addressed in the ABC statement.

The NIMH critique dismisses criticisms regarding the definition and measurement of violent behavior despite the fact that this is a crucial aspect of the issue. If scientists claim that television viewing leads to aggressive or violent behavior, the assumption is that they are accurately and consistently measuring that behavior. Scientists do not actually measure violence at all; they measure a variety of substitute behaviors that are either socially sanctioned (such as in laboratory experiments) or are, at the very most, behaviors that can be more accurately classified as "incivility" rather than as violence.

Scientists cannot measure real violence, and this is noted in our previous statement. It follows that the NIMH cannot conclude that television causes violent behavior without having actually measured that behavior. In the absence of a proper measurement of the specific behaviors that the NIMH claims are associated with exposure to television, there is no justification for reaching the conclusion about a cause-effect relationship.

The critique misquotes references to the Belson study. We did not dismiss that study as merely correlational. We noted that the primary criticism of Belson is that the findings run counter to the NIMH conclusions. Belson found that light viewers and heavy viewers were less likely to engage in aggressive behavior; moderate viewers were more likely. Thus, the Belson study does not support the NIMH claim of a linear, causal relationship between television viewing and subsequent aggression.

The NIMH contends that the Belson study is a notable instance in which research has explored the connection between televised violence and real "violent behavior." When assessing the validity of this study we must realize that no observations of violent behavior were employed. The researchers relied upon self-reports. Involvement in violent behavior was measured by asking the boys in the study if they had committed any of fifty-three violent acts in the last six months. The validity of these reports is limited by the veracity of the boys' statements and their ability to accurately recall their past behavior. Many people would have trouble believing the self-reports of juvenile delinquents.

The NIMH critique's discussion of correlation underscores the way in which the use of the statistical technique in the report is misinterpreted. Correlation must exist in order to find a causal relationship. This means that before cause and effect can be demonstrated, it must be proven that two variables are co-related; but the statement cannot be reversed. For example, even though all oceans are bodies of water all bodies of water are not oceans. A correlation is necessary to prove causation, but finding a correlation in no way assumes causation. Correlations are highly susceptible to misinterpretation, especially when investigators do not control for third variables. The NIMH critique never addresses the correlation issues that are raised in our statement regarding spurious correlations, the insignificant amount of variance accounted for by the correlations (which are often approximately 1 or 2 percent of the total), and that many so-called significant correlations disappear with the use of third-variable controls.

The NIMH critique suggests that we "invented" the notion of convergence. In the summary volume of their report, the NIMH states: "the convergence of findings supports the conclusion of causal relationship." Regarding the issue of convergence, consistency in prior research findings does not eliminate the possibility of drawing erroneous conclusions. In order to appropriately apply the convergence approach to research conclusions, one must assume that different studies do not have any systematic biases that operate in the same direction and that no invalid measurement techniques are employed. Our review of the NIMH research indicates that many studies share a number of significant flaws that are simply perpetuated from one study to the next. The NIMH critiques misses this point and instead suggests that we are engaging in a "head count" of individual studies. This was not done at all. The point is made that every research study must be individually evaluated for its strengths and weaknesses before determining how much credibility to place in its results and conclusions. Using the convergence approach eliminates this crucial evaluative element and leads to distorted conclusions.

The statement about 95 articles supporting the cause-effect conclusion is not true. There are only 14 studies that lead the NIMH technical chapter author to the conclusion: "the evidence seems overwhelming that television violence viewing and aggression are positively correlated in children." The remaining studies, which are referred to as the "95 studies," deal with other issues such as catharsis, attitude change, and observational learning.

The exclusion of the Milavsky study is extremely important despite the critique's protestations to the contrary. In arriving at the ultimate conclusion of cause-effect, it is unfortunate that the NIMH technical report author never considered a major study that did not support his contention of a causal link. The Milavsky study is included in a completely separate chapter where it is essentially ignored in the NIMH's review and evaluation of relevant literature. The Milavsky study results are dismissed in the summary report.

The purpose in citing the Bybee study was not to provide a definitive poll of the scientific community, but to put forth the only empirical evidence which was available at the time regarding the issue of consensus in the research community. Rather than making a statement without substantiation regarding consensus, as the NIMH report does, we felt that it would be useful to indicate the degree to which there is a continuing debate among researchers. Regarding Bybee's methodology, we find another instance in which the critique offers a misleading statement. According to the critique, the sample consists of many irrelevant individuals with expertise outside the mass communication field. According to Bybee's own paper, which was presented at the annual convention of the American Association for Public Opinion Research in 1982, the sample was a poll of "mass media scholars" who are members of the mass communication division or the theory and methodology division of two nationally recognized professional organizations. They are actively involved in these research issues.

The Bybee study shows tremendous variability among researchers' agreement with the cause-effect conclusion posited by the NIMH. Less than 1 percent believed television was "the cause" of aggressive behavior, another

21 percent believed it was an "important cause," and another 44 percent considered television a "somewhat important cause." Twenty-four percent said television had "no relationship" and 11 percent "didn't know." We do not suggest that the Bybee study is without flaws. The questionnaire's wording was biased in the direction of a positive relationship; of the five possible answers only one states "no relationship." Thus, the survey most likely overestimates the number of researchers who report a positive relationship at all. In spite of this, we find fully one-third of all researchers questioned do not report a relationship at all, and only one-fifth—at most—concur with the NIMH claim of a strong and direct causal relationship. This is not a consensus.

The assertion regarding publication policies is not raised solely by us but is supported by and credited in our original statement to Krattenmaker and Powe. The issue of publication policy is extremely significant, especially when evaluating a large body of research as the NIMH report attempted. Despite the critique's remark that studies can be published which do not disprove the "null hypothesis" of "no findings," this is exceedingly rare. There is a distinct bias in the academic literature against publishing any study that supports the "null hypothesis"; that is, a study in which no effect or relationship is found. In an article entitled "Prejudice Against the Null Hypothesis," published in *Psychological Bulletin,* Greenwald demonstrates that scientific publications are far less likely to accept null findings, and this to Greenwald, "can be very detrimental to research progress."

The reason for bias against the null hypothesis is that many researchers in this field assume that there are significant social effects from television and fail to question that assumption. As scientists who work in an area of investigation that is frequently described as "the social effects of television," it is clear that these researchers come with the underlying assumption that television does have profound and significant social effects. As we have demonstrated, many of the "effects" the NIMH panel suggests support their claim of causal link between television and violence are extremely small. In many social science disciplines they would be considered to be a finding of "no effect." Because some researchers studying television have accepted *a priori* the premise that effects do exist, their interpretation of the data leads them to an erroneous conclusion of profound and significant effects. The result of this reasoning is to view a study that fails to find an effect as either poorly designed or executed; the implication is that if it had been properly designed the effects (which are assumed to exist) would be apparent. This circular reasoning results in the inclusion in the academic literature of far fewer studies that find no effect than those that find an effect.

Seven literature reviews originally cited by us conclude that television and violent behavior are not causally related. These are not seven individual studies, but a compilation of many independent studies with conclusions that run counter to those of the NIMH. We never suggested that the ABC statement was designed to be an exhaustive review of the literature. It was the NIMH—not ABC—that claimed to conduct a "comprehensive" and "integrative" review of the relevant literature. Yet this comprehensive review failed to cite or to mention over forty published articles, dissertations, and papers with conclusions running counter to the cause-effect relationship claimed by the NIMH report. These studies and literature reviews are not simply dismissed by the NIMH; they are completely ignored.

Our preceding statement devotes considerable attention to the Cultural Indicators project simply because the NIMH relies on it so extensively in support of many of their conclusions. George Gerbner—who is the director of the Cultural Indicators project—is a member of the seven-person advisory panel responsible for reviewing and assessing the available research in the field. NIMH accuses ABC of ignoring the "many publications" of the Cultural Indicators project. They have not been ignored. These studies form the basis for our criticism of two of the NIMH report conclusions.

The NIMH contends that any study conducted or reviewed by social scientists working in the television industry is either biased or mistaken and is the result of an obvious vested interest. They imply that research by academic researchers is without error or bias and does not reflect an established viewpoint. This argument has no validity. Social scientists working in industry are subject to the same professional peer review and evaluation of their work as any other scientists and researchers.

Relevant to the issue of bias is the composition of the NIMH advisory board and the individuals who were selected to review the articles in the technical report. Four of the seven advisory board members had taken a strong public position on the violence issue before the NIMH panel was formed. A number of individuals who were asked to comment on and evaluate the research were placed in the position of assessing their own research or research of a colleague with whom they had collaborated. For example, in the chapter evaluating and reviewing the Cultural Indicators content analysis studies, of which the work of Gerbner and his Annenberg colleagues plays a pivotal role, the authors—Signorielli, Morgan, and Gross—were three of Gerbner's colleagues and/or former students who developed and continue to work on the content analysis research that they were asked to evaluate. Not surprisingly, they found the research to be scientifically valid. Similarly, in the chapter developing the argument in support of the cause-effect relationship, the author, Huesmann, cites eight of his own research studies in support of his contention. It seems inconceivable that any researcher who is asked to evaluate his or her own work will be in the best position to uncover unintended flaws or systematic biases that can detrimentally affect the conclusions reached. It is difficult to believe that the NIMH was unable to find a sufficient number of scientists competent to evaluate their colleagues' work without being placed in the difficult position of assessing the strengths and weaknesses of their own research. This review procedure is not conducive to a rigorous and objective analysis of the research and its conclusions.

The critique's criticism that the controversy surrounding the Gerbner content analysis is artificial is a misstatement of the facts. The "perennial network objections" they dismiss are actually made by nonnetwork representatives Krattenmaker and Powe, and by Owen, in addition to the sources that they acknowledge. These sources are clearly referenced in our original statement. The critique also summarily dismisses a number of critics without ever indicating why they believe the criticism is invalid. For example, Newcomb is dismissed as a "humanist scholar." Coffin, Tuchman, and Blank are accused of bias because they are working for the television industry. At no time does the critique ever address the merits of their specific criticisms.

Astonishingly, the NIMH authors failed to note that an entire section of our statement is devoted to the ABC Incident Classification and Analysis Form (ICAF) system. The ICAF system is explained in detail in an article appearing in the 1984 *Journal of Broadcasting*.

Despite the NIMH critique's assertion, we did not deal solely with primetime television or with any particular part of the day. We dealt with the research into television and its impact on behavior and attitudes. The critique suggests we misrepresented the data from Gerbner's table 67 in the 1972 surgeon general's report; the table clearly indicates that for all programming, one-third of the violence attributed to network programming is not committed by human agents.

Even if one accepts the arbitrary delimitation to prime-time programming the critique asserts, for the three-year period shown in table 67 (1967-69), the range of violent actions caused by nonhuman agents ranges from 9 percent to 20 percent. The Gerbner report acknowledges that fully one-fifth of the violent action recorded was categorized by Gerbner as being "mostly light, comic, humorous."

We cannot find any breakdown of violent agents (human vs. nonhuman) in any subsequent Gerbner report. Consequently it is impossible to ascertain to what extent nonhuman agents (such as fantasy characters or acts of nature) are contributing to the violent scores of programs more current than those of fourteen years ago. This is only one illustration leading to the conclusion that the Gerbner system is idiosyncratic and produces results that distort the actual amount of violence on television.

The NIMH critique refuses to address the issues we raised. They refer to ABC's argument as "claims by network publicists." The statement was written by social scientists, and it makes reference to sources from the social science literature to substantiate its arguments. The comment referred to by the critique regarding the "idiosyncratic and arbitrary nature" of the Gerbner Violence Index was a criticism made by Krattenmaker and Powe and by Owen. It was clearly referenced in the original statement.

The Violence Index may meet the "statistical and empirical requirements of unidimensionality and internal homogeneity" as the critique suggests. This does not indicate whether it meets minimum requirements of validity; in other words, does it measure what it purports to measure?

In defense of the use of one week's worth of programming to represent the content of a fifty-two week season, the critique relies upon the evaluation of Gerbner's former students and colleagues. The wide variation in programming on the three networks today no longer enables a sample of a single week to be representative of an entire season. The Gerbner data assessing the validity of the one-week sample were obtained more than ten years ago and do not reflect contemporary program scheduling.

Two examples of the "extensive work" that the critique refers to in support of its evaluation of content analysis methods include one study in which the researchers determined program content by using synopses from *TV Guide* and another that used a total sample of twelve television programs. The ABC statement extensively reviewed the material and indicated clearly why the various content analysis methods provide a distorted view of the violent content on network television.

The NIMH critique insists that "causal direction" is not an issue in the cultivation hypothesis. On the "Viewpoint" show on February 24, Gerbner was quoted as saying:

> Media violence is a demonstration of power. There is direct causal relationship, our 15 years of research has shown, between exposure to violence and one's feeling of where one belongs in the power structure—one's feeling of vulnerability, one's feeling of insecurity. That is the direct relationship.

The notion of cultivation does indicate that a causal relationship exists between exposure and impact, with Gerbner stating that one's perceptions of reality are distorted in direct proportion to the amount of exposure to television. Thus, causal direction is the issue involved, and on this the NIMH report states: "the evidence is not sufficient for strong conclusions."

The advisory panel employs a quote by Hawkins and Pingree to establish the validity of a relationship between viewing television and perceptions of social reality. The quote, taken from the NIMH report, omits the paragraph that follows immediately after: "There does seem to be a relationship then, but is it real or is it an artifact of some third variable? The research does not easily answer this question."

Our review of the arguments put forth by the NIMH critique demonstrates that they are without merit. Significantly, the critique ignored a number of additional points made in our statement that are crucial to the central issues. A detailed analysis of each of the fourteen studies in which we raised questions regarding sampling, statistical methods, violence measurement, and interpretation was never responded to by the NIMH. We discussed various problems in laboratory or field experiments including atypical violence stimuli, the inappropriate use of certain statistical techniques, and the refusal to acknowledge the impact of controlling for third variables in correlational studies. The NIMH completely ignores the extremely small effect sizes that their studies report and that variance accounted for rarely reaches 3 or 4 percent in most cases.

In many social sciences, statistical results of this magnitude would lead to a conclusion of "no significant relationship." In the NIMH studies the same small correlations are interpreted as signifying very important behavioral and attitudinal relationships. Social science depends heavily on the interpretation of data in order to reach conclusions and to determine implications. That the behavior observed in these research studies does not constitute real violence and the statistical correlations are extremely low, suggests that conclusions and inferences are being drawn that go far beyond what the empirical data warrant. In ABC's view, the research is being interpreted and used in a way that is not consistent with the rigor and objectivity of the scientific method.

The purpose of research is to investigate questions with rigor and objectivity. A continuing exchange of viewpoints is crucial to this scientific process. In the NIMH report, Eli Rubinstein, one of the seven scientific advisers, stated that the cause-and-effect issue of television and violence "is still subject to honest disagreement." Our intention in writing a research perspective on television and violence was to address a number of fundamental research issues and to contribute to the scientific dialogue.

14

Proliferating Violence

George Gerbner

Since 1967 my colleagues and I at the Annenberg School of Communications of the University of Pennsylvania have been engaged in the scientific study of media content and effects. As part of this ongoing work we have conducted and issued a series of reports, most recently Violence Profile No. 8 in March 1977. These are the highlights of our Violence Profile No. 8, a study of trends in network television drama and viewer conceptions of social reality for the 1976 television year.

Increasing Violence

Television violence increased sharply in all categories, including "family viewing" and children's program time on all three networks. The increase resulted in the highest Violence Index on record. The only score that comes close to the current record of 203.6 was the score of 198.7 in 1967, the year of turmoil that led to the establishment of the Eisenhower Violence Commission and our TV Violence Index.

Other components of the TV Violence Profile confirmed previous findings of the unequal structure of power and risk in the world of television drama, and showed children's particular vulnerability to the effects of television. Heavy viewers revealed a significantly higher sense of personal risk, law enforcement, and mistrust and suspicion than did light viewers in the same demographic groups, exposed to the same real risks of life. The results also showed that TV's independent contributions to the cultivation of these conceptions of a "mean world" and other aspects of social reality are not significantly altered by sex, age, education, income, newspaper reading, and church attendance.

The Violence Profile is a cluster of indices sensitive to different aspects of the nature and effects as well as the amount of violence on television. The Violence Index itself is a composite of measures of the prevalence, rate, and characterizations involved in violent action.

The latest Violence Index was based on the analysis of a fall 1976 sample of prime-time, late evening, and weekend daytime network television dramatic programming. The analysis focused on clearcut and unambiguous physical expressions of overt violence in any context. Available evidence suggests that violence in a humorous or fantasy context may be at least as effective a demonstration of some of its social lessons as "realistic" or "serious" violence.

The percentage of characters involved in violence and killing rose to the second highest, and the indicator of violent action in programs to the highest, point on record. Three-fourths (74.9 percent) of all characters were involved in some violence, compared to 65 percent in 1975. Nine out of every ten programs sampled (89.1 percent) contained some violence, compared to 78.4 percent in 1975. The saturation of programs with violence, indicated by the rate of violent episodes, rose to record heights of 6.2 per play and 9.5 per hour, compared to 5.6 and 8.1, respectively. Only killing declined slightly. The cumulative effect of the increases resulted in the unprecedented jump in the composite Violence Index.

Rating the Networks

The increase in violence cuts across program categories and times. The context of dramatic programming did not change significantly, eliminating the possibility that the upsurge of violence was due to a sudden jump in the number of action programs, or late evening, cartoon, new, or "serious" programs in the sample. All three networks increased their overall mix of violence but stayed in the same violence rank order as in 1975, with NBC the highest, ABC second, and CBS third.

Data from the past ten years show that NBC is the "leader" in overall violence and in both children's hours and late evening violence. ABC is in the middle in overall violence, due to a decline in late evening violence (in which it had been the highest before) and despite increases in family viewing and children's hours. CBS, leader in the family viewing concept, lifted its two-season lid on family viewing time violence, but still held the lowest family viewing time, late evening, and overall violence scores. Children's hour violence on CBS rose to above that of ABC, but below that of NBC. The Violence Index ranks CBS least and NBC most violent overall, CBS least and ABC most violent in family viewing time, CBS least and NBC most violent in late evening, and ABC least and NBC most violent in weekend children's program time.

Violents and Victims

Other components of the Violence Profile deal with the structure of power demonstrated in TV violence and with conceptions of social reality that television viewing cultivates in the minds of viewers.

The most elementary—and telling—social structure involved in a violence scenario is that of violents and victims. The ratios of those who inflict and those who suffer violence provide a calculus of life's chances for different groups of people in the world of television drama. These Risk Ratios are obtained by dividing the more numerous of these two roles by the less numerous within each group. A plus sign indicates that there are more violents or killers than victims or killed, and a minus sign indicates that there are more victims or killed than violents or killers.

The overall Violence-Victim Ratio since 1969 (when this measure was developed) is -1.21, meaning that for every violent there were 1.21 victims. However, while the overall victimization ratio for men is -1.20, for women it is higher: -1.32. Even more striking are the differential risks of fatal victimization. There were nearly two male killers for every male killed (Killer-Killed Ratio of $+1.96$). However, for every female killer one woman was killed (K-K Ratio of 1.00).

Particularly high risks of victimization (relative to the ability to inflict violence) are borne by children (-1.73), old women (-3.00), unmarried women (-1.50), lower-class women (-2.25), nonwhites (-1.40), and particularly nonwhite women (-2.50). "Good" characters were more likely to be victimized (-1.28) than "bad" characters (-1.02), although the latter were more often fatal victims. "Good" women were even more likely victims (-1.47) than "good" men (-1.24). But "bad" women had the most favorable (and only positive) Violent-Victim Ratio of all groups ($+1.16$). Committing violence seems more likely to mark a female than a male character "bad" in the world of television. Exceptionally high relative risks of fatal victimization are borne by the old and the poor, particularly among women.

The patterns of viewer responses to questions about social reality given by different groups of children and adults confirm previous findings that the cultivation of fear and mistrust may be among the most pervasive effects of heavy exposure to the violent and risky world of television drama. In giving the "television answer" to questions about violence, law enforcement, and trust, children tended to score higher and learn more from television than adults. Heavy viewers in all sex, age, education, income, reading, and church attendance groups were more imbued with the television view of a "mean world" than were light viewers in the same groups.

CBS Criticisms

The CBS answering report of April 1977 deals with two of three areas of the annual Violence Profile. It discusses the Violence Index and the Risk Ratios showing relative levels of victimization. It is unfortunate that the third area of our research, that of television's effects (or Cultivation Analysis), is ignored. The answers to some issues raised in the CBS material come from our study of television viewers rather than from program content alone. By omitting results that would answer its questions, CBS serves its own convenience rather than the need for objective judgment based on all available evidence.

Organized in logical order, the CBS report focuses on four main criticisms:

- The Violence Index is deficient because it defines violence too broadly and because it is composed of "an arbitrarily weighted set of arbitrarily chosen measures of violence on television, whose meaning is totally unclear."
- The Violence Index employs faulty units of analysis because "it counts as multiple acts of violence, single incidents which should be counted as single incidents."
- A single week's sample is inadequate for representing an entire television season.
- "The Risk Ratio analysis is equally defective" because it measures relative rather than absolute victimization which "in all likelihood" does not correspond "to viewers' perceptions."

Each of these claims rests on erroneous—if convenient—assumptions and results in highly misleading conclusions.

Violence Index

CBS claims that the Violence Index is deficient because "it includes kinds of dramatic incidents which should not be included—comic violence, accidents, natural disasters." The report suggests the unlikely example of a "pie in the face," and amplifies its conception of what *should* be included: violence "which might conceivably make potentially wayward youths wayward" and violence "in what reasonable citizens would consider to be potentially harmful dramatic forms."

The fact is that our analysis of television content as reported in the Violence Index does not presume effects—useful or harmful. The reporting of trends in the Gross National Product, the Employment Index, or in weather conditions, cannot depend on the presumed effects of the facts being reported—be they good, bad, indifferent, or mixed. CBS confuses communications *content* with the scientific study of communications *effects* and thus ignores our study of television viewers. Yet only by studying the conceptions and behaviors of the public, rather than speculating about "wayward youths" or what seems "potentially harmful," can one determine the actual consequence of exposure to any form of violence.

CBS would also prefer to discount all violence in a comic context, which is especially frequent in children's programming. But CBS recently published *Learning While They Laugh*, a public relations booklet extolling the educational virtues of its children's programming, including cartoons. The weight of scientific evidence, including the recent Rand Corporation research summaries compiled by George Comstock, indicates that a comic context is a highly effective form of conveying serious lessons. If CBS wants to maintain that comedy teaches only what they wish for it to teach, the burden of proof lies with it.

Overall, the Violence Index for fall 1976 shows that violence occurs at the average rate of nearly 10 incidents per program hour. Yet CBS—and other industry spokesmen—typically attack these findings by the supposedly disarming example of the "pie in the face." First, we do not think there has been "pie in the face" in one of our samples of TV drama in a long time. Second, the Violence Index rules specifically exclude any non-credible comic gesture or verbal abuse. We classify as violence only the credible indication or actual infliction of overt physical pain, hurt, or killing. Thus, if a pie in the face does that—which depends on the actual incident—it is violence and should be so recorded.

The contention that "serious" violence is only what "reasonable citizens would consider harmful" is equally specious. It again confuses communication content with the assessment of effect. For example, we know from independent studies of the physical environment and of foods and pharmaceuticals that citizens are not necessarily aware of the full range of consequences of many of our industrial activities and products, including the products of the television industry. That is why independent research is needed. That is why the scientific diagnosis of a complex cultural-industrial phenomena—such as television—cannot be left to conventional wisdom, and even less to rationalizations by the corporate interests involved.

CBS also argues for the exclusion from the definition of TV violence dramatic incidents portraying "accidents," and "acts of nature." But there are no "accidents" in fiction. The author invents (or the producer inserts) dramatic disasters and "acts of nature" for a purpose. The pattern of violent victimization through such inventions may be a significant and telling part of television violence. It is hardly accidental that certain types of characters are accident-prone or disaster-prone in the world of television. Such TV content patterns may have significant effects on some viewers' conceptions of life and of their own risks in life. These patterns are, therefore, important to report if one is concerned with the full range of potentially significant consequences.

Another objection raised by CBS is that the Violence Index includes a set of measures rather than only a single indicator, and that different measures may move in different directions. The CBS report also cites a paper by

Bruce M. Owen as complaining that the index "involves adding apples and oranges." CBS could just as easily criticize any set of comprehensive indicators such as the GNP, labor statistics, or the weather report.

As pointed out in our response to the Owen paper, the usefulness of any index is precisely that it combines measures of different aspects of a complex phenomenon. One *must* add apples and oranges if one wants to know about *fruit*. The Violence Index reports all its components separately as well as in combination. That has made it possible for any user of the Violence Index, including CBS, to observe the movement of each component, and to weigh each as it sees fit.

The CBS report correctly notes that the absolute number of violent incidents in CBS family hour programs declined in 1976, while other components of the index showed an increase. CBS fails to discuss the nature of these other measures. It also ignores the reasons for including them in the index. John A. Schneider of the CBS/Broadcast Group further confuses the issue by claiming that the index rose "apparently because we had the 'wrong people' involved in the action."

The *kind* of people involved had nothing to do with it. As Violence Profile No. 8 clearly shows, 23.1 percent of *all* leading CBS family hour characters were involved in violence in 1975, compared to 31.8 percent in 1976. Even more important, violence was more broadly distributed in 1976 CBS family hour programming, making it more difficult for viewers to avoid (or have their children avoid) violence during family viewing time. While in the 1975 sample only 27.3 percent of CBS family hour programs contained violence, in the 1976 sample 62.5 percent contained violence. So, although the number of violent acts was reduced in 1976, the percent of leading characters involved in violence increased and violence was found in many more programs. Much as we empathize with the CBS attempt to get credit for partial effort, we cannot agree that such contrary evidence should be covered up or omitted from the index.

Units of Analysis

The CBS complaint about counting multiple acts of violence when single acts should be counted is unfounded. In the tradition of such research since the first studies of the 1950s, our coding instructions specify that a violent act is "a scene of some violence confined to the same agents. Even if the scene is interrupted by a flashback, etc., as long as it continues in 'real time' it is the same act. However, if new agent(s) enter the scene it becomes another act."

The CBS coding instructions define a violent act as "one sustained, dramatically continuous event involving violence, with essentially the same group of participants and with no major interruption in continuity." The two definitions are similar except for the ambiguous CBS qualification of "essentially." Since the criteria for determining the "essential" set of agents are not specified, the CBS rule permits the arbitrary and subjective manipulation of the unit of violence. Such ambiguity not only tends to reduce the reliability of the measure, but also gives the coder employed by CBS the opportunity to stretch the rule on which all other measures depend. For example, under the CBS rule it would be possible to ignore shifting participation in a long series of violent scenes, possibly involving an entire program, as not "essential" and thus to code the whole program as a single violent incident. Such a defective measure cannot be accepted as the basis for the sole standard of network performance.

Sampling

CBS asserts that we measure only one week of television, which can lead to "statistical errors of horrendous proportion." Elsewhere its report states that CBS research found wide variability in its own count of violent incidents.

Plausible as that claim seems, in fact it reflects the limitations, instabilities, and ambiguities of the CBS definition. Our own interest in assessing the representativeness of the one-week sample led to an initial analysis in 1969, to repeated spring-season test samplings in 1975 and 1976, and to an analysis of six additional weeks of fall 1976 programming. These studies indicate that while a larger sample may increase precision, given our operational definitions and multi-dimensional measures that are sensitive to a variety of significant aspects of TV violence, the one-week sample yeilds remarkably stable results with high cost-efficiency.

With respect to the number of violent actions per program (the measure of most concern to CBS), our six-week analysis found the same rank-order of the three networks no matter which week was chosen, except for one instance when ABC and CBS were tied. CBS claims it found that the week with the highest number of incidents on any network had 2.5 to 3 times the number of incidents of the lowest week. We found in our six-week test that this multiple was 1.98 to 1 for CBS; for the others, it was even less: 1.29 to 1 for NBC, 1.23 to 1 for ABC.

The explanation for the discrepancy between our results and those of CBS lies more in differences of methodology than of sampling. CBS limits its observation of violence to those acts its coders presume to be intentionally harmful and excludes the majority of violent presentations they judge to be "comedic" or "accidental." These arbitrary limitations involve much subjective speculation and introduce variability and instability leading to gross statistical aberrations.

Sharply reducing both the number and potential reliability of observations, and then limiting the analysis to a single unstable measure, do indeed lead to "statistical errors of horrendous proportion." These are the errors that our broadly based and precisely operationalized methods are designed to overcome.

Risk Ratios

The Violence Index reports absolute as well as relative risks. It makes clear, for example, that women are less likely to get involved in violence on television than men. But it also finds that, when involved, relatively more women than men end up as victims. CBS claims that relative victimization (that is, victimization compared to the commission of violence across different social types) is difficult to grasp, and is, therefore, a "meaningless statistic."

We must repeat that the validity of a TV content indicator does not depend on viewers' conscious understanding of its meaning. Our Cultivation Analysis shows that exposure to violence-laden television drama cultivates a sense of exaggerated fear and mistrust in the minds of heavy viewers. Young women—with an especially unfavorable Risk Ratio—are particularly affected, despite the fact that in absolute terms they are not as likely to get involved in violence as are the men. What CBS terms a "meaningless statistic" turns out to be potentially important in its consequences.

Our analysis of the CBS report and methodology confirms the judgment of social scientists, legislators, and the general public that only a scientifically tested, independent, and comprehensive set of indicators, measuring both TV content and effects, can be the basis for judging network performance. Our experience indicates that the Violence Index and Profile provide such a set of indicators. For independent confirmation we recommend the findings of an international panel of distinguished industry-affiliated and academic social scientists. This group's recommendations provide broad scientific support for the general direction and methodology of the Violence Index and Profile and offer advice which is directly opposed to the CBS methodology.

Inadequate Research

We have subjected the CBS materials and methodology to careful analysis and have found important features of the CBS methodology unreliable. That may account for the widely fluctuating results. The CBS objections to our Violence Index and Profile stem from an inadequate conception of the task of scientific research. They reflect a corporate defense mechanism rather than a broad and multifaceted investigation into the nature and effects of television violence. That basic misconception, coupled with questionable methods, makes the CBS contentions scientifically unacceptable.

The claims that all components of an index must move in the same direction, that a solid week sample cannot be representative of a season's programming, that "comic" or "accidental" violence should be ignored, and that relative victimization is a "meaningless statistic" represent confusion and wishful thinking. Congress and the American public need not revert to the era when self-serving claims and public relations gestures were the only bases for judging network performance. Our analysis of the CBS claims and complaints confirms the position that only an independent and scientifically tested comprehensive set of measures, such as the Violence Index and Profile, can do justice to the need for an objective standard of network performance in the public domain.

Much as we empathize with the CBS attempt to reduce indicators of network performance to the narrowest and most manageable basis, we cannot agree that such limitations would yield a valid measure of television violence. Network executives have long complained about "mechanical counts" of violence divorced from meaningful social and dramatic context. The Social Science Research Council and the National Institute of Mental Health committees of experts examined our methods and commended the use of a multidimensional profile sensitive to a variety of important aspects of violent representations. It is ironic that CBS now wants to go back to a one-dimensional count of a single and highly unstable measure.

Our methodology was developed and tested over many years both before and after the start of the current series of television violence studies in 1967. It was designed to avoid the sorts of flaws and errors typified by the CBS methodology. For example, it uses a more precise and comprehensive definition and a multidimensional set of indicators. Each component is reported separately so that any single measure (including the one to which CBS would like us to limit the entire research) can be seen by itself, as well as in combination with others.

It is true, of course, that some measures may show a decline while others increase, whenever that is in fact the case. Violence Profile No. 8 reported a decline in CBS family hour violent acts but an increase in the percentage of programs in which violence occurred. In other words, violence was reduced but spread to more programs. Thus viewers who wished to escape violence by turning to what they assumed to be nonviolent programs found that now those programs had some violence. This spreading of violence to more programs is a significant fact that should be reported regardless of whether CBS finds the results convenient.

We agree with previous statements of CBS and other television executives, writers, and analysts that meaningful and responsible analysis of television violence is not a simple matter. Thus it should not be dealt with by a simplistic count. Violence is a social relationship whose full and responsible understanding requires a multiple analysis of perpetrators, victims, actions, and consequences. But we must emphatically disagree that the study of TV violence should be reduced to those areas that are easily perceived by the average viewer or that have led to criticism of network policy. Indeed, the less readily detectable long-range consequences may be the most important to illuminate. All significant lessons of exposure to violence—be they good, bad, or indifferent to corporate interests—should be scrutinized.

Insuring Proper Standards

A comparison of the CBS methodology with that of our study shows that, in fact, it is the limitations of the CBS method that lead to the "fatal flaws" of which Schneider complains. Had we followed the CBS method of measuring violence, we might indeed be subject to those "statistical errors of horrendous proportion" that Schneider attributes to our study.

The Violence Index is in fact a valid and reliable indicator of television violence. True, it is more broadly based than CBS would like. But to reduce it to a single narrow measure of questionable reliability would be a disservice to the Congress, the public, and—in the long run—to the industry that also needs an independent and objective standard.

Instead of trying to explain away findings when they happen to be inconvenient, CBS should take the lead in responding to our call for pooling research data in the national television archive of the Library of Congress. Librarian of Congress Daniel Boorstin is receptive to such a project, and Congress could expedite such collaboration in the public interest. That would be a truly fruitful and productive way to compare methodologies and to reach an open consensus on the most appropriate indicators and standards of network performance.

15

Networks Hold The Line

John A. Schneider

Each year for almost a decade George Gerbner and his associates at the Annenberg School of Communications have produced a report on depictions of violence on network television, entitled the Violence Profile. The current March 1977 Violence Profile No. 8, reporting on fall 1976 television network programming, incorporates three distinct areas of study. The first is the well-known Violence Index, the second deals with so-called Risk Ratios, and the third is Gerbner's Cultivation Index. The CBS report of April 1977 deals with the first two areas of Gerbner's study.

Defective Measurements

With regard to the Violence Index, our review at CBS indicates that the index itself is not a measure of the amount of violence on network television; that it may, and in fact often does, change over time in different directions from the changes in the amount of television violence; and that it is, in substance, an arbitrarily weighted set of arbitrarily chosen measures of aspects of violence on television, whose meaning is totally unclear. It cannot be used as a measure of the trend of televised violence over the years, or as an indicator of whether that violence is increasing or decreasing.

Gerbner's count of violent incidents, which is only one component of the overall Violence Index, has numerous and fatal deficiencies. It includes kinds of dramatic incidents which should not be included—comic violence, accidents, natural disasters. It counts as multiple acts of violence, single incidents which should be counted as single incidents. And most important, it rests on a single week's sample at a time in the television industry's history when programs are constantly changing and when there are no longer any typical weeks.

The Risk Ratio analysis is equally defective. Instead of directly measuring relative risks among various population segments, Gerbner devised indirect measures which do not reflect the differences in actual risk among differing population segments; nor, in all likelihood do they correspond at all to viewers' perceptions. Simpler and more direct measurements of risks often show a totally different relationship among social groups from the Gerbner measures.

Violence Index

The Gerbner Violence Index is deficient in a number of important ways and is, in fact, very misleading. First, the Violence Index itself is not, and does not purport to be, a measure of the amount of violence on television, although that is the way it is generally interpreted. The Violence Index is the sum of a number of measures, only one of which is Gerbner's count of violence. Another measure included in the index, for example, is the proportion of leading characters engaged in violence. Because the Violence Index is composed of a number of factors in addition to the violence count itself, it is quite conceivable that the Violence Index could show a rise in a given year at the same time that Gerbner's own count of the amount of violence goes down.

That, in fact, is exactly what happened in the family viewing hour on CBS in the fall of 1976. Gerbner's Violence Profile No. 8 states that "CBS ... lifted its two-season lid on 'family viewing time' violence in 1976." In fact, the number of incidents of violence on CBS in the family viewing hour actually declined in 1976, according to the same Gerbner report. In the fall of 1975, according to Gerbner, family viewing hour programs on CBS contained 20 incidents of violence; CBS family viewing hour programs in the fall of 1976, again according to Gerbner, contained only 11 incidents of violence! So the Violence Index is a measure which simply does not tell anyone whether violence on network programming is increasing or decreasing.

Other components of the Violence Index include measures of the proportion of programs that week containing any violence, of the rate of violence per program and per hour, and of the proportion of all leading characters involved in killings. These measures are combined by the use of a set of arbitrary weights. Indeed, the index is composed of so many varied and incomparable elements which are combined in such an arbitrary fashion that it is difficult to know what it means.

Bruce M. Owen of the Office of Telecommunications Policy, in a staff research paper which addressed the meaning and validity of the Gerbner Index, stated that "this exercise [that is, combining and arbitrarily weighting the various components of the Violence Index] involves adding apples and oranges. . . . One is always free to add apples and oranges if one wishes,

Networks Hold the Line   165

but it isn't all clear what the result means, and some people may take it seriously." Unfortunately, many people have taken Gerbner's Violence Index seriously.

When Gerbner's violence count itself is examined, a variety of deficiencies are apparent. Violence is counted presumably to measure the number of incidents depicted on network television which might conceivably make potentially wayward youths wayward. On this view Gerbner includes a number of kinds of dramatic action which clearly ought not to be included in a count of violence. Thus he includes comic violence and injuries caused by accidents or acts of nature. None of these are included in what reasonable citizens would consider to be potentially harmful dramatic forms.

A second difference in definition is related to a very complex set of social hypotheses which Gerbner superimposes upon his violence counts. Because Gerbner's hypotheses relate to the power relationships among individuals, he counts as new violent actions a period of violence in which a new person enters the action. Thus if two men are fighting in a restaurant, and one of them knocks down a waiter while trying to escape, Gerbner would count this as two separate episodes of violence. Since the count of violence should not be distorted by extraneous social theories, the proper count is the number of violent incidents themselves, not affected by changes in the participants of the action.

The results of these differences between the Gerbner measure of violence, and what we consider to be the more rational measure that we use, is that Gerbner's count results in a much higher number than is valid. Furthermore, it may often move in an opposite direction than to that indicated by the count one would get on a more reasonable basis.

A final deficiency of the Gerbner violence count is the size of the sample Gerbner uses. Since its inception the Gerbner effort has measured violence during one week a year. In the last two seasons he has added a second week in the spring, purportedly to verify the results of the fall count, but he does not use this week in his year-to-year comparisons of the magnitude of violence.

From the beginning of our monitoring we felt that there was too much change between fall and spring network schedules to permit reliance on a single week's results. So we always measured two weeks a year, one in the initial network season and one in the so-called second network season. Several years ago, as the network schedules became increasingly variable from week to week, with series being canceled and new series being brought on board all through the year and with mini-series becoming a new programming category, we decided to review the statistical basis of our count. As a result of this review, we concluded that one could no longer make statistically valid comments about the level of violence on network television without a much larger sample of weeks. Accordingly, in the fall of 1975 we began to monitor 13 weeks a season and have continued that practice.

We have measured violence on the television networks for 13 weeks in each of two years; on the basis of these data we have learned that estimates of current year-to-year changes in television violence, based on single-week samples, are normally subject to too much random error to be valid. For we have found in the 1976-77 season that the range in the weekly number of incidents of violence on individual television networks is on the order of 2.5 or 3 to 1; that is, the week with the highest number of incidents of violence on any network was 2.5 or 3 times the number with the lowest number of incidents. Accordingly, for statistical reasons we cannot accept the Gerbner violence counts even if we waive the deficiencies of his definitions.

Risk Ratio

Since 1969 Gerbner has made much of a statistic to which he variously refers as the "Victimization Ratio," "the Risk Ratio," the "Violence Victim Ratio," and which will here simply be called "RR." This statistic is obtained by noting, in reference to specific population subgroups, the number of such characters in "principal roles" who are depicted as "violents" (aggressors), the number who are depicted as victims, and dividing the larger number by the smaller. If victims exceed violents, the figure is preceded by a minus sign; if violents exceed victims, by a plus sign.

Gerbner considers that these RRs "provide a calculus of life's chances for different groups of people in the world of television drama." He occasionally modifies this description in an important manner by stating that the RRs are indices of "risks of victimization (relative to the ability to inflict violence)." As the terms "Victimization Ratio" and "Risk Ratio" suggest, he is primarily interested in the groups with minus sign RRs—that is, those in which victims exceed violents. He considers the RRs indexes, or at least clues, to "conceptions of social reality that television viewing cultivates in the minds of viewers" regarding "the structure of power." In the highlights of TV Violence Profile No. 8 he notes especially the high negative RRs of women, children, old women, unmarried women, and various other groups. Explicitly or implicitly, Gerbner regards the RRs as either distortions of social reality or perpetuations of existing stereotypes regards negative RRs as reason to believe that viewers regard such groups as relatively powerless and believes that viewers themselves become fearful of becoming victims of violence.

At least two important questions arise regarding the meaning of the RR and its presumed effects. First, the RR is not a measure of simple risk, in reference to which the number of "violents" is irrelevant. If, as Gerbner's data show, 243 of 697 women (34.9 percent) in "principal roles" across 10 sample weeks since 1969 were depicted as "victims," what matter whether the number depicted as "violents" is, as he indicates, 184, or whether it is 284 or 26? The "risk" is the same. The RR is also not a measure of "victimization (relative to the ability to inflict violence)," since the *ability* to do so is not normally a theme of television drama. The fact that 513 of the 697 women were not portrayed as inflicting violence is not an indication of their *inability* to do so. What the RR actually measures is victimization relative to the *commission* of violence. The implications of such an index are somewhat difficult to conceive.

Second, it is very difficult to believe that viewers would become aware, consciously or unconsciously, of the differential RRs—that is, the relative proportions of different groups which are depicted as violents or victims, and the differences between groups in this regard. It is not at all difficult to believe, however, that viewers would become to one or another degree aware of something much simpler and more easily statistically stated: that certain groups are more often victims than others (or more often violent than others, or more often involved in violence, one way or another, than others). Maintaining the emphasis on risk, the more telling statistics would seem to be the simple number of persons in that group who are depicted as victims, or, for somewhat greater refinement, the percentage so depicted (the number of victims divided by the total number of persons in that group who are depicted at all). These are, to the best of our knowledge, the measures used in calculating risks of contracting given diseases, the likelihood of being in an automobile accident, and other "risk" statistics.

When Gerbner's figures are examined in terms of these simpler statistics, what emerges is often a very different picture from the RR. Briefly, it is frequently found that a group with a *higher* RR than other groups is both numerically and proportionately *less* often depicted either as involved in violence at all or as victims. By way of example, women have a higher RR (-1.32) than do men (-1.20).

The simpler statistics reveal that Gerbner observed 2,328 male characters, of whom 1,604 (68.9 percent) were involved in violence and 1,400 (60.1 percent) depicted as victims. In comparison, 697 females were observed, of whom 311 (44.6 percent) were involved in violence and 243 (34.9 percent) depicted as victims. Of what is the viewer more likely to become aware: the complex fact that female victims outnumbered female violents to a greater degree than male victims outnumbered male violents, or the simpler facts that, both in terms of absolute numbers and proportionately, women were less often than men involved in violence at all, and far less often than men depicted as victims?

This same sort of situation applies to various other groups which Gerbner notes as having high RRs. Thus the RR is not a measure of *risk* as such, and the simpler and more telling statistics often reveal that groups with *higher* RRs than others are in fact *less often* than the others depicted as victims, both numerically and proportionately to their depiction.

Extent of Violence on CBS

The results of thirteen weeks of monitoring prime-time television show that, for the 1976-77 season, CBS was the lowest of the three networks in violence. As in the 1975-76 season, CBS is at its lowest level of violence since our monitoring activities began in the 1972-73 season. CBS continues to have little violence in the pre-9:00 P.M. period; specifically, an average of three incidents of dramatic violence per week, or 10 percent of all incidents, occur in the family viewing period.

Violence was defined as follows: "the use of physical force against persons or animals, or the articulated, explicit threat of physical force to compel particular behavior on the part of a person." As in the 1975-76 season, 13 weeks of prime-time television (or half the season) were monitored in order to obtain a reliable measure that made allowance for week-to-week variation in the incidents of dramatic violence.

The violence tabulations for the 1976-77 season, covering 13 weeks of prime-time programming for each network, indicate that CBS and ABC have remained at essentially the same level as last year, while NBC has increased in violence from last season's averages. Of the three networks, CBS has the lowest rate of violence and is still at its lowest level of violence since these tabulations began in 1972. As a result of the increase in violence on NBC, the combined three-network total has risen. In both number of incidents and rate of violence, the three-network total is higher than last season.

Week-to-Week Variation

Both in 1975-76 and in this season, 13 weeks of programming were monitored for each network, providing considerable information on the extent of week-to-week variations. In earlier tabulations, which included only two weeks of programming, an effort was made to select weeks that represented as little variation from regularly scheduled programming as possible. The decision was made in 1975 to expand the sample to a longer time interval that would more closely approximate the true average incidence of dramatic violence in prime-time programming. This was done because in recent years television prime-time programming has become less constant, as "specials" have become more frequent and program changes more rapid.

This season in particular was characterized by frequent changes in scheduled program series and numerous "specials." Replacements were made throughout the season, and such unusual practices as the preemption of an entire week's programming for a special series (*Roots*) also occurred. Additionally, some scheduled programming (such as NBC's *Big Event*) included a variety of programs under one rubric. Thus it is even more difficult than in previous years to define a "typical" week in this year's season.

Another source of week-to-week variation derived from differences in the nature of the films shown. Each of the networks had some weeks in which films with little or no violence were shown; conversely, each of the networks had at least one week characterized by more violent film content. "Action" programs were more stable in rate of violence (averaging between 3-5 violent incidents per hour), but even here there was some week-to-week variation. In addition, in some weeks preemptions have resulted in the showing of fewer "action" programs than were scheduled.

Because of all these factors, the week-to-week variation in the extent of dramatic violence becomes quite large. For each of the networks, one or more individual weeks varied considerably from the overall 13-week average. On each network there was at least one week that had more than double the violence of the lowest week. If only one or two weeks had been selected to represent this season, the outcomes might have been considerably higher or lower than those obtained. The expansion of the number of weeks monitored results in a much more realistic appraisal of the amount of violence on prime-time network programs.

Pre- and Post-9:00 P.M. Violence

CBS still has very little violence in the family viewing period. Specifically, there is an average of three incidents of dramatic violence per week before 9:00 P.M. on CBS, constituting 10 percent of the total violence on the network. Most of the pre-9:00 P.M. violence this season has occurred on NBC and ABC, which have average 14 and 11 incidents per week respectively in this time period.

For the three networks combined, the extent of violence in the pre-9:00 P.M. family viewing period has increased from last season, though it still is lower than in previous years we have monitored. In the 1976-77 season the average number of incidents of dramatic violence in the family viewing period for the three networks combined was 28 per week, as compared to 14 in the 1975-76 season.

The proportion of all dramatic violence that occurred during the family viewing period has also increased over last season. In the current season about one-fifth (21 percent) of all dramatic violence occurred in the pre-9:00 period. This is less than the proportion of violence that would occur pre-9:00 if programs involving dramatic violence were evenly distributed over the prime-time period, but it is higher than last season. Only 11 percent of dramatic violence occurred in the pre-9:00 P.M. period in the 1975-76 season.

Changes in Amount of Violence

In general, a major share of the dramatic violence that occurs in prime-time entertainment programming consists of incidents in regularly scheduled "action" programs. However, action programming this season accounted for less than its usual share of total violence. Only slightly more than half (56 percent) of the incidents of dramatic violence noted occurred in "action" programs (crime, mystery, adventure series), as compared to 71 percent in the 1975-76 season.

This season was notable for the development of several nonaction dramatic series, such as dramatizations of popular novels, which included some violence in their story lines. While the number of incidents of violence in "action" programs on the three networks combined declined, the number of incidents in other programming showed a marked increase. The amount of violence accounted for by made-for-TV and feature films also showed an increase, despite the fact that there was no increase in the amount of time devoted to films on the three networks.

For each network the average number of hours of "action" programming tabulated has been less than the number of scheduled "action" hours. This is to be expected in a sample carried over many weeks, since the regularly scheduled "action" programs are occasionally replaced by specials and other preemptions. With regard to the rate of violent incidents on "action" programs, CBS and ABC have stayed at the same level as last year, while NBC "action" programs have shown an increase. Each network averaged about four violent incidents per hour of "action" programming this season.

Duration of Violent Incidents

As an additional indicator of the extent of violence, the duration of violent incidents was introduced as a supplementary measure in this season's monitoring. As would be expected, there is a substantial relationship between the total number of minutes devoted to violence and the number of incidents of violence, but there is some variation among program types.

Violent incidents in film material tend to run longer, averaging close to two minutes in length; incidents of violence in action programs average slightly over a minute, and the occasional episodes of dramatic violence in other types of programming usually run slightly less than a minute.

Reducing Television Violence

We at CBS regard the issue of violence on television as a most serious matter, and we try to deal with it in a responsible manner. We have pursued a course of action that has greatly reduced the number of violent incidents portrayed—and greatly altered the depiction of those incidents—on the CBS Television Network.

Our initial approach, in the late 1960s, was to change our Saturday morning programming for children. The superheroes were phased out, replaced in part by entertainment programs carrying prosocial and informative messages. Our efforts—and successes—in this area were recently summarized in a booklet that we published, *Learning While They Laugh*.

We also began to make changes in our prime-time schedule. This activity was intensified after the issuance of the surgeon general's report in 1972. We reduced the number of incidents of violence. Equally important, we drastically changed the portrayal of those incidents.

The CBS Office of Social Research started counting the actual number of incidents of violence, as various social scientists have done. We have made one major change in this approach, however. Although most other violence counts are based on monitoring one or two weeks of television annually, CBS now measures alternate weeks over a period of 26 weeks, for a net of 13 weeks. The reason for this approach, quite simply, is that there is no typical week of television.

Our monitoring clearly demonstrates a decline in the number of incidents of violence in CBS prime-time, dramatic programming. For the last full season—1975-76—there was a 36 percent decline in the number of such incidents over the previous season. Our preliminary figures for this season show that we have maintained this same low level. While our actual numbers may differ with other studies, the end result does not. Various organizations and individuals active in the monitoring of violence have also reported that the CBS Television Network is lowest in violence.

As an additional step, in 1974 CBS proposed the institution of the family viewing concept for television. This was to provide an early evening period in which the family could watch television together without embarrassment to either young or old. Despite controversy and unfavorable court rulings, we continue to believe that the adoption of the family viewing proposal represented a significant step in fulfilling our programming responsibilities. We believe that family viewing is in the public interest, and we will continue to adhere to that principle.

Unfortunately, the efforts of broadcasters in reducing the incidents of violence on television have seemingly gone unnoticed. We may not have made enough of a reduction in violence to satisfy everyone. But it is important to emphasize that the total elimination of violence is a goal that few have suggested, since violence has been part of every art form for centuries. The goal of CBS has been the elimination of gratuitous and excessive violence.

Responsible Actions

Unfortunately, some have adopted a simplistic approach to an obviously complicated problem. There is, for example, talk of boycotting sponsors of violent programs. We have moved from the scientific to an emotional level.

Some people talk about "too much violence" on television. If we do indeed present "too much violence," then what is an acceptable level? There are no easy answers. Given the subjective nature of this issue, perceptions and definitions of violence differ. Indeed, if we were to poll the viewing public as to programs to be banished for excessive violence, I doubt that we would find any unanimity of concern.

We at CBS have reduced the amount of violence and we have altered the nature of that portrayal. CBS will continue to act in a responsible manner.

16

Assessing Academic Achievement

Bert Briller and Steven Miller

Are American school children learning more or less well than they used to? If there is a decline in their ability to read and in their academic achievement, is it the fault of television? These and similar questions have been raised by news reports that "Johnny can't read" and that there is a long-range decline in Scholastic Aptitude Test (SAT) scores. In 1982 the College Entrance Examination Board announced that for the first time in nineteen years SAT scores rose, but the upturn is marginal and we will have to await further reports to learn whether a turning point has truly been reached.

Over the years, a number of theories have been offered to explain the decline in academic achievement. One of the most prevalent is the attempt to assign substantial blame to heavy television viewing. This report addresses that thesis and considers studies by the California State Department of Education, the National Assessment of Educational Progress and other groups, and a discussion of falling SAT scores. Clearly, television does attract children's attention. According to Nielsen survey data, the average child aged six to twelve watches three and a half hours a day; some watch very little and some watch considerably more than the average. Does this viewing hamper their education?

The California Survey

A major study often cited as confirmation that heavy viewers are also likely to be low academic achievers was undertaken a few years ago by the California State Department of Education. That study, "Student Achievement in California Schools," frankly states the conclusion that "preliminary results by no means prove that television watching causes lower test scores." It, however, presents its data in a way that places the blame on television, leading seekers of a quick remedy for scholastic shortcomings to claim that television is the cause of the problem. In discussing the relationship between heavy viewing time and lower test scores, the report claims that "the relationship was very strong, and none of several other factors—such as socioeconomic status and English language fluency—that were analyzed substantially affected it."

Analysis of the data shows socioeconomic factors to have been one of the major—if not *the* major—influences on test scores results. This can be seen in the study's graphs which show that children of professional parents do best; the gaps grow bigger as one goes down the socioeconomic levels. In the California survey, children of professionals and semi-professionals, even those that viewed four or more hours a day, did much better than children of the skilled and unskilled, even those that watched little or no television. Among the skilled and unskilled groups, there is almost no decline in reading scores as viewing increases to three to four hours daily. There is a decline, albeit relatively slight, for those viewing four or more hours a day. The same pattern is repeated throughout the survey, whether the subject matter is reading achievement, mathematics, or written expression. For example, a student with a parent holding an advanced degree watched six or more hours of TV daily and still scored five points higher (sixty-five vs. sixty) than a student who watched TV only zero to one hour daily but in whose family neither parent was a high school graduate.

David A. England, associate professor of curriculum and instruction at West Virginia University, criticized the California study in the 1981 *American School Board Journal*. He pointed out that the weak relationship between viewing and low achievement was called "strong" and that the socioeconomic factor was ignored. He also cited other relationships in the California data which the report did not comment on:

> Test scores of students from lower socioeconomic levels often tended to rise in all three skill areas as television viewing *increased* up to three or four hours daily. . . .
>
> As television viewing for students with limited English increased—up to four hours daily—so too did scores on reading examination.

Despite the significance of the socioeconomic background, the headlines reporting on the California study proclaimed heavy television viewing as the culprit. There are weaknesses in the study because the data on viewing was self-reported. Students were asked to report how much time they spent on viewing and how much on homework. Data given in a classroom setting on such questions should be taken with a grain of salt. Families with more education may place greater stress on academic achievement and families with less education may think television is more beneficial. This thesis, borne out in findings by Robert T. Bower, suggests that students from homes in higher socioeconomic strata may tend to underreport their television viewing. This would place more high achievers in the light-viewing category.

In an article in *Reading Teacher* in 1980, Susan B. Neuman, a teacher of reading courses at Eastern Connecticut State College, assessed the relationship between TV viewing and reading achievement. She analyzed the findings of twelve studies undertaken between 1951 and 1976 and found that regardless of the measures or research designs used, "the relationship between the amount of television viewed and reading achievement in the schools was *not* significant." Neuman stated that this should not come as a great surprise: a child's pattern of influences, such as heredity and family environment, are already present when television viewing habits are formed. Compared to these more important factors, "the number of hours of television watched appears to exert only a minor influence on achievement in reading and success in school."

Lilya Wagner, an English teacher at Union College in Lincoln, Nebraska, reported similar conclusions in the *Journal of Reading* in 1980. She examined some of the same studies as Susan Neuman, as well as later surveys on TV and reading. Her verdict: "A student's academic standing in an educational system based largely on reading does not appear to be greatly influenced by TV."

Explanations of Declining Scores

Why have academic standards fallen over the past two decades? Indicative of the range of discussion is a recent article in the educational journal *Phi Delta Kappan* which suggests that young people were affected by the aboveground nuclear tests of the 1950s and early 1960s. In 1977, the College Entrance Examination Board and the Educational Testing Service revealed the findings of a two-year study to determine the reasons for declining SAT scores. Among the causes cited: (1) lack of proper training in reading and writing; (2) less demanding textbooks and homework assignments; (3) high rates of absenteeism, condoned by the schools; (4) an increase in the proportion of children living in one-parent homes; and (5) upheavals in American society which have led to distraction and a lack of motivation. Television was also listed as a possible factor, but only one of many and definitely not the major cause.

"Teaching and testing methods in American schools may be partly to blame" for below-average performances in our schools. That was one of the conclusions reported by the National Assessment of Educational Progress

(NAEP) in its 1979-80 study of young people's reading habits and responses to literature. The survey, "Reading, Thinking and Writing," was funded by the National Institute of Education. The NAEP report placed part of the blame on poor reading habits and attitudes and a lack of homework assignments that required reading. It also noted that in all fields assessed, advantaged urban students consistently outperformed disadvantaged urban students.

Another interesting insight disclosed by the survey: "although television appears to consume much more of their [the students] time than reading, both television and reading have low priority compared to movies." When asked what they would like to do if they had several hours of free time, nearly twice as many nine-year-olds said they preferred reading a book to watching TV. Nearly three times as many opted for going to a movie instead of watching TV. For the older age-groups tested (thirteen- and seventeen-year-olds) the preference for going to a movie led watching TV by a better than three-to-one margin. Among thirteen-year-olds watching TV was only seven percentage points higher than the choice of reading a book. Among seventeen-year-olds, TV viewing was the preference over book reading by only two percentage points. The inference may be drawn that if TV watching is cut down, movies may gain rather than reading.

Socioeconomics and Educational Innovation

In 1978, The Roper Organization asked a national sample of parents whether their children's teachers ever assigned a television program as part of their homework. Nationally, under half—48 percent—reported that their youngsters had been asked to watch a TV show as a learning experience. Looking at the demographic breakdown, among low-income families the figure was only 34 percent compared with 59 percent for families in the upper income brackets. Among black families, the figure was also below average, only 40 percent compared with 50 percent for white families. The idea that TV viewing can enrich classroom instruction and motivate learning seems to have greater acceptance in schools teaching the more affluent than in schools serving blacks and the poor. At the very best, one can infer that schools serving the more affluent are more likely to employ newer teaching strategies.

In another study, also conducted by the California State Department of Education, the conclusion was reached that children "who watch "M*A*S*H" tend to have higher achievement and those who watch "The Dukes of Hazard" tend to have lower achievement." Some suggested that "M*A*S*H" is raising achievement and "Dukes" is lowering it, but there is no justification for claiming a cause-and-effect relationship. A more valid explanation appears to lie in the socioeconomic makeup of the audience. The "Nielsen National Audience Demographic Report" for February 1982 shows that 54.3 percent of children aged six to eleven in lower income households watch "Dukes" compared with 25.6 percent in upper income households. The same disparity exists for teenagers aged twelve to seventeen (26.8 percent in lower income homes to 10.5 percent in upper income homes). In contrast, "M*A*S*H" viewing families have a much greater upper income slant than the audience for "Dukes." We should expect the lower income "Dukes" viewers to have lower academic scores than the higher income "M*A*S*H" viewers. The programs are not affecting academic performance; they are being selected by viewers whose tastes are associated with different levels of academic performance.

In reporting the 1982 Scholastic Aptitude Test results, the College Entrance Examination Board divulged for the first time the performance of minority students. Blacks scored on average about 100 points lower than the national norm. The board also found that "as students' family income and the level of their parents' education rise, so does the average SAT score." Average scores rose from 336 in verbal testing and 374 in math for those with household incomes below $6,000 to 460 in verbal testing and 509 in math for students whose parents earned $50,000 or more annually. The socioeconomic factors are much stronger predictors of academic performance than hours of TV viewing.

Frequently voiced is the argument that heavy television viewers spend less time on schoolwork and thus receive lower test scores than they otherwise might. There is little evidence to support this view. More likely, children having difficulty with classroom study and with homework will turn to television more often because of their reading difficulties. It is likely, too, that they will have fewer recreational facilities and outside resources.

In 1978, The Gallup Organization conducted a survey on reading habits and library usage for the American Library Association. They asked: "If your children watched less television, do you think they would read more, read less, or read the same amount?" While half the respondents (49 percent) with children aged seven to seventeen guessed their children would read more if they watched less, almost as many (45 percent) said their children would read about the same amount even if they watched less television.

Television's Contributions

Even as the controversy about television has continued, the medium has made significant contributions to children's education. Much of this takes place before the youngsters begin their formal schooling. Programs such as

"Sesame Street" help children learn such basics as the alphabet and counting to ten before they enter kindergarten. Syndicated programs like "Romper Room" and local shows for children teach more general knowledge such as safety and hygiene. Children learn much from the general and family programs they watch. John Culkin of the National Council for Children and Television notes that children entering the first grade today are able to recognize about 10,000 words used in sentences, compared to 1,000 at the turn of the century.

In an article in *Language Arts* in 1979, Darryl S. Strickler and Beverly Farr of Indiana University discuss how television helps develop communication skills. They comment that even though preschoolers may not understand all they see on TV, "most are probably aware of the fact that it is, at least, potentially meaningful." Because of this, "they are able to understand whatever is within their experience." TV thus helps to broaden their experience by exposing them to "situations and events to which they might not otherwise have access." Strickler and Farr claim that instructional television programs "can increase the range of language experiences that children have in school and can be highly motivating." As with preschoolers, the expansion of experience enables children to communicate more effectively.

In a study of television's effects on reading, published in the 1978 *Phi Delta Kappan*, teacher Jackie S. Busch reaches the same conclusion. She observes that because the medium exposes youngsters to so many new words, "television's effects on reading for the preschooler and first-grade reader is of major proportions." This is echoed by a Virginia librarian interviewed by Busch. The librarian maintains "in her 25 years of experience, the TV-viewing first grader had a richer vocabulary" than the non-viewing first graders. Busch also discusses TV benefiting older students. She found that many TV programs that appealed to ten- to twelve-year-olds were science-oriented. This is a subject, she believes, which is more easily introduced to intermediate students by television than by printed materials. TV also stimulates the reading habit through its airing of stories adapted for television. Busch reports that 57 percent of the students surveyed in grades four, five, and six "stated that a television story had caused them to read a book."

The war between educators and television is becoming a cautious but optimistic alliance. Experience and the yearly entry of younger teachers into the system have caused a shift from intuitive but pervasive negative attitudes to more realistic appraisals of television's place in the educational scheme. Teachers' guides to programs and reading scripts related to specific programs have been supplied to schools by networks and stations. Reading is urged in broadcast announcements; TV games related to the news are provided by many stations. All these activities have required substantial funding by broadcasters. Critical viewing skills are being taught more widely, based in many cases on materials funded by broadcasters, but prepared by educators.

Television is here to stay. It is the chief entertainment and informative medium of our time. In blaming television for low test scores and poor academic achievement, critics ignore other, more compelling factors that should be addressed. The quest of educators should be for more and better ways to capitalize on the useful aspects of the child's viewing experience. To this experimentation and exploration, broadcasters have brought their own expertise and support while recognizing that the essential challenge must be met by the educational community.

17

Facts, Fantasies and Schools

*George Gerbner, Larry Gross, Michael Morgan,
and Nancy Signorielli*

Whether television harms, helps, or has no effect on academic achievement is a question of long-standing scholarly and popular debate. As with the issue of television's impact on aggressive behavior, it provokes strong opinions on all sides. These are often based more on wishful thinking than on objective, scientific analysis. As with television and violence, the issues and the research are often more complex than they appear at first glance. In some ways, these concerns are nothing new. We do not have to look far back to find the most popular mass media of earlier days accused of causing similarly dire consequences—whether the medium was movies, comic books, or even fiction (the reading of which is generally endorsed today).

Television is different from other media in some important ways. The television set is on in the average American home more than six and a half hours a day. Children are born into a new symbolic environment and grow up absorbing thousands of stories told by television each year. There is no longer any need to go outside of the home—to church, to school—or to learn to read in order to encounter the broader culture. The ritualistic nature of the activity and the quantity of time children and adolescents spend watching television makes it a historically unprecedented phenomenon. We assume that there might be equally unprecedented consequences.

Some claim that television has created a brighter, more aware generation, with greater knowledge of the people and the cultures of the world. Some argue television can stimulate reading, increase vocabulary, expand general knowledge, and help develop critical faculties.

Many who view the medium's effects as negative tend to be far more vocal, outspoken, and adamant about their position. To support their case, they are also more likely to cite research studies or reports of those studies in the press, which, unfortunately, often exaggerate or sensationalize the data. Some of these critics point to troubling social developments, such as the steady decline in Scholastic Aptitude Test (SAT) scores and the existence of millions of functionally illiterate adults. Critics note that the longer we live with television, the worse these situations become. Similarly, veteran teachers complain about new crops of bleary-eyed pupils with short attention spans, whose frames of reference seem entirely determined by television. There is no potential source of these ills as easy to target for the blame as television.

It is tempting to connect the apparent decline in school performance with the rise of television and let that be the end of the discussion. The problem with such "self-evident," "commonsense" conclusions is that many other things have happened in the last thirty years that might account for the decline. A recent attempt to point this out is the preceding article by Briller and Miller, which states the views of the Television Information Office (TIO) of the National Association of Broadcasters. It attempts to refute the often heard claim that television adversely affects academic achievement. It criticizes one well-known study that purports to show that heavy viewers get lower test scores; discuss other studies that show no such relationship; considers other factors that negatively affect school achievement; and presents research that implies television has made "significant contributions to children's education."

The central flaw in the TIO presentation is the way in which it frames the issues. It asks, in essence, whether television is *the* cause of declines in academic performances: "If there is a decline in . . . [children's] ability to read and in their academic achievement, is it the fault of television?" The answer is, "Of course not." The question that should be asked—one that leads to a sharply different answer—is: "Does television viewing exert an independent influence on academic achievement, and if so, for whom, under what conditions, and in which direction?"

What the Research Says

Research on television's effect on school achievement dates back to the earliest days of television. The past few years have seen a rapid increase in the number of studies on the topic and in-depth reviews of those studies. Within the past two years alone, the question has been the focus of special sessions at conferences of the American Educational Research Association, the Conference on Culture and Communication, and the International Communication Association. The amount of attention paid to the subject shows no signs of diminishing.

In addition to the work done by academic researchers, the Departments of Education in various states (including Rhode Island, Connecticut, Pennsylvania, Texas, and California) have attempted to determine whether amount of television viewing relates systematically to students' achievement scores. These state assessment programs have provided results from many thousands of students. Taken all together, they point to a firm conclusion: Those students who say they spend relatively more time watching television are more likely to get lower scores on achievement tests. There can be no doubt or disagreement about the consistency of this finding across numerous studies all over the country. Even the TIO acknowledges the basic finding that heavy viewing tends to be associated with lower test scores.

The controversy is not over whether or not students who watch more television get lower test scores. It concerns the kinds of interpretations and inferences that have been (or may be) drawn from that finding. Specifically, these revolve around two central issues that are tightly intertwined: (1) the size of the relationship, and (2) the impact of controls for important background factors.

The TIO charges that the relationships found in one highly publicized study (conducted by the California State Department of Education) were termed "very strong," but are more properly characterized as weak. We do not disagree, but we also do not share the conclusion that weak relationships are irrelevant, and that television is somehow "off the hook" just because the observable relationships between television and achievement are weak.

The size of an effect is less important than the direction and consistency of its contribution. Small effects may have far-reaching consequences, in spheres ranging from consumer product sales to election results to geothermal temperature changes. There is a wide gap between small effects and no effects. Small overall effects may also hide larger ones for statistical reasons. For example, most American children may be so heavily exposed to television that our instruments are only able to detect the tip of the iceberg. More importantly, small effects observed over an entire population may be masking much larger effects in certain subgroups; these may show systematic evidence of greater susceptibility.

The TIO attempts to bolster its case for minimal television effects by citing two articles, one by Susan B. Neuman and the other by Lilya Wagner. Both of these discuss, in very general terms, about a dozen studies conducted between the early 1950s and the mid-1970s.

Neuman is quoted as concluding that, across all studies, regardless of the specific research designs or measures being used, "the relationship between the amount of television viewed and reading achievement in the schools was *not* significant." This is not quite accurate; several of the studies cited by Neuman show significant correlations between television viewing and numerous areas of achievement. The Neuman article (and the TIO report) ignore other studies which find substantial associations. The criterion of statistical significance can be misleading, since many of these studies were based on small numbers of children; the same coefficients, if found in larger samples, would have generated the opposite conclusion. The Neuman paper is of remarkable little value in attempting to understand research findings, since none at all are presented beyond the unqualified statements that we quoted. Neuman mysteriously contrasts "survey" and "correlation" as opposing research designs and misrepresents the use of controls for intelligence quotient in these studies, claiming that all but two used such controls. Virtually none of these studies even considered controlling for IQ.

TIO quotes Wagner's "verdict" that "A student's academic standing in an educational system based largely on reading does not appear to be greatly influenced by TV," but ignores the next sentence: "Creativity does seem to be hampered because of television's one-way transaction." Wagner's also notes:

> Students of lower intelligence watch more TV while those of higher ability turn to reading with increasing frequency as they mature. However, if they continue their extensive TV viewing, their ability to achieve declines.

Some studies Neuman and Wagner cite are seriously flawed. One, for example, asked students for their own subjective judgments of how television has affected their reading habits. Such data could hardly represent convincing evidence one way or the other.

Others have reviewed the same (and more) research evidence in considerably greater detail and come up with different conclusions. Robert Hornik discusses most of these same studies in a 1978 article in the *American Educational Research Journal*. He points out critical methodological and analytical limitations that severely challenge their validity. He notes that the strongest of these studies reveals negative trends and that one "cannot help but wonder whether inadequate design or measurement, whether failure to introduce the right control variable, might not have resulted in underestimates of these negative trends." In a 1979 article in the *Review of Educational Research*, Hornik evaluates evidence from more studies:

> There are a few studies which find inconsistent relationships between television use and schooling outcomes.... However, the great majority of studies find a negative association between number of hours of television watching and level of school achievement or reading ability.... In particular, when

students beyond the fourth grade level are tested, hours of television watching is always negatively associated with achievement and reading skills.

Even more recently, in the *American Educational Research Journal* in 1982, Patricia Williams and her colleagues published the results of a "research synthesis" on television and achievement. This study systematically consolidated the data from all available studies on the topic as of 1979, about twice as many as either Neuman or Wagner considered. (Some of the studies relied upon by Neuman and Wagner were discarded by Williams et al. because they provided inadequate statistical information.) In this synthesis, the authors find a preponderance of negative associations and conclude that there is a small but overwhelmingly consistent negative association between viewing and achievement.

Their research synthesis does not include a half dozen or so recent studies, all showing consistent negative relationships, such as the California Education Department project. References to even more studies showing comparable negative relationships can be found in a review of the research by Michael Morgan and Larry Gross in the National Institute of Mental Health's report on *Television and Behavior: Ten Years of Scientific Progress and Implications for the Eighties*. That review also presents data from a national sample of adults, showing that those who watch more television have significantly lower scores on a verbal intelligence test. None of these reviews, nor the implications of the studies they evaluate, are acknowledged in the TIO report.

We have been considering only the overall association between amount of television viewing and scholastic achievement, but neither television nor its consequences operate in a vacuum. Television viewing is part and parcel of various constellations of factors, many of which also affect achievement. Many of the early studies of television and achievement failed to control for these factors.

Controls for such factors as IQ and social class must be implemented for two reasons. First, even if there is a demonstrable and stable association between television viewing and achievement, it may be spurious; that is, some other variable, such as IQ, may be the true cause of both amount of viewing and achievement, and thereby be responsible for any apparent relationship between them. When the true cause is statistically removed, the association may disappear entirely. Second, whether or not various background factors account for the observed relationship, there may be systematically different associations between television and achievement within different subgroups in the sample. There can be a strong negative association within one subgroup and a positive association within another. These different patterns would then cancel each other out in the overall comparison and lead to the misleading conclusion of a small negative association.

The TIO report muddles and confuses these concepts. In discussing the California Education Department study, TIO states that

> The report claims that "the relationship was very strong, and none of several other factors—such as socioeconomic status and English language fluency—that were analyzed substantially affected it."
>
> Analysis of the data shows socioeconomic factors to have been one of the major—if not *the* major—influences on test scores results.

This rebuttal is a nonsequitor. We live in a universe of multiple causality. To say that automobiles are the major cause of air pollution is not to say that factories have no effect. Similarly, whatever the impact of variables such as social class and IQ on achievement, they have no necessary, intrinsic bearing on whether or not television also has an influence. Controls for those background factors would have to be shown to eliminate the relationships between television and achievement—that there are no such relationships within any of the different IQ or social class groups. This is not the case.

Other variables have profound but subtle effects on the relationship between television and achievement, in ways not dealt with by TIO. Intelligence quotient is probably the strongest known predictor of achievement scores. In an article in the *Journal of Broadcasting* in 1980, Michael Morgan and Larry Gross point out that there appears to be no dispute over the relatively strong relationship between television viewing and IQ: heavier television viewers have lower IQs than light viewers, and those with higher IQs watch less television. Apparent relationships between viewing and test scores may be merely an artifact of IQ: high-IQ students watch less and score better, low-IQ students watch more and score worse. In some areas of achievement (especially mathematics skills) this seems to be the case; television has no independent relationship to achievement above and beyond the effects of IQ. In some other areas, notably reading comprehension and language usage, significant associations between television and achievement persist even after IQ is taken into account.

Most importantly, the associations are not the same at all IQ levels. These overall assessments mask systematic variations within different subgroups. The figure graphs the relationship between amount of viewing and test scores in reading comprehension, and does so separately for boys and girls of low, medium, and high IQ. These data show an enhanced negative relationship between television and achievement among high-IQ students, and a small positive association among low-IQ students, especially among girls. The resulting pattern is one of convergence among heavy viewers of otherwise divergent groups, with heavy viewing being associated with the "center" of achievement. In each IQ group, heavy viewers have the score that is closest to the midpoint percentile.

This is exactly what the California Education Department study found, using controls for social class and English fluency, for most areas of achievement and at most ages. The relationships between amount of viewing and achievement were slightly positive among students from lower socioeconomic levels and for students with limited English fluency; in their counterpart subgroups, stronger negative associations emerged. The TIO report interprets these patterns as evidence for no effects.

More researchers in the field are uncovering the same results. Jerome and Dorothy Singer, in a paper presented at the 1983 Conference on Culture and Communication in Philadelphia, found this type of convergence when their sample was partitioned according to social class divisions. Richard Kohr, in a 1979 presentation to the National Council for Measurement in Education, found stronger negative associations between television viewing and achievement among students whose parents have more education (based on data from 90,000 Pennsylvania students). The research synthesis by Patricia Williams and her colleagues also concluded that the negative associations between television viewing and achievement are strongest for high-IQ students.

These findings are paralleled in research conducted by our Cultural Indicators Project at The Annenberg School of Communications, University of Pennsylvania, on television's contributions to viewers' conceptions of social reality. In this work, the process of convergence among heavy viewers has been called "mainstreaming," on the premise that television's portrayals of life and society represent the mainstream of our culture. In general, stronger evidence that television cultivates conceptions of reality has been found within groups who, as light viewers, are least likely to be part of that mainstream. The result is a homogenization of heavy viewers from otherwise different groups; television viewing seems to override or diminish the effects of other factors. The phenomenon of mainstreaming has been found to explain group differences in cultivation patterns in terms of images of violence, sex-role stereotypes, health-related beliefs and practices, science, and other issues. In articles in the *Journal of Communication* and the *Public Opinion Quarterly*, we extend the theory of mainstreaming to television's contributions to political orientations and attitudes.

Variables that mediate relationships between television viewing and achievement in ways that reveal mainstreaming are not limited to social class and IQ. A whole range of personal, social, family, and other factors have been found to make a difference in systematic and theoretically meaningful ways. These are some of the major results we have found:

- Students with higher educational and occupational aspirations get higher achievement scores, but they show stronger negative associations between amount of viewing and those scores.
- Students who devote most of their attention to television while they are watching reveal stronger negative relationships between viewing and achievement; students who engage in many activities while viewing show smaller associations.
- More studious, home-oriented students, who spend more time on homework, chores, religion, art, and music, show stronger negative associations between television and achievement.
- Students whose parents are less involved in their viewing show stronger negative associations. Parental involvement in the viewing experience—whether restrictive and protective or characterized by an active, critical viewing orientation—reduces or eliminates the associations. The more students argue with their parents about how much television and what shows they watch, the greater the negative associations.
- The more socially isolated the student, the stronger the effect. Students who are more integrated into cohesive peer groups reveal weaker relationships between television and achievement.

When we talk about television's implications for academic achievement we are not talking about any simple clear-cut associations. The TIO report's contention that television viewing is not "the" cause of scholastic decline is correct; but contrary to TIO's interpretations, the bulk of research evidence supports the argument that those who spend more time watching television will get lower test scores and that some groups of students are more vulnerable. In study after study, reading skills in particular are negatively associated with heavy viewing.

18

Reading Performance

Susan B. Neuman

Television's potential effect on children's reading performance has become an issue of concern among educators. The estimate that by the end of the high school years, children will have spent more time watching television than attending school is frequently quoted and has both alarmed and intrigued researchers. Such a ubiquitous phenomenon as television is presumed to have effects on the child.

The research literature, for the most part, consists of small-scale studies conducted with different age-groups and using diverse methodological strategies. As a result, there has been a lack of convergence across studies regarding the relationship between television and reading. Two schools of thought have emerged: one that claims there are no apparent effects, and the second that suggests the strength of the effects have been masked because of procedural problems. Unfortunately this polarization has led opponents and proponents of the television medium to interpret research findings according to their specific self-interests.

These are difficult phenomena to study. Television and reading activities tend to be episodic in nature. The amount of time devoted to each activity is likely to vary considerably from week to week, depending on such factors as availability of materials, current interests, alternative attractions, amount of homework, and time of year. Also limiting progress in the field is what Hornik describes as "the fly by night" character of the research. The field tends to attract "instant experts" who claim that without television children would, as Winn states "calmly spend more time looking for something good at the library."

Historically, media innovations have not been introduced without concern for displacement of other activities. Controversies are being raised today regarding new cable technologies, videogames, and teletext/videotex. Concerns arise over the belief that these take children's time away from other activities thought to be more constructive such as reading, homework, and sports. Mike Royko's prediction in the *Chicago Sun-Time* is probably more accurate:

> Given a choice between doing something constructive (like homework) and something useless, 98 percent of all teenagers will choose to do something useless. If you make it impossible for him to do one useless thing, he will find some other useless thing to do.

The presumption that television displaces reading activities, that it thereby contributes to declining Scholastic Aptitude Test scores, and to a lack of skills for concentration is most likely a simplistic response to a complex problem.

A relationship between television and reading is not disputed. The large majority of studies suggest that children who view an excessive amount of television tend to score lower than students who watch a more moderate amount. Some studies demonstrate that up to ten hours of television may actually enhance achievement slightly. In an analysis of the Connecticut statewide reading assessment of fourth, eighth, and eleventh grade students, Prowda and I noted a slight negative trend in television's relationship to reading performance. Reading scores for the fourth graders seemed relatively unrelated to TV watching, but for eighth and eleventh graders, there was a weak negative correlation. Some might conclude that these data represent evidence of a cumulative effect of TV viewing over time. Others might suggest that the data reflect a subtle personality factor. The less able students, showing little initiative, continue to be heavy viewers while their peers are finding greater challenges in social and school-related activities. Himmelweit, Oppenheim, and Vince, for example, found that students who were heavy television viewers were generally shy, retiring, lacking in security, and characterized by a need for ready-made entertainment which demanded little effort.

Studies of television viewing and reading have, for the most part, examined the relationship between the number of hours viewed and performance scores on reading achievement tests. These studies have not addressed how television might affect the process of developing mature readers—those people who not only can read, but do read to broaden interests and develop improved patterns of thinking and behaving. In an analysis of four groups reflecting distinct media preferences, I found that after controlling for sex, socioeconomic status, intelligence quotient, and reading achievement scores, those students who were inclined to watch a good deal of television (three or more hours per day) and read little (less than two books per month) chose books of significantly lower quality than others in the sample. The scores of students who were heavy TV viewers and heavy readers were not differentiable from those who did not choose to watch TV. Again, factors other than media patterns appear to influence reading behavior, including such variables as home environment, role models, and personality characteristics such as energy and perseverance.

The kinds of interpretations and inferences that Gerbner and his associates have drawn from research findings should be critically reexamined. Their assertion that weak relationships may have far-reaching consequences and that the use of statistical significance may be misleading, allows them to support or reject hypotheses at will. They criticize my use of the criterion of statistical significance as the means for concluding no relationship between the two media; however, in one of their own papers by Morgan and Gross, they report a small, but significant finding of $-.08$, clearly indicating the deleterious effect of television viewing on achievement. Given a large enough sample size, weak findings may indeed be statistically significant but theoretically insignificant. The Williams meta-analysis reported in the preceding article is yet another example. Gerbner et al. interpret these findings as indicating a small but overwhelmingly consistent negative association between viewing and achievement. Williams reports a different conclusion: "Television accounts for little variance in achievement. It is neither the villain nor the redeemer some have claimed." Morgan and Gross's review of the research in the National Institute of Mental Health's report on television and behavior reports that the more one views, the lower the intelligence quotient, attributing this finding to Schramm et al. That study indicated that the children with lower IQs tended to watch more television than others, and those young children learned most from television fare.

Despite rising concerns over test scores and literacy, Americans are reading as much as ever. The *New York Times* recently reported: the total daily newspaper circulation is now 62.5 million; library circulation has grown at twice the rate of population growth in the last four decades; and 50,000 book titles are being published each year. Paradoxically, the electronic revolution has generated new demands for reading material, including videogame books, computer magazines, and books advertised on television. We should not retreat from research on television and reading, for the complexities of the relationship still remain. Rather than a moral crusade against television, we need to use new sophisticated theoretical models.

Bibliography

Himmelweit, H.; Oppenheim, A.N.; and Vince, P. *Television and the Child*. London: Oxford University Press, 1958.

Neuman, S. "Television Viewing and Leisure Reading: A Qualitative Analysis." *The Journal of Educational Research* 75 (May/June 1982).

Neuman, S. and Prowda, P. "Television Viewing and Reading Achievement." *Journal of Reading* 25 (April 1982).

Schramm, W.; Lyle, J.; and Parker, E. *Television in the Lives of Our Children.* Stanford, Calif.: Stanford University Press, 1961.

Winn, M. *The Plug-in Drug.* New York: Viking Press, 1977.

19

Dubious Facts and Real Schools

Lilya Wagner

Television has had a pervasive influence on schooling and scholarship. Any article about television and its relationship to school achievement therefore has guaranteed readership among many parents and teachers. A title referring to facts and fantasies about television and school achievement places that article among the top ten of the plethora of articles and discussions on the topic. Unfortunately, the promise of the article by Gerbner and his associates is not fulfilled.

We have to read only down to the second sentence before confusion strikes. What is the antecedent of the pronoun "it"? Television's effects? Popular debate? Academic achievement? Problems such as these abound throughout the article. How can a point be made clear when such grammatical difficulties, coupled with faulty sentence construction, detract from the essence of the piece? What is the message of the piece? Paragraph after paragraph gives vague promise of focused and centralized discussion while nothing concrete surfaces. One might assume that the question, "Does television viewing exert an independent influence on academic achievement, and if so, for whom, under what conditions, and in what direction?" hints of thesis, yet when the subsequent sections are perused, the question nudges the mind: "Just what are these authors trying to discuss?"

Even if the thesis were clear, the vagueness of statements such as "in the past few years" adds doubt and confusion about the purpose. A few years make a significant difference when research studies are considered. When the years are not defined in number, the statement loses significance. Most freshmen college students are taught about loaded words and their use and abuse. Scholarly discussion should stand on its own merit and not have to delve into the netherworld of loaded language. Why then, do Gerbner et al. make statements about Neuman "mysteriously" contrasting two ideas, or Wagner stating a "verdict," or that the Television Information Office report "muddles and confuses these concepts"?

I find the references to my article of half a decade ago to be both curious and puzzling. The authors state that it is tempting "to connect the apparent decline in school performance with the rise of television . . ." and point out problems with such "self-evident," "commonsense" conclusions. Vast differences in learning styles might result in misinterpretation of the purpose and contents of my article. I had attempted to collect research findings available at that point in time, which related to a narrow topic. I was reporting along defined lines, not drawing "self-evident" and "commonsense" conclusions. Since I was reviewing research relative to a clearly defined and narrow topic, I find it puzzling that Gerbner et al. chide me for citing only "about a dozen studies conducted between the early 1950s and the mid-1970s." The authors also state that Neuman "ignored" other studies that they find significant. I have yet to find an author, particularly one who reviews research, who has access to all material on a topic. The wealth of literature on almost any given topic precludes such a luxury.

Gerbner and his associates castigate me because I quoted a statement I thought relevant from an article but ignored the subsequent sentence about creativity. Do the authors realize that I was concentrating on television and its possible effects on reading and not centering on creativity? Had I quoted that sentence, would they have found fault because I was not sticking to my topic? Neuman and I are said to have cited some studies that are seriously flawed. It would be interesting to have these listed. I wrote my article early in 1979. Time generally does reveal flaws in almost everything. Often studies will be inaccurate when new research and new knowledge surface. The authors state that I supposedly attempted to present some "convincing evidence." I do not recall that this was the implication of my article. I presented cautions on interpretations of research until more convincing evidence could be found.

The authors appear to place much significance on controls for factors such as intelligence quotient. The IQ test and resultant score has for some time now been designated as a dubious measure of intelligence, and its relationship to achievement is not clearly definable. Several scores must be compiled and averaged to be used as a significant measure, and the information is most valuable when combined with other relevant data such as school achievement.

In their conclusions the authors state that "we are not talking about any simple, clear-cut associations." Neither was I. Did they notice? Regrettably the confusion, lack of focus, and negative tone of the article preclude its being a significant contribution to the literature. Scholarly discussion is stimulating; vague nitpicking is not.

20

Mass Media Values

Gaye Tuchman

Television entertainment is a highly political method of social control. Seemingly fantasy-like material, it is charged with information about the appropriate structure of society, the appropriate distribution of goods and power, and appropriate motives for behavior. Contemporary television programming helps maintain the existing political, economic, and social systems by refusing to question basic American assumptions about social arrangements, preferring to take these arrangements for granted as the natural condition of human life. These characterisitcs are particularly clear in its treatment of both property and sex roles.

Critics and Charges

Critics have leveled such charges against popular entertainment for centuries. Eighteenth century tracts, penned by social critics, attacked the moral degeneracy of the newly popular novel. Early twentieth century critics blasted comparable charges against radio. By the 1940s such charges were more explicitly political. In a 1948 essay published in *The Communication of Ideas* (edited by L. Bryson) Harold Lasswell noted that a primary function of communication, whether in so-called primitive or advanced societies, is to pass the social heritage from one generation to the next.

More recently, George Gerbner, Larry Gross, and William Melody argue in *Communications Technology and Social Policy* (1973) that American culture always conserves society, and that "the dominant image patterns" produced by mass communication "structure the public agenda of existence, priorities, values and relations." And, in an essay to be published in a forthcoming anthology edited by Gaye Tuchman, A.K. Daniels, and J. Benet entitled *Women and the Mass Media*, Gross and Suzanne Fox insist that television is a "system of messages to which total communities are exposed and which provide bases for interaction and common assumptions and definitions... among large heterogeneous publics." Culture helps structure social life.

Other researchers have also challenged the assumption that TV entertainment is apolitical fantasy. Such a challenge is explicit in McLuhan's work, and all can quickly provide their own illustrations. For instance, in his research for the surgeon general's report on television and violence Gerbner points out that television entertainment tends to place social problems involving violence in another time and place, letting us watch those fictionalized characters search for solutions to our problems in settings safely removed from our own.

Hegemony and the Consciousness Industry

Calling one kind of program "factual news" and another "nonpolitical entertainment" is to accept a socially imposed and taken-for-granted distinction, a distinction as dependent on social structured learning as the ability to know that a film actor plays a role and can rise to play another role after a seemingly brutal cinematic death. These ideas may not be new, but it is only within recent years that Americans have begun to use such ideas to speak of the political impact of such factualized fiction and fictionalized fact as the maintenance of hegemony by the consciousness industry.

Both the term "hegemony" and the notion "consciousness industry" were introduced by European Marxists to talk about the political domination of the spirit, that phenomenon that in an earlier and more religious age was called "soul" and—in a more rational era—"mind." According to Gramsci, hegemony is "an order in which a certain way of life and thought is dominant, in which one concept of reality is diffused throughout society in all its institutional and private manifestations informing with its spirit all social relations, particularly in their intellectual and moral connotations." The German poet Hans Magnus Enzensberger speaks of the consciousness industry as the "industrialization of the mind," the use of the electronic media to shape consciousness and serve as "pacemaker for the social and economic development of societies in the late industrial age."

As the Finnish sociologist Kaarle Nordenstreng points out in Gerbner, Gross, and Melody's anthology *Communications Technology and Social Policy* (1973), both notions are opposed to the Anglo-Saxon tradition in which "culture is understood as a largely independent realm of human society and [mass] communications is similarly perceived as a kind of stream of isolated elements of consciousness." Instead, both terms refer to "psychological phenomena as an integral part of the total material structure" and view these phenomena and their accompanying world views as a cohesive gestalt.

Values, Ownership, Programming

Let us return to Gramsci's definition of hegemony and Gross and Fox's conception of television entertainment as a series of messages. How might we characterize this system of messages? How is it produced? Does this system necessarily uphold views of life and society that serve the interests of American monopoly capitalism? Or is it more accurate to suggest that American entertainment expresses middle-class American values and lifestyles because the producers of the programs are themselves middle class and are expressing the values they hold?

It is clear that the ownership pattern of the three billion dollar a year television industry reflects the ownership pattern of the American corporate economy. It is characterized by local monopolies, regional concentration, multiple ownerships, multimedia ownerships, and conglomerates. The most profitable stations appear to be those owned and operated by the networks, and the networks themselves are units of larger economic entities. The revenues of the three networks (including those of their owned and operated stations) have exceeded those of all television stations (excluding the network owned and operated) and their income before taxes is rapidly approaching those of all television stations (excluding again the owned and operated).

The profitability of individual programs is the product of the interaction of networks and stations, as the approximately seven hundred affiliates dicker with their respective networks about the programs for which they will provide clearance. Additionally, and most important, profit is also determined by the participation of other actors in the corporate world, as advertisers and agencies choose the programs near which their commercials will be positioned.

But these patterns cannot specify the exact impact of corporate industrialism on the content of programs. They "merely" indicate that television programming is designed to be profitable and that "least objectionable programming"—the industry term for content that will offend the least number of people while attracting the largest possible audience—is preferable. A closer look at the production of programs yields more information about least objectionable programming.

In a study for the surgeon general's report on television and violence communications researchers Thomas F. Baldwin and Colby Lewis point out that economic considerations guide the creativity of writers and producers charged with producing acceptable network and syndicated fare.

Take the task of the writer. Hired on a free-lance basis to formulate in sequence a story idea, an outline, and a finished script, he (rarely she) is not paid for revisions; objectionable material must be rewritten without remuneration. By occupying time that could be spent on other potentially profitable assignments, rewriting shrinks possible income. Equally important, rewriting slows production schedules and so potentially alienates the free-lance writer from producers who might otherwise have hired him again. As one producer explained to Baldwin and Lewis, "the producer looks for a writer who can meet deadlines and give him material that he can shoot in six-and-a-half days, within his budget and without any trouble." "Trouble" refers to objections from the network.

Producers, themselves dependent on the goodwill of the networks, are loath to initiate battles in support of supposedly objectionable materials. As Muriel Cantor explains in *The Hollywood Television Producer* (1971), producers have limited notions of professional autonomy. Filmmakers (Cantor's term for producers concerned with acquiring and developing technical skills with which to break into the cinema) and old-line producers (experienced men who subscribe to the adage that box-office success measures artistic worth) do not defend their ideas against network onslaught. Writer-producers (recruited from script writing) retain a notion of professional autonomy from the days when they objected to criticisms of their work, but they quickly learn to bow to network reservations or seek their livelihood elsewhere.

It is difficult to gather examples of network objections. Some are known to concern excessive sexuality or overly excessive violence. Some are known to be rejections of unusual family relationships—such as the amicable concern for one another displayed by divorced spouses in the rejected pilot of Norman Lear's "One Day at a Time". (Such friendliness was held to encourage the notion that divorce is preferable to marriage and to discourage the notion that divorce must be prompted by hate). Most examples become public accidentally or because of a writer's rage.

The difficulty in locating freely discussed examples of objectionable materials (with which to explicate the rules of acceptable content) does more than tell us that writers and producers have learned their lessons well. It forces researchers to use content analysis to explicate the "least objectionable" version of social life, a procedure that Gerbner and his associates refer to as the development of "cultural indicators." These more systematic characterizations can go beyond impressionistic observations and reveal the ways in which entertainment programming hides the pernicious effects of American capitalism. Consider two basic components of any society—relationships to property as revealed by treatments of crime and violence and relationships between men and women.

Crime and Violence

Ignoring the violence inherent in slapstick comedy, Gerbner finds that television tends to banish violence to other times and other places. When violence occurs in a contemporary setting it is generally the product of the interaction of police and criminals, a variation on the traditional climax of Westerns in which the posse smokes out and battles the gang of outlaws. It is removed from the lives of the good citizenry.

Crimes against citizens, such as murder, are also removed—placed behind the doors of homes where murderers kill out of greed or to insure that the skeletons of their lives will remain safely in their closets. Indeed, it seems that TV criminals are *not* lower-class individuals for whom crime is an economic necessity or the only available path of economic mobility. Instead, crime is the creation of individuals who are not satisfied with the obvious sufficiencies of their lives and want to grasp even more. The popular police show *Columbo* is a particularly apt example.

The frequent observation that the world of television is peopled by the middle and upper classes provides additional evidence that factualized-fiction avoids the realities of class in America: that we are a blue-collar society. The patterns of crimes presented provide yet more. Comparing the rankings of the frequency of serious crimes in American society and the frequency of serious crimes on American television in *Public Opinion Quarterly* (Summer 1973), Joseph R. Dominick reports an inverse correlation: crimes against property dominate in the society; crimes against persons dominate television. It is as though television cannot face either the economic motivation of robbery by the poor or the passion of murder.

And so fictionalized fact—news programs—teach the audience that "crime in the streets" is a concern of politicians and populace, while factualized fiction—least objectionable entertainment—instructs that the greed of gangs and illegal greed of corrupt upper-middle-class citizens (folks rarely, if ever, encountered) are to be feared. Factualized fiction encourages psychological displacement or hegemony, for it encourages us to take for granted that the motives and settings of televised crime are natural—the way things are and have always been.

Men and Women

Television's presentation of men and women also encourages hegemony. For instance, as the major figure in a program women—like racial minorities—are banished to the ghetto of comedy. When they appear in the dominant type of program—action/adventure—they are either assisted by a white male or require the assistance of white males to be saved from the rigors and dangers of their work. On action/adventure programs women are victims, not perpetrators, of crime, a generalization that also holds for the anthropomorphic animals of cartoons. Victimization occurs in comedy too; there women are more likely to be the butt of jokes. Similarly, when a man and a woman interact the man is more likely to dominate the conversation. In soap operas this dominance extends to the use of close-ups; the camera lingers longer on the male.

But then all studies report that television has more men to linger on. Gerbner and Gross report in the *Journal of Communication* (Spring 1976) that there were four men to each woman in a study of televisions plays between 1970 and 1975. Of the characters located in a 1974 study of prime-time television, 72.2 percent were men. Children's programming is less bleak: among major characters there are only two men for every woman. And soap operas approach the proportions found in the country's population, although the occupations of men—but not those of women—are skewed toward the professions. (It is again noteworthy that television places the men in the entrepreneurial profession, not in the corporate office). Television is a male world.

Viewer Characteristics

Of course the "real" world is a male world too. Males hold the powerful positions in society, so television "merely" takes for granted the ongoing nature of social relationships. But, as women's groups and feminist research have consistently found, television also encourages its audience to overestimate male dominance.

Gerbner and Gross's work suggests that heavy TV watchers, particularly women, exaggerate interpersonal violence in society, the role of women as victims, and the proportion of the populace employed by law enforcement agencies. Gross and Fox find that teenage girls who are heavy TV watchers are significantly less likely to aspire to college than boys who watch heavily. This pattern is much stronger for children whose parents are college educated, indicating that the pertinent variable is TV viewing, not class.

The impact of television viewing on sex-typing is underscored by a recent study regarding television characters as models for children: children exposed to women portrayed in "male occupations" were more likely to believe that "real" women held these jobs and that it was proper for them to do so. And work by Michael J. Robinson and Clifford Zukin published in the *Journal of Communication* (Summer 1976) stresses the overall conservative impact of TV: heavy viewers are more likely to support George Wallace than light viewers, and this effect is most pronounced among the college educated.

Television and Popular Attitudes

In the two spheres, crime-violence and gender, television entertainment perpetuates male superiority and discourages a concern with class. Yet some readers may object that an analysis of these dominant patterns does not necessarily mean that the television industry is the consciousness industry; it may simply mean that television influences attitudes. Further, it has yet to be established that television forms those attitudes. It may simply give people what they want.

Attitudes do not exist in either a psychological or social vacuum. More important, when those attitudes concern such basic components of social life we may take them for granted: they act as background assumptions that we do not expect to see violated. They are conditions of our daily life against which we plot the foreground of our daily activities and future projects. Without these stable background assumptions we would have to perpetually reinvent social order. Most important, insofar as we are social beings, background expectancies help make us what we are. They help us think about ourselves and know what is good or bad, beautiful or ugly, or that profit is a proper motive for human behavior.

It is difficult to prove that television deliberately sets out to mold conceptions of self and society. Indeed, it is improbable that somewhere in New York an executive is sitting in a suite on the Avenue of the Americas plotting which characteristics he will inculcate in viewers. However, data indicate that cycles in programming are functions of the search for profit, not a cynical attempt to give viewers what they want and deserve. This situation is also evident in another branch of the consciousness industry—popular music.

Search for Profits

William H. Melody's *Children's Television* (1973) provides further evidence that changes in entertainment are informed by a search for profit, not by consumer taste. He points out that children's programming has gone through several cycles. First, the networks carried a glut of children's programs, 42 percent of them on a "sustaining basis" (without ads) in order to induce families to buy television sets. Once the country had been converted to television, children's programs were eschewed. Prime-time had become too economically valuable to be wasted on children. "Family programs," representing millions of mesmerized eyeballs, were more valuable as vehicles for advertising.

The invention of the filmed program, accomplished by "I Love Lucy," had also opened the profitable overseas market. In 1953 the ABC-Paramount merger and the demise of the DuMont network introduced a new cycle. ABC banded with Disney, initiating alliances with Hollywood that changed both children's programming and the whole program-supply market. As this market developed emphasis on adult and family shows increased, and children's programs were banished to local stations ready to appeal to local spot advertisers with syndicated cartoons. When the networks again wrested control of programming from the sponsors and advertising agencies, they invented the family-oriented animated cartoon series.

By 1963 specialized audiences had been discovered: housewives inherited daytime television to become the backbone of industry profits. Children's shows were grouped on Saturday morning to appeal to toy manufacturers who had recently adopted year-round advertising budgets designed for children, not their parents. Additionally, these Saturday morning programs are contrived to fit the commercials.

Teaching Audiences

All this evidence indicates that programs are the by-product of the television industry, its marketable industrial waste. The primary product is the audience sold to advertisers. Audiences, today conceived as differentiated by demographic characteristics, are developed, not found. This situation is seen most clearly in the master's thesis of television's former wunderkind Fred Silverman, who writes of "program philosophy" as the development of audiences. We can see a parallel to an earlier era, when industries fought to teach workers new modes of behaving in work settings and a passive acceptance of close supervision and expanded management.

Part of developing audiences is to teach them to want—to want advertised products that will make them as attractive as the characters who people their sets. Part is teaching a way of life, and acceptance of male dominance and an ignorance of the perniciousness of class. Television teaches a manufactured consciousness, a social and political adherence to the supposed glories of American life. Factualized fiction—fiction-fact—is not politically neutral. It is, rather, a method of social control.

Bibliography

Enzensberger, Hans Magnus, *The Consciousness Industry: On Literature, Politics and the Media.* New York: Seabury Press, 1974.
Gerbner, George and Larry Gross. "Living with Television: The Violence Profile." *Journal of Communication* (Spring 1976): 172-200.
Gerbner, George, Larry Gross, and William Melody, eds. *Communications Technology and Social Policy.* New York: Wiley, 1973.
Tuchman, Gaye. *The TV Establishment: Programming for Power and Profit.* Englewood Cliffs, N.J.: Prentice-Hall, 1974.

21

Television: Mass Communication and Elite Controls

by Emile G. McAnany

For most of this century, America has enjoyed a dominant position internationally. We have exported goods as well as capital, technology and technical know-how, films and television series to the rest of the world. We have had a proportionate amount of power and influence internationally and specifically a great deal of influence in both the economies and cultures of many countries.

Because of this, it may be hard for Americans to understand the strong reaction of other countries that may be in a more dependent situation to television programs for direct-broadcast satellites. If we can envision having most businesses in the United States owned or partly owned by foreign interests and viewing mostly foreign films and prime-time television, we might be able to empathize with the opposition of other countries to a laissez faire attitude about satellites and television.

The elements of the debate over satellites on which the United States was so overwhelmingly outvoted recently concerned two basic principles: the sovereignty of countries and the free flow of information among people and nations. The debate about national sovereignty is complex; there are arguments about the influence that our political power exerts on other nations, not to speak of the economic power and influence multinational corporations may wield within other sovereign states. Television is an information channel in the same way that books, musical records, tape recordings, radio, film and telephones are. Some information may be exchanged electronically; other information may be exchanged physically.

A principal assumption of the free flow of information is that it is a free exchange. If there is an imbalance in this information exchange, where one partner controls the communication channels as well as the ability to produce messages, then there cannot be a genuine free exchange, but only a reinforcement of the imbalance.

Certain aspects of television as an information technology make the free flow principle difficult to foster. The use of direct-broadcast satellites only adds to these difficulties. Basically, television is an expensive and complicated technology, which fosters centralization and control by a few groups that have the money and influence to create and send messages. On an international level, this means that a few wealthy and technologically advanced countries have control over television messages and their distribution. Television's expense has meant that poorer countries have had to commercialize their broadcasting to a great extent and have been forced to buy cheap program series from dominant producer countries. The experience of many countries has been to watch television messages generated from outside their cultures; to have relatively little input at a national level and even less at a local level and to witness the fostering of consumer aspirations among its populations, for whom such habits were often inappropriate. Satellites only increase centralization and demand even larger audiences for cost-effective use. A few senders dominate the present television system; satellites will be developed and promoted by this same group of gatekeepers and will only increase the present one-way flow of information.

Imbalance of Power

Given this situation regarding transmission of television messages, many people are concerned about the influence that continuation and reinforcement of this imbalance can exert. The argument is that television programs are either produced by the United States or imitative of them; consequently, the impact of television is to induce people of other countries to think and act in conformity with messages from outside their own country. This influence is due to a one-way flow of information that hurts, rather than helps, the development of other countries and ultimately is an infringement of their sovereignty.

Several basic assumptions on which the validity of this argument rests must be examined: the first concerns the messages, that they exist in sufficient quantity, are produced by certain structures and are broadcast widely enough to cause concern to governments. The second concerns the audience, that there are people who are exposed to these messages, that this exposure is widespread and extends over a long enough period to have an impact. The third concerns the nature of the influence that television has on these audiences, while the fourth deals with the value judgment of the influence. In order to judge the validity of arguments concerning television and satellites, the evidence on each of these assumptions requires review.

Impact of Television

We have all heard or read many arguments about the effects of television. Critics blame it for national crises, children's failure to achieve more in school or erosion of cultures and values. Proponents see it as a technology that, if used well, holds great promise for informing and educating great masses of mankind. Both sides present evidence to buttress their positions; both deny the legitimacy of contrary evidence.

An illustration of two groups speaking at cross purposes over this issue is found in *Television and Social Behavior: Reports and Papers,* the Surgeon General's report of 1971 on the impact of violence on television. Television industry spokesmen tended to dismiss the forty-two studies as not having "proved" the ill effects of television violence on audiences, especially children. Social scientists said that the weight of the evidence, although not containing "proof" in an absolute sense, certainly indicated that television violence had an impact and a bad one. What this debate demonstrates is that so-called objective scientific evidence is often interpreted to support a political position and is not as objective as some suppose.

Evidence about television and other mass media messages concerns the quantity, structure and direction of the flow of these messages. Regarding the quantity of television in the world, the evidence clearly shows an exponential increase worldwide. The United Nations Educational, Scientific and Cultural Organization's (UNESCO) most recent survey (in *UNESCO Statistical Yearbook, 1971*) of mass media gives national figures for radio and television transmitter-receivers and hours of programming. There are comparative figures for 1960 and 1970. Even taking these figures as approximate, it becomes clear that electronic media have increased enormously over the last decade, radio even more so than television in Third World countries. In a survey of 110 countries, there were approximately 250,000 hours of radio programming a week. Others have estimated that the United States alone airs about 5,000,000 hours of television a year. Clearly, the amount of media production and hours of transmission is large and growing rapidly.

Another area of message production critical for the free flow of information argument is the structure and flow of television between nations. In a recent study by the University of Tampere in Finland and a subsequent symposium on the topic, a great deal of new evidence has been gathered concerning this structure and flow. The authors of the study showed quite clearly what most people knew already: that "the United States is still the biggest TV programme exporter in the world and in most countries of the world American TV programmes compose a major part of all of the imported programmes." By contrast, the import of foreign television programs by the United States is negligible. This one-way flow of television is not a new phenomenon, nor is its origin obscure. It was built during the 1950s on the foundations of the United States film industry's distribution system developed before World War II. The Tampere study begins to document not only the structure of television production, its distribution and the direction of its flow, but also the kind of programs that get into the pipeline. The bulk of these are entertainment programs like "Peyton Place," "I Love Lucy" or "The Untouchables." The cultural values reflected in these programs do not conform to those of the importing country. Recently, the British Broadcasting Corporation found that their television imports (almost exclusively American) contained twice as many incidences of violence as British productions.

The Tampere study has documented the details of a picture that others began to sketch some time ago. Herbert I. Schiller, in *Mass Communications and American Empire* had already indicated the American dominance in international mass communications. Alan Wells, in *Picture Tube Imperialism? The Impact of U.S. Television on Latin America*, corroborates Schiller's findings. This particular kind of evidence documents the large amount of influence United States private enterprise has in the international communication field, especially in distribution of television. This is not in dispute, but the influence of this dominance through television messages is most in need of study and interpretation.

Television is an addictive habit. Estimates of television viewing have been made for years by commercial firms in the United States and Western Europe. One recent estimate in the United States was that the television set of the average family operated about six hours every day. Even though audience research is less regular and television less saturated in many underdeveloped countries, exposure to television is a daily phenomenon for those who have access to a set. The UNESCO evidence also indicated that the number of sets, even in poor countries, is increasing rapidly. Use of satellites would make widespread distribution much more rapid among large rural areas of these countries.

Media Influence

Although there is little dispute about whether the mass media, and especially television, influence people, there is a great deal of disagreement as to how this takes place. Television may contribute to change in many aspects of people's thoughts and actions, in what they know and how they know it and in their attitudes and opinions as well as behavior. There have been attempts to disentangle the mass of variables that go into the complex relationship of media exposure and human knowledge, attitude and behavior, but no model has explained more than a part of the change. Neither experiments nor field studies have come up with a completely satisfying solution. This relative inconclusiveness in research is not only true of the impact of commercial or entertainment television programs, but also of educational television.

What is discouraging to people who see the potential of the mass media for beneficial social change is the contradictory phenomenon between commercial and educational media in many countries. Many underdeveloped countries have been unsuccessful in using media to promote social welfare among their people: at the same time, there is a widespread and growing use of commerical media whose audiences are faithful to soap operas, quiz programs or modern music in a way they are not to farm forums or health programs. Two radio audience studies, in Mexico (by the Fredrick Ebert Foundation Seminar on Rural Radio) and the Philippines (by the Institute for Communication Research, Stanford University), illustrate the unequal competition between information and entertainment programs. Both studies showed the audiences were almost unaware of important health, educational and even economic information, but were heavy listeners to music and entertainment. An interesting phenomenon in the Philippines study was that, in the relatively rural region where the study was done, eighteen different radio stations competed for audiences and advertising support. All tried to be "popular," carrying programs to which people would listen. Even when audiences do pay attention to information relevant to their own betterment, a great deal of evidence indicates that attitudes and behavior are slow to change.

Governments facing such contradictions may attempt to solve them by blaming the inroads of outside values (which may be true) instead of finding out why people do not pay attention to and use the information offered to them over the mass media. To understand this situation better, we must view the mass media as part of a total social and cultural system and not as isolated phenomena unrelated to the environment.

An important breakthrough in mass media research came with a study of voting in the 1940 United States Presidential elections. In *The People's Choice,* Paul Lazarsfeld and his colleagues showed that the media were not so much like a hypodermic needle, directly affecting the individual, but worked through leaders who paid closer attention to the media and passed along information to others in an indirect or two-step manner. Thus, the media exerts influence through personal contact between the individual and his social group. The study also showed that voting habits were slow to change, but when they did, it was a result of the personal influence of opinion leaders and not directly through the media. This marked the beginning, in communication research, of seeing mass media as part of the larger system and the effects of the media as systemic ones reinforcing social and cultural change, but not directly causing changes.

By reversing the question of the social effects of the media to ask where important social and cultural change is found and then what role the media have played, we are more likely to discover the true role of the media as a contributor and not the root cause of change. Three examples are illustrative.

The People's Republic of China presents one of the most dramatic cases of profound social and cultural change in a society. Although not much direct information about communication in China is available, the pattern of change and media's role are beginning to emerge. Radio and the village amplifiers, along with newspapers and wall posters, played an important role in relaying certain messages to large groups. Still, media were not the central factors of change. Face-to-face communication and persuasion was a more critical element. Change was reinforced by strong support from the central political power along with a restructuring of institutions to accommodate the change. What seems clear from the China case is that there was a systemic social change in which the media played a reinforcing, but not causal, role.

Although the media may contribute to changes in social systems, its use alone will not cause these changes. A radio school project in Honduras was geared to provide the motivation and basic education for rural people. After ten years of effort, an evaluation showed that the results, in terms of social change, were discouragingly small. The evaluator concluded that many of the changes advocated by the radio school project had little effect on the individual because the system of underdevelopment was unchanging despite appeals to the individual. As long as structures remained the same and political power did not encourage change, the media could do little to influence change.

A final example comes from Brazil, where a social change oriented radio project called Movement for Basic Education had begun to attract a large audience of rural listeners before the military coup in 1964. It was subsequently changed and lost almost all of its audience and influence. What many media people ignore in this case are the origins of such a media-based movement. Only after a great deal of political ferment in rural areas and the beginning of the peasant leagues in the late 1950s was this radio project, as well as the Paulo Freire method, developed as a means of helping rural people change their situation. The effective use of media was, in this case, clearly subsequent to the beginning of social change due to political factors.

The media alone do not cause social and cultural change. The greatest impact of the messages of television or radio will be in reinforcing values that are already present or are being introduced through other forces in society. For educational use of the media, the lesson is clear. Social change for rural people, for example, will not take place simply because it is advocated by radio schools or on televised farm forums. Unless there are structural changes and backing by political power, the media are creating irrelevant messages that will largely be ignored.

Many have argued with some persuasiveness that American television programs reinforce a set of consumer values upon which our own social and economic system is based. In other countries, where the majority of audiences do not have consumer goods available, the result is the creation of a false and disruptive aspiration or a predisposition to become consumers of goods that large international companies are promoting. The amount of economic and political influence that such commercial interests wield is not easily measurable, but if these interests also control media messages (whether directly through foreign companies or indirectly through elite national groups) the elements for change are present. The problem for most governments is that the direction of social change and development advocated by official plan and that of outside investors may often be contradictory. Advocacy of rural development and dedication to self-sacrifice for one's country through a government media program may stand in sharp contrast to life-styles and values advocated by prime-time television imports (not to say the obvious life style of the elite in the big cities). Viewers are going to respond to the more credible message and accept the consumer message that their leaders have chosen to follow.

Value Judgments

Different sides of the controversy over the media do not dispute whether television has an effect, but rather whether a particular effect was observed and if that effect was good or bad. In many countries, there are nationalistic arguments about the influence of foreign television, even that which purports to be educational. Peru was the only South American country to reject a Spanish version of "Sesame Street," saying that the program's values were not those that Peru wished to promote among her young children. Others have argued even more strongly that educational media like "Sesame Street" are less acceptable than entertainment programs like "Bonanza" or "Mission Impossible," simply because they more directly affect younger and more impressionable audiences. Many would dispute this judgment, but it is indicative of a basic problem in the use of media produced by outside sources. These media inevitably reflect the values of the social and cultural system where they were produced. Many countries cannot afford to produce programs to fill up their television schedules so they buy relatively cheap series from the United States and help make foreign source's product even more profitable. The dilemma is that the

United States government does not control media production and yet receives the brunt of the criticism for its effect in other countries.

Since part of the problem is the influence of the United States in the cultural arena of other countries, the ultimate solution will come from the countries themselves. Given the structure of international communications, immediate solutions will not be easy, but countries could respond in several ways. Many countries are anxious to develop a positive policy concerning television and satellites. They are not convinced that the technology is the problem, but the costs of both hardware and software are high, perhaps too high for them to afford. At the same time, they believe that television is potentially a very powerful medium of communication for development. In the face of this dilemma of high costs and potential benefits, many countries hesitate to make a decision.

New Cultural Models

For most countries, the simple alternative is to fill their hours of broadcasting with cheap American series or broadcasting only a minimum time each day. Most countries have chosen to use the expensive hardware and provide set owners with entertainment, even though it comes from outside their cultures. Given the structure of television production and its international distribution, the choice to fill screens with imported material has meant that most of it has been American, with the British and French in distant second and third place. Historically, most countries have chosen a full television schedule at relatively low cost, but they have done so at cultural and political costs.

Today, many countries would like to change this situation. Instead of obeying the pressure to fill up their television screens with many hours of imported programs from the United States, they would prefer a more balanced diet. The model of "cultural openness" to whatever the market situation offered is no longer acceptable to many countries that feel vulnerable to unwanted cultural influence. For years countries like Mexico and Canada were prime markets for United States films and television series. Although much still remains unchanged, there is strong political feeling about controlling the media so that they reflect the national culture more. Most smaller countries share these feelings, but have fewer means than Mexico and Canada to become culturally independent.

Alternative models of cultural independence for different countries to follow are not clear, but only a gradual solution to the problem seems likely. The goal is to become culturally independent or at least less dependent on one dominant culture—that of the United States. The first stage might call for a model of cultural pluralism. This stage would assume that a country could not simply blacken its television screens. On the other hand, it could not produce enough programs for local consumption. A trade-off of less programming time and more careful attention to purchasing would result in a better mix of television fare. Such a policy would cost more in time for purchasing programs, as well as increase the cost of series, since few other countries can compete with the price of American series. However, more countries would be encouraged to enter the international producing market, and purchasing countries, by thinking out more carefully what they want on their screens, would better define their television policy for a time when they can become more truly independent.

The second stage might be called cultural self-reliance because it would be a time when a nation could take care of most of its major television needs. This stage has both policy and technical requisites. Countries must have a clearly defined set of goals for their television capability as well as a trained group of producers to help achieve these goals. A few countries have refrained from getting into the television sweepstakes altogether. Tanzania has refused to use television because radio seems to be a more appropriate means of achieving the mass education and rural development goals it has set for itself. Niger has television, but uses it only for educational programs in schools. The few elites who bought sets years ago in anticipation of the usual influx of French entertainment programs are still waiting. Peru has tried recently to move into a more self-reliant position, but still depends on outside sources for programming.

The reaction of some in the United States to this increasing reluctance to use American products on the television screen has been to invoke the First Amendment or the principle of free flow of information. Self-reliance is seen as a form of cultural protectionism and some think we should respond with pressures on countries to remain contented consumers of our media messages. But the principle of free exchange of information depends on the ability of each country participating to share in this exchange. No one can truly share unless he is independent and has something to exchange. Given the virtually nonexistent flow of television programs or even news from most countries to the United States, promotion of a better balance of information transfer is a first, vital step in genuine free flow of information.

The communication industry in the United States is only under indirect control or influence by the government. Yet, the government must negotiate our position on the satellite question in the United Nations (UN). Whatever the future of United States commercial dominance in international communications, the American government should demonstrate, by positive action, its commitment to the use of communication technology for the benefit of all and not simply the profit of a few.

There is no panacea for many nations' mistrust of the dominating influence of the United States. Nor is there a panacea in communication technology for solving deeply ingrained social and economic problems in other countries. Still, making sure that this technology is shared among nations would do much to advance the standing of the United States in the eyes of other nations.

Positive Alternatives

Some policy suggestions for this positive action are as follows:

- Before seeking solutions, we must be sure of the nature of the problems concerning free flow of information and the impact of communication technology. First, the appropriate United States government bodies (e.g., the State Department, Agency for International Development (AID), Department of Health, Education and Welfare and so on) should continue to inform themselves on the definition and explanation of these problems by:
(1) Having access to research information in this field through universities and other sources;
(2) Continuing to sponsor discussion and debate of the problems in seminars of this kind;
(3) Listening to the points of view of scholars and decision makers from other countries so that wider cultural views might be represented.

The AID, National Aeronautics and Space Administration (NASA) and other similar agencies, should foster better uses of communication technology for purposes of social development. AID and others, through multilateral agencies of the UN, could help countries develop self-reliance in mass media so that they would have genuine options to buying software from dominant communications countries. The promise of television for education and information has yet to be fully realized; the promise of less costly and more flexible technology under the control of each country may be an even more promising avenue for future development. Regardless of strong United States economic interests in large communication technology, the United States should be open to alternative technologies which offer better solutions to educational problems.
- The United States, through its appropriate agencies, should promote tests of television and satellite technology in experimental ways that might help solve pressing social problems, such as health care for the most isolated and poorest populations of countries. Field research should be carried out on the social impact of satellite television for such uses so that not only the hardware system is tested. This kind of information is important for countries to have when they are considering the decision of using satellite technology. However, "experiments" should

not be used to dodge difficult problems through use of operational satellites.
- The recent emphasis by the United States, in its international aid, on the social and economic development of the least developed nations and concern about equity and income distribution, should also include the use of communications. The potential of communication technology should be promoted for the benefit of the least developed and the most oppressed. This principle is not easily promoted with a technology developed for profitable urban countries, such as the United States, and will take thoughtful consideration from the United States, lest it simply aggravate problems of dominance of marginal people, whether by America or the elite of other countries. Satellite-conveyed services of television, radio or telephone will not automatically improve the lot of isolated rural people in underdeveloped areas, but as part of an integrated plan to better distribute services of education, health and information, satellites can improve the quality of life for such people.

Finally, the United States must recognize that the problem of communications involves power. No individual or country likes to always receive, but never send messages. Whether it concerns control of television in the United States by three major networks, world news flow by a handful of international news agencies or dominance of satellite technology by the United States, the problem is not essentially changed. There are always the few generating messages for the many. Man has the right to information, as well as *unbiased* information, which means at least some choice among different sources. Man also has the right to privacy, to not being invaded by persistent and unwanted messages from the outside by a group controlling the messages, whether this be a government or a commercial interest.

The United States can work positively to share satellite and communication technology with other nations. These steps should help counterbalance attitudes of distrust among other countries. Imbalances of power, whether economic, military or technological, will still remain and no external aid program will entirely eliminate them. The long-term solution is to help all people attain a more equitable share of this power in the economic and technological resources that can improve the quality of life for everyone.

22

Fantasy and Culture on Television

Ben Stein

There is, on prime-time television, a unified picture of life in these United States that is an alternate reality. For hours each day, people can leave the lives they are compelled to lead, lives whose limitations and frustrations hardly need to be detailed, and enter a different world that is more pleasant and less difficult in almost every way—life on television.

Most TV shows are set in the present or in a time within the memory of the viewers. All of the characters are supposed to be types we are familiar with. While that familiarity may be more imaginary than real, we do see a world on television with which it is not difficult to a feel a distant kinship. More than that, we see a world that is extremely appealing in a whole variety of ways. Again, these ways have to do largely with simplification. Life on television is in many ways a schematic of real life.

The whole alternate reality that television creates is not a coincidence or a result of random chance. It is the product of the thinking of TV producers and writers about life. We can see reflected on our video screens the attitudes of TV creators. More than that, we can sense the experience and "feel" of a city replicated on television. For what we see on prime-time television is nothing less than the apotheosizing of Los Angeles, and the spreading of the Los Angeles experience across the TV screens of America.

It is important to realize first that television is indeed creating a unified experience, a consistent alternative world. There is no contrast on television such as there is between a Dostoevsky and a Gogol, between an Osborne and a Stoppard, between a Mailer and a Didion, or between a Chandler and a Dunne. There is no major difference in texture or attitude between a "Baretta" and a "Happy Days," which is to say, between a show about a street cop in a dangerous and violent city in 1978 and a show about an utterly happy family in a small Wisconsin town in 1956. Both shows have the same optimistic, cheerful attitude about life, the same utterly unshakable premise that everything will come out right in the end, the same absence of anxiety or worry about daily life or death, the same feeling of life's infinite potential. With the exception of "Mary Hartman, Mary Hartman," there is no major show that says anything the slightest bit pessimistic about the potential for happiness of daily life. ("Mary Hartman" was not on during prime time in most locales). No show challenges the assumption that the unexamined life is the only life worth living.

No show displays a kind of life that is anything but immaculately clean and neat, in which people are anything but well-groomed and hygienic and their motivations anything but straightforward. Certainly, this has partly to do with the exigencies of a mass culture. Traditionally, the dramas of folk culture are not as complicated as those of high culture. Yet that does not account for everything. In movies (the mass culture of another era) there was dirt and tragedy and complexity, even in films with enormous appeal to mass audiences. The dirt of Tara, the sweat and grime of Scarlett O'Hara's brow, the tawdriness of John Garfield's apartment in *Body and Soul*, the grim grayness and ambiguity of 50 detective stories of the 1940s *film noir* genre are only a tiny fraction of the available evidence on that score.

Even in the early days of television, before it moved so completely to Los Angeles, there was complexity and sadness. When reruns of "Your Show of Shows" appear, their sad endings are almost shocking. The truly frightening and earthy quality of some early "Playhouse 90" and "Kraft Theatre" shows is amazing when compared with the cheerfulness and antisepsis of the present day's fare on television.

Today's television is purer, in terms of backdrop and story endings, than the lines of a Mercedes convertible. Every day's shows bring fresh examples. Recently I saw an episode of "Charlie's Angels" about massage parlors that were really whorehouses. The three beautiful "angels" of the show were compelled to pretend they worked at massage parlors in seamy areas. (On this particular show, the girls are almost always compelled to act as prostitutes or prisoners or lesbians or nymphomaniacs). Anyone who has ever passed by a massage parlor knows that they are invariably dirty, shabby places, with pitiful and degraded denizens. On "Charlie's Angels," the Paradise Massage Parlor compared favorably with the surgical theater at Massachusetts General Hospital. The girls were immaculate and well-groomed, soft of speech and clear of eye and skin.

On "The Waltons," we are supposed to believe that we are in a Depression-era farming town in backwoods Virginia. Anyone who has been to a backwoods farming town in the South knows that whatever else may be said about them, they are invariably dirty and bedraggled. On "The Waltons," even the barnyard is immaculate. Marie Antoinette could not have asked for more agreeable play-farm quarters.

Fantasy and Culture 217

The grittiest TV show is generally believed to be "Baretta." Yet even there, the supposedly, shabby boardinghouses are neat, bright, and cheery. Even the junkies wear fresh clothing and sport recent haircuts.

Why is television so clean? Why, when a recent show dramatized living conditions on New York's Lower East Side during the early twentieth century, did every apartment look like something that a DuPont great-grandson had recently redecorated?

The answer is simple. TV writers and producers replicate the world in which they live in their art, and the world they live in is the super-clean, super-bright world of Los Angeles, where even the slums are spotless and have palm trees in front. The world on television is the world south of the Tehachapi and north of Frontera.

Until I moved to Los Angeles, I had no idea where the images of television came from. Where on earth, I wondered, were pastel drug stores, low stucco apartments with balconies overlooking artificial waterfalls in the poor neighborhoods, and bars with almost pitch-black interiors, opening onto glaringly bright sidewalks, utterly without litter or refuse? Drive along any boulevard in Los Angeles. There is block after block of pastel drug stores and apartment houses with balconies and artificial waterfalls. Close by are the bars with pitch-black interiors.

When I lived in Washington and in New York, I wondered where in America were all cars bright and shiny, unspattered by mud, with their original colors gleaming in the sun. Where did people have new cars even if they were secretaries or rookie policemen?

In Los Angeles, where everyone spends a few hours a day in a car, everyone has a shiny new auto, even if it is a financial sacrifice. In Los Angeles, where the sun shines every day and rain never falls, cars never get muddy.

Where are policemen handsome, thin, neatly dressed and polite? They certainly were not in New York or Washington or New Haven or Santa Cruz or anywhere else except Los Angeles. In Los Angeles, the policemen look like male models, except that they do not look effeminate. They are the models for the ruggedly modish cops on a dozen TV shows.

Artists re-create their experiences, and the Los Angeles experience is one of cleanliness, brightness, shininess, and handsomeness. The artists of television do not live in drafty garrets. An artist for television simply never can experience the grittiness of daily life that might be experienced in any other city.

Among the TV writers and producers I interviewed, whenever people spoke of Los Angeles they spoke of a "fantasy land," "plastic paradise," "wonderland," "sterile concrete," "lotus land," and similar hackneyed phrases that are nevertheless accurate. The writers and producers see and experience a life of cleanness and emphasis on good appearance that would be unbelievable to anyone who did not live in Los Angeles. That has become their image of life, so that when a world is recreated on television, the Los Angeles world, the one in the creators' minds, is the one that comes out. However much the writers and producers may mock and decry the sterility and cleanliness of Los Angeles, it is Los Angeles they are broadcasting around the world as the model environment, The faces, clothes, haircuts, and cars of people on television are the faces, clothes, haircuts, and cars of people walking down Rodeo Drive in Beverly Hills.

All of this has nothing to do with politics of left, right, or center. It does have to do with the control that the Los Angeles TV community has over television's content. It illustrates powerfully the influence that the experiences in the producers' and writers' minds has over what goes out over the airwaves. Television is not creating a world that reflects a composite of the American experience. Nor is the TV world the result of random chance. Television is what comes out of the Los Angeles TV community's heads, and since Los Angeles is what goes into their heads, Los Angeles is what comes out.

But this applies only to the question of appearance and graphics. There is also a moral and philosophical world on television, and that, too, has to come from somewhere.

Beyond the physical and visual cleanliness on television is an attitude appealing far beyond most of what real life has to offer. On television, everything ends happily, which might be a way of summarizing the TV climate. There is far more, however. Every problem that comes up on television is cured before the show is over. No one suffers from existential terrors. They are not even hinted at.

On a smaller-scale, people on television are not small-minded, nasty folks. If they are murderers, at least they are polite. No waitresses neglect to take a diner's order. No busboys spill Coca-Cola on anyone's lap. No one cuts a driver off and makes him slam on the brakes. Clerks in stores are polite and helpful. No one gets caught in traffic jams. There are no blackouts. No shopping-bag ladies, reeking of urine, stalk a traveler in a crowded subway. No snarling teenagers threaten and mock on a deserted sidewalk. Instead, people move along rapidly on highways and byways. Impediments are cleared out of the way, both visually and psychologically. At the end of 60 minutes, at the most, everything has come up roses, even if there were a few minor thorns along the way.

On television, people get things done. No one spends all day in a windowless office going over musty volumes of figures and regulations, seeking to comply with guidelines and plans laid out by persons long since dead.

No one on television spends all day in bed, too lethargic or depressed to get up. On television, in fact, there is no such thing as depression. That most widespread of modern psychic ailments simply does not exist in the alternate world of television. Everyone, good or bad, is charged with energy. If someone wants to do something, he or she simply goes out and does it. There are no mental blocks working to derail the TV hero or villain.

Further, people on television think big. They are no longer concerned with telling Ricky Ricardo how much they spent on a hat. Instead, they think about making a million by selling heroin, or about ridding Los Angeles of the most vicious killer of the decade. In a comedy, a poor family thinks of getting rich. A middle-class family thinks of getting into the upper class. A black family thinks of overcoming racism. Nothing trivial occurs as a main theme any longer.

"Out there," for the folks on television, is a big world, full of possibilities. Here, a sharp distinction needs to be made between social activism and personal ambition. The people on television are never interested in social movements. They may want to be more well off themselves, but they are never interested in a political try at massive and immediate redistribution of wealth. Similarly, Edith Bunker may make a stab at social accommodation by accepting the fact that a relative is a lesbian, but she will never march for gay rights. J.J. on "Good Times" will do his best to make a killing in faulty underwear, but he will not demonstrate against double taxation of corporate dividends. Tony Baretta will extend himself to catch a murderer, but he will not agitate for a return of the death penalty. Charlie's Angels will coo with sympathy over the plight of a hooker, but they will never carry placards asking for repeal of laws against prostitution.

People on television want money and happiness for themselves. They want to be great sleuths or great criminals. But they are never interested in social movements. They have big plans and hopes for themselves, but not for society.

This entire psychic galaxy is, as far as I can tell, a reflection of the psychic makeup of the Hollywood TV producer and writer. Before I came to the world of TV production I never would have imagined that a group of people as psychologically successful and liberated as TV writers and producers existed. It is their mental world that is up there on the TV screen.

In the world of television are people who are financially successful, creative, living in comfortable surroundings, and generally quite happy. Around a successful TV production company (and the unsuccessful ones quickly vanish) there is an air of confidence and self-satisfaction that is rarely encountered anywhere else.

Those people are highly unusual folk, operating in a highly unusual milieu, and it shows. In the eighth decade of American life in the twentieth century, the working situation of Americans has become steadily more bureaucratized. Almost everyone coming out of school goes to work for a large enterprise of some kind, finding a spot on a bureaucratic ladder. The worker must flatter everyone over him and worry about everyone under him. His real rewards come not from producing anything, but from pleasing those above him on the ladder.

Workers derive their security and status from the bureaucratic structure in which they find themselves. They are cogs in a vast machinery. There is little or no creativity in their daily lives. Advancement comes with infuriating slowness. To reach a position of financial independence or modest wealth is almost impossible. Getting that extra few thousand a year in wages becomes the key goal, and few see further than that.

On the other hand, the bureaucratic structure provides a protection against having to actually produce anything. Simply serving one's time at the office is all that is required to get by. Eventually, however, that too takes its toll. The realization that one is doing nothing but serving out a life sentence results in devastating blows to one's self-esteem.

The whole process of the engorgement of institutions and the swallowing up of the individual into large enterprises leads, in my experience, to a smallness of mind. Bitterness and pettiness are generated by the unmixed frustration that is each day's portion.

Imagine, on the other hand, the world of Hollywood. It is a throwback to the world of individual entrepreneurs. Each writer sinks or swims on the basis of his product. Those people do not have to wait in a bureaucratic holding pattern all of their lives. If their product is good, they become successful and important immediately. They are not judged by how well they can accommodate themselves to a paranoid boss's suspicions. Rather, they move along or fall out depending on what they get done. They are immediately able to make themselves independent by having a skill that is in great demand and correspondingly highly paid. They float from contract to contract. Each time they begin a project, they have the opportunity to become millionaires, and many of them do.

The economics of TV production are such that successful writers can demand and get proprietary interest in the shows they write. If the show is successful, the rewards become staggering. Each successful TV writer becomes an entrepreneur on some scale. The money comes pouring in. A story about Bob Dylan comes to mind. When Dylan started out, he wrote about depressed, crazy people suffering daily crises. After a few years, when his income had risen to eight figures left of the decimal point, he started to write only about happy, cheerful subjects. When asked about the change, he is reported to have said. "It's hard to be a bitter millionaire."

So it is with the people on television. They have many firm and negative opinions about various groups within the society, but they are basically fairly satisfied with life. There may be, and probably are, starving would-be TV writers in North Hollywood and Studio City who are filled with rage and anger. But the ones who have made it, the ones who are working regularly for many thousands a week, are quite content for the most part.

TV writers are not like novel or play writers. They are simply not allowed to become depressed and unproductive. They must get out a show every week. No sulking or brooding is permitted. To get out a new teleplay each week is not the pastime of blocked people. Those who sulk all day because they get a rude remark from a waiter are not successful TV writers and producers. Those who cannot drag themselves out of the house because of existential dread do not get to see their names in the credits. Life's annoyances and pitfalls are not permitted to throw the train of creation off the tracks.

Imagine, if you will, a Texas wheeler-dealer who is also able to write situation comedies and adventure shows, and there you have a good idea of the personality type of the successful TV writer and producer. He is a person who gets things done and who feels good about it. After spending years in bureaucracies of various kinds, I found it staggering to see how much each individual writer and producer got done each day. In Norman Lear's TAT Communications, there is a full-time staff of fewer than 50 to get out hundreds of millions of dollars worth of TV product. If the government had a department of TV comedy, there would be at least 75,000 employees—and they would do nothing. Naturally, each of those few people who is producing so much feels good about it and about himself. The exact opposite of small-mindedness is generated.

No one is completely or even mostly happy, but the Hollywood TV writers and producers that I have met went a long way along that line. They were, and are, people who take risks and live successfully. Their horizons are broad. The small annoyances of life do not faze them unduly. They see life not as a prison sentence but as a garden of rich potentialities.

TV writers and producers are not starving in garrets, cutting off their ears to send to prostitutes. They are generally far more prosperous than the bankers they hate, far more energetic and entrepreneurial than the businessmen they hate, and infinitely more effective than the bureaucrats they tolerate. They lead fulfilled, productive lives, by most standards. They live those lives in an attractive, uncluttered world of immaculate sidewalks and gleaming new cars, pastel storefronts, and artificial waterfalls. They have been a party to striving and success in their own lives, and they have not missed the lesson of the possibilities of life. And it is this way of life that has been translated into the flickering colorful images on hundreds of millions of TV screens.

To set forth a way of life on television is not necessarily political in terms of left, right, or center. Still, it has some policy content. To replicate one's life and tell the world that it is the model of how life should be lived is a normative statement with some degree of power and forcefulness. The people who have created that model world on television are telling the rest of us—that we should try to conform to that model—implicit though the demand may be.

America, like every country, has a folk culture. This is made up of the lore of the folk, the great mass of people, those who are not part of the more elevated areas of culture and society. Long ago, it consisted of folk tales and traditions and stories. Now, since the age of mass literacy (an age which may be coming to an end), the folk culture is largely bound up in books. It is also on display in movies, which show, by their durability and acceptance, how well they are loved by the American people.

One takes one's life in one's hands when trying to summarize the mass culture of America. There is simply too much of it and it is too varied. However, some common elements stand out. From the time of James Fenimore Cooper to the time of Joan Didion, from the lore of Thomas Jefferson to the lore of James Earl Carter, from Mark Twain to Ernest Hemingway, from Mary Pickford to Doris Day, small towns have been seen as wholesome, decent places, the wellsprings of America's best virtues. It is from small towns that innocence issues to be subverted by the city. It is from the city that corrupted innocence departs to be cleansed in small towns.

The appeal of the small town in the American heart and imagination is older than the Republic. To this day, it is used as the backdrop for commercials that want to emphasize the wholesomeness or cleanliness of a product. To this day, the president of the United States cannot get enough cornpone in his mouth when he wants to appear sincere. And to this day, while most Americans do not live in very small towns, more than half live in cities other than the largest 25.

Yet the image of the small town has been frontally and continually attacked by TV culture. Television repeatedly shows the evil, conspiratorial, murderous small town, and no other, so that in the alternate world of television, "small town" and "evil" are synonymous.

This means something quite interesting and fundamental. Because the TV community is using the dominant folk culture medium of television, it might be expected to carry the message of the traditional folk culture. Far from it. Instead, the dominant folk culture medium has been captured by a group whose view of small towns is opposed to that of the folk tradition. To oversimplify somewhat, the folk culture is in service against the views of the folk, in terms of its views of small towns.

The case of businessmen is more complicated. Men of business, if thought of as robber barons of the gilded age, have never been wildly popular in American thought. Probably only a small fraction of the population ever loved the Rockefellers. On the other hand, there is a tradition of respect for the successful man of affairs. In the work of writers from Horatio Alger to F. Scott Fitzgerald to Irving Wallace, businessmen are put on show as successful achievers of the American dream, people to be envied and emulated. While the movies of Depression-era America often showed crude, rapacious businessmen, they were usually foiled by more high-minded businessmen.

Certainly we can see that, on a national scale, there is more interest in becoming a successful businessman than a successful professor or archaeologist. At any rate, more people make the effort in business, which apparently signifies something about the loathing or lack of it that Americans have for business. Even the high poobahs of government go into business as an American tradition—once they have finished their tours of duty.

So, while there is a mixture of admiration and fear surrounding businessmen, they are far from being universally despised. Except in the works of a few reform writers like Sinclair Lewis and more notably, Upton Sinclair, businessmen are a mixed group—not all good or all bad, and certainly embodying many worthwhile characteristics. No tradition of American folk culture that I know of depicts businessmen exclusively as murderers and drug dealers and fools.

Again, as in the case of small towns, the picture that comes over the chief folk culture medium, television, is far different from the traditional folk concept. The new molder of folk wisdom, television, tells us that businessmen are dangerous, homicidal frauds or buffoons. And while that is different indeed from what the tradition was before, who is to say how long any idea or concept challenged so often by television can survive?

The picture of rich people in America's folk culture is slightly complicated as well. There has always been respect and admiration for people with old money, especially money derived from the land. Indeed, the father of our country was supposedly the richest man in the colonies. For the first several decades of national life, all of our presidents and statesmen came from moneyed backgrounds.

An image of the patrician farmer or plantation owner surveying his holdings, dispensing justice and largesse, is a fixture of folk culture. One need only think of the colonel in *Birth of a Nation* or of Scarlett O'Hara's father in *Gone With the Wind*, not to mention Ashley Wilkes in the same book and the film, to see that we have placed rich people of the land on a pedestal.

It is hard to think of any instances when rich people, as opposed to grasping people on the way up, are depicted as bad or unworthy. The picture of Lionel Barrymore nobly suffering the slings and arrows of the parvenu Wallace Beery in *Dinner At Eight* comes to mind as a model. Rock Hudson standing up for right and decency in spite of the fabulously newly rich James Dean in *Giant* is a similar ideal.

The confused but richly decent people of Henry James also appear in literature as people we might all wish to imitate, as do the characters of Marquand. On a more folksy level, we have to recall that Batman was in reality a wealthy and (seemingly) indolent young gentleman of means. Even in the early days of television, the only stupendously rich person we met, J. Beresford Tipton, who made millionaires at the wave of a hand, was a generous and kind soul, somewhat Olympian in stature and mental bearing.

The TV picture in 1977 could hardly be more different. If J. Beresford Tipton were to reappear on "Kingston: Confidential," he would be using his money to bring about the American Reich. If Lionel Barrymore were on an episode of "Columbo," he would have killed Wallace Beery and tried to cover it up.

Whatever respect there is in the folk culture for the rich is completely and totally gone from television. "Rich" equals "murderous" in the TV world of today, or at least "rich" equal "means" (if we are looking at a situation comedy).

Military men's role in the American folk culture is straightforward and highly complimentary. It does not take much recollection to bring out the memories of movies about great soldiers of America's past. It is even clearer in the history we all learn in school. America has no tradition of an elite and repressive military system, and we have loved our citizen soldier heroes from Mad Anthony Wayne to Douglas MacArthur and beyond. I never saw any signs on bumper stickers saying "Leave Our POWs in Hanoi." Military men are our defenders and protectors, from John Wayne to John Wayne. Except for comic sallies like *Dr. Strangelove*, attacks on military personnel as being fools and conspirators are uncommon, and, before the nuclear age, generally unrecorded.

On television the picture, while mixed, is far more negative. On shows for children, there are still good automatons of soldiers. But when soldiers appear elsewhere, they are not the kinds of people you would want to have as close friends. Again, the medium of television is at work against the wisdom of the folk culture.

Something similar is happening in the subject areas of criminals, poor people, and religion. Americans have traditionally had little sympathy for criminals. There is no *Les Miserables* in the American folk tradition that says that the peccadilloes of criminals are caused by the relentless cruelty of society. (The movies that comes closest, *I Am a Fugitive from a Chain Gang*, is about a man who in reality committed no crime but was framed, and the literature of all countries abounds in those stories). Criminals have been people to find out and put in jail. Yet on television, criminals are simply concealed so thoroughly that they do not appear at all except in a complete social and class disguise. (Here one enters a complex area. In certain types of middlebrow lore, crime has always involved primarily the upper classes. The novels of Arthur Conan Doyle and Agatha Christie are but two well-known examples of a vast genre. On the other hand, American movies during the Depression—the classic era of gangster movies—did show gangsters as gangsters and not as the presidents of utility companies. Thus while television's exclusive depiction of criminals as well-to-do people is not unprecedented, it is also a departure from mass culture).

When someone is daily confronted on television with crimes committed only by men in three-piece suits and women in tennis outfits, he will eventually begin to wonder who the criminals in the real world are. And the focus of guilt may well shift from the man holding the gun to the man holding the mortgage. Against a mass medium that says that the individual criminal is not responsible for his actions, there stands a folklore that says that he is.

The question of the poor is entirely different. There, television's image has much in common with folk wisdom. Traditionally, there has been a great deal of sympathy from people who are not poor toward people who are poor—at least in folk culture. Social Darwinist thought floated through American business and universities but never made much impact on popular culture. There are endless stories about the deserving poor and very few about the people who deserve to be poor. So in that particular respect, television does not challenge the folk culture.

However, the folk culture has also traditionally placed heavy emphasis on working one's way out of the morass of poverty and into wealth and success. That is, after all, the American dream. On television, the folk idea has been changed, so that while it is good not to be poor, it is bad to be rich.

America has no established church. Even so, men of the cloth have traditionally been highly thought of in the folk culture. One need only remember Bing Crosby as the lovable Father to get the idea, while a Norman Vincent Peale or a Billy Graham would make the point even more clearly. On the other hand, leaders of sects somewhat off the beaten track, the Billy Sunday and Aimee Semple MacPherson crowd, have never lasted in public admiration. Sooner or later they become kooks and crackpots in the public mind. On television, the religious picture is mixed. There is a strain of priests and nuns who are fine, solid people. There is also a strain who are lunatic hypocritical cranks. It simply cannot be said, in this particular case, that the TV culture is at war with the folk culture.

There is a final struggle between TV and the folk culture, which is the least explicit. It is over lifestyles. Once upon a time there was a national legend that the best life was a quiet, unassuming one, spent in cultivating friends in a corner of the world and trying to be thrifty, considerate, and careful. Those are, in fact, widely called "the old-fashioned virtues." That whole concept is at odds with TV life. On television, life is lived in the fast lane. The motto is to live it up, right now. Forget about quiet living. There is no wisdom in one's elders, and the past offers no guides to the present. That is the lesson of TV situation comedies and adventure shows. If you want to be cool, drive fast and speak in monosyllables, and if you hold back, you are hiding something. The new folk medium says that the old-fashioned virtues are for racists and conspirators—people who get small children hooked on drugs. Old-fashioned people are not to be trusted. The life to live on television, is the life in Los Angeles.

To put it more clearly, if you come across someone who is full of folk wisdom and homilies, he may be: an Archie Bunker racist slob, however lovable; a con man, *à la* innumerable adventure and comedy shows; a small-town sheriff out to murder the innocent, a staple of any TV show about crime; or a fool, like the senator of "All's Fair." The good people on television are slick-looking men and women, up-to-the-minute, lithe and thin, in flashy cars and flashy clothes. The kindly housewife of "Ozzie and Harriet" has been utterly displaced by Farrah Fawcett.

Television shows on prime time are a new folk culture, energized by the most powerful media tool of all time, contending with the time-honored wisdom of the folk. This new folk culture is relentlessly attacking the old, not in every area, but in every area in which the TV-making class can be benefited. Against the once-mighty fortresses of the rich, small towns, and business success, the battering ram of a new and militant medium—television—has been unleashed.

It is not too early to see some of the consequences. Television, which can reverse an entire nation on a political issue of the greatest moment (who to have as president, for example) which can move a lot of soap and underarm deodorants, is at work on the national mind on a whole variety of subjects.

Already, scientists have found that the TV news, with its constant diet of sneers and negativism, makes regular viewers hostile and apathetic. What must be the views of people exposed to the far more massive doses of political and social advertising on shows that are not expressly or openly political and social? To deny that there is some effect is to deny a great deal.

However, even if the effect is difficult to measure, the effort of the TV shows and their makers is still interesting as an indication of what is on the minds of a powerful and little-known group. Siegfried Kracauer's thesis in *From Caligari to Hitler*—that popular culture represents and reflects national dreams and nightmares—is untrue in the case of prime-time television. Television in this case represents nothing more than the views of a few hundred people in the western section of Los Angeles. It is a highly parochial, idiosyncratic view of the world that comes out on TV screens, the world view of a group whose moment has come.

It is not clear that it is good or bad that the views of the TV community get the prominent display they do. I have certain opinions, which are undoubtedly revealed in my writing, but I have no overall feeling that something terrible is happening. In a free society, different groups will obtain power over different institutions at different times. Certainly the government should do nothing to stop it. But then again, no one should be stopped from pointing out what has happened in Hollywood.

23

Direct-Broadcast Satellites and Cultural Integrity

Ithiel de Sola Pool

Direct-satellite television broadcasting has been alleged to represent an active threat to the integrity of national cultures. It is hard to take this allegation seriously when there is no imminent prospect of direct-satellite television broadcasts to countries that do not wish to receive them. Other media pose more significant threats to the integrity of national cultures, such as syndicated reruns of television tapes. Nonetheless, many people are alarmed by the prospect of direct-satellite broadcasting and thus it becomes a political, if not physical, reality.

A sharp distinction should be made between direct-television broadcasting with the cooperation of the receiving country and direct broadcasting to a country that does not wish it. The former may be practicable in the visible future; the latter probably not. Any economically rational use of direct broadcasting requires that the receiving country allocate one of the few suitable wavebands to that purpose and distribute sets and antennas designed appropriately to receive such signals. The sender must choose to launch a large satellite capable of radiating much more power than required for broadcasting to sophisticated earth stations.

For American domestic communications, a national satellite television distribution system could be created by placing 10,000 current, $3,000 antennas around the country so that in every city and town, broadcasters and cablecasters could pick up national programs and redistribute them over the air or by cable. Another system would require only a $100 to $300 antenna and amplifier at every set, i.e. 50 to 100 million of them. The latter (or direct broadcast) system is ridiculously expensive, costing perhaps 100 times as much as the former.

There is no reason to expect direct-television broadcasting in the continental United States, but it does make sense for other countries and situations. For remote sparsely populated areas like Alaska or Siberia, it may be economic to provide each of the relatively few, scattered sets with antennas and other special equipment at a cost of several hundred or even thousand dollars apiece so as to eliminate the need for ground stations and re-transmitters. In India, if the policy of one set per village can be enforced, then in the parts of the country where villages are widely scattered, direct broadcasting to enhanced community receivers makes sense. Such situations favorable to direct broadcasting are few. Most satellite broadcasting will be distribution-to-redistributiuon ground stations, not just for the near term, but for the indefinite future.

Under those circumstances, a country that wished to disseminate direct television to others would have an extremely small audience, limited to those few individuals who possess their own enhanced receivers. To reach those few persons, the sender would have to launch a large, expensive satellite capable of beaming high radiation—if to more than one country, then with different standards of signals to different countries—and in each case on a band (a) not otherwise in use in that area, but (b) suitable for satellite transmission and (c) receivable by sets currently in use. These requirements would rarely be met on any significant scale. To invest in direct-satellite television broadcasting to countries that do not cooperate would therefore require great expenditure for trivial results. The situation is entirely different from shortwave broadcasting which takes little bandwidth, relatively cheap transmitters and cheap receivers, which many people own for other purposes than to listen to the propagandist. Direct-satellite television broadcasting to countries that do not wish it is not an attractive option for either governments or commercial broadcasters.

Cultural Intrusion

Whatever one's value position, the fact is that in the modern world, there is international cultural intrusion. Foreign influence, it can be argued, is but a special case of the disruptive impact of intellectual and cultural media in general. All through history intellectuals have been called subversive and their products attacked as assaults upon the established culture. Poetry, philosophy, literature and the media are perennially labeled immoral, corrupters of youth, disrespectful of tradition. Those conservative charges have an element of truth. Intellectuals are gadflys. They claim a right to seek the truth and evaluate the good on their own, other than by the writ of established authorities. They are also, and always have been, conduits for foreign ideas. From the days of Greek slave tutors in Rome, to the wandering bards and scholars of the Middle Ages, to the refugee or brain drain scholars of today, communicators and men of intellect have been rootless cosmopolitans and introducers of alien ideas.

Phenomena that have been with us from time immemorial are magnified by the emergence of telecommunications and the mass media. That is a quantitative change so great as to become a qualitative change too. Mass media and electronic communications obliterate many of the impediments that once served to slow down changes in ideas and mores. Barriers of time and space that once protected the status quo are easily penetrated or jumped over by modern media. These eliminate the cushion of time between when an event happens and when it is known worldwide. People have become ringside observers to dramatic news events, be they wars, moon landings, hijackings or riots; the public follows events as they unfold, while the outcome is still unknown. Thus, the barrier of distance is gone.

Electronic communication and mass media also serve to widen the units in which political, economic or social action takes place. A peasant who sells his crop in the local marketplace may ultimately be linked to the world market by a series of trading intermediaries, but that is quite different from the situation of the farmer who receives world price quotations on the morning newscast. He operates directly in a regional or national, if not world, market. The village leader who established his legitimacy by his ties to local lineages and shrines operates in a very different way from the national politician who has to formulate issues as abstract platform planks that will be meaningful in national journals or national broadcasts.

The important point about the way in which electronic and mass media operate is the fact that, as new sources of information or belief, they create counterweights to established authorities. Simultaneous radio coverage of war, a moon walk or whatever absorbs and fascinates the mass audience directly, cuts out traditional local purveyors of information and interpretation. It is not the imam or the chief of state who tells the people what happened and what it means. The people were there, along with the camera crew. The broadening of the arena of action transfers authority from the village bigwig returned from a visit to the district town, to nouveau powerful national leaders and eventually beyond them to world figures.

In the 1950s, Daniel Lerner in a classic study of communication and development, *The Passing of Traditional Society*, described the difference between three types of men and three orientations found in the Middle East. He described illiterate villagers as traditional men. The world they could understand stopped at the limits of their firsthand experience. They could not conceive what national politics was all about. Recent migrants from country to city, were described as transitional men. They relied heavily on radio even in that pretransistor era, but they selected domestic broadcasts with familiar themes. They knew about national politics, but only as it affected them. A good ruler was one who got them jobs or repaired their town. Lerner called educated urbanites modern men. For them foreign radio was a major medium.

They understood the issues of the cold war and ideological movements and followed world affairs with interest. World media enabled them to raise the scope of their empathy well beyond their personal experiences.

Lerner related this in the 1950s without reference to direct-broadcast satellites. The process was taking place without them. Every year the world communication system becomes more integrated. However, a worldwide focus on common news is not the kind of homogenization which exercises those who are alarmed about violation of national cultures. The examples they typically cite are movies, television, literature, songs, hairstyles, clothing styles, patterns of respect and etiquette and religious observances.

Assimilation

Popular songs are a common issue between upholders of tradition and its violators. Stylized traditional music tends to give way to more expressive modes, such as jazz, rock or film songs conveyed on radio, records or movies. In India, to preserve traditional musical forms, the All India Radio has put quotas on film songs—the most popular program item—a genre which crosses familiar indigenous ragas and the soupy, personal sentimentality of Western popular songs. India is not unique. In Japan and most non-Western countries, tin pan alley has proved to have a wide appeal, often in the same hybridized way.

Dance manifests similar tendencies toward cultural assimilation. The dance is generally a stylized, controlled indulgence in taboo behavior, whether in male-female relations or in expression of other passions. New-style dances, imported from or influenced by the West, express feelings and break taboos in ways that are bound to shock many who see them. This also applies to dress; it symbolizes one's identity. To refuse to wear one's proper tribal or caste dress, to assume the dress of a foreign elite or to bare one's legs in a miniskirt is to express a challenging assertion of changing identity.

Eating habits, manner of address and place of residence often become highly charged items in the conflict of generations. In most countries, the principal battle between traditional culture and modernity is fought over the independence of the young from parental authority. The battle most often reaches its zenith on the issue of arranged marriages and the locus of habitat of the new household, but skirmishes are fought over every sign of self-assertion by the young: impoliteness, staying out late, wearing their hair oddly, drinking coca cola or reading bad books. The central issue is the power of the old vs. the autonomy of the young. In a traditional economy, the social security of the whole family and the maintenance of its elder members may depend upon carrying out family obligations. At the same time, the chance for the young to get ahead depends upon their being able to free themselves from such family obligations.

Religion is another area in which the conflict between tradition and innovation takes expression. Piety is the most common rationale offered in defending established relations of respect. Reformations, skepticism or militant atheism are common attacks upon the traditional culture.

New tastes created in the process of social change provide an economic opportunity for merchants. Commerce seizes upon the chance to stimulate tastes for what it can sell, and to produce for sale what people will buy. Thus, advertising and the money economy become major agents of the process of change, and serve to undermine family-centered traditional culture. The marketer is a willing panderer to the tastes of transitional men moving naively into a cash economy. Those merchants who sell what is popular among those new strata are in turn attacked by traditional authorities as unscrupulous corrupters who will do anything for a price.

Excellence vs. Mediocrity

The usual charge by the defenders of the integrity of national cultures is not only that the new mass media material is new, but also that it is "junk." That it will violate existing cultural taboos, whether on violence, sex, politeness or sacrilege is clear. An additional charge is made that the shocking mass media material is also without artistic merit and has no redeeming qualities of excellence. Intellectuals in the West join in that chorus of complaint and not without reason. The kitsch dispensed in recently modernized countries is often a horror compared to the art of the traditional culture.

A case to be made for the mass media is that cultural products previously available only to the few are brought to the masses. Stage plays are rare events; movies can be shown in every small town or village. Orchestras and performances by great musicians are luxuries of the capital; records and radios bring them to every home. But the obvious critical comment, which can hardly be rebutted, is that standard mass media bring but little of such quality in relation to the amount of "junk." Thus, defenders of cultural integrity may argue that they are defending the excellent against the mediocre.

Finally, and most important of all, the defenders of cultural integrity against free-flowing information point to the one-sided balance of exports and imports of mass communication. The developed countries and particularly the United States export messages, while less developed countries import them. The best documentation of this fact is the University of Tampere's "International Inventory of Television Programme Structure and the Flow of TV Programmes Between Nations." In that study, Tapio Varis estimates total foreign sales of United States program material at 100,000 to 200,000 hours, about one-third to Latin America, another one-third to the Far East and East Asia and the rest mainly to Western Europe. The dollar amounts look different because the rates charged Europe are much higher than the rates charged less developed countries.

Television export sales by the United States fell from about $100 million in 1970 to $85 million in 1971. In general, the dominant role of American material is declining, as one would expect. The United States was the first into the massive television production business; gradually other countries built up their capabilities. The Tampere report tries to reject this interpretation of the data, but the data show a gradual decline in United States dominance. They also show that there is a continuing imbalance in the direction of flows, with large and more advanced countries being producers and small and less developed countries as importers.

There is enormous variation in the proportion of programs imported. A few countries show shockingly low figures: United States, 1-2 percent; Union of Soviet Socialist Republic, 5 percent; Japan, 2 ½ percent. On the other hand, about half of Latin American programs are of foreign origin; the figure is similar in the Middle East and in Asia, excluding Japan and China. In Western Europe, 30 percent are imports as compared to 24 percent in Eastern Europe. Similar, though less lopsided data, could be compiled on motion pictures, print syndication and publishing. To cite some 1967 United Nations Educational, Scientific and Cultural Organization (UNESCO) figures: of 39,483 titles translated in that year, 15,279 were from English, 5,368 from French, 3,892 from German and 3,822 from Russian. All other languages ran far behind.

The facts as of the early 1970s are clear. Underdevelopment means underdevelopment in media production as in everything else. More important than the facts, which could be taken as simply an injunction to get on with the work of development, are the emotional reactions to them. One could fill a volume with heated quotations from unhappy nationalists, guilt-ridden Westerners, worried reactionaries and angry radicals attacking the free flow of information as a Western plot to impose its culture on helpless people. Paranoid fantasies on the subject, particularly by some American writers, leave the realm of serious discussion.

UN Debates

Suggestions that satellites might be used to broadcast directly to home receivers in foreign countries first appeared along with Sputnik. Then suggestions of new things to come were expressed with some enthusiasm by writers in the Union of Soviet Socialist Republics. Attitudes more like those now heard in the UN began to be expressed from various sources in the 1960s. In 1962 and 1963, the dangers of foreign propaganda broadcasts were discussed in the UN. Brazil raised the issue in November, 1963. Active debate on the issue in the reported proceedings of the UN began two years later at the time of the discussion of the Outer Space Treaty.

The lineup of the subsequent debate forecast many more debates. On July 26, Hussein Khallaf of the United Arab Republic submitted a new article for the treaty to provide worldwide regulation of direct-satellite broadcasting and that the nations should "undertake to refrain from using communication satellites for direct broadcasting until such regulations are set by the competent international organizations." He was backed by P.D. Morozov of the Union of Soviet Socialist Republics, who raised the argument that would repeatedly again appear as an appeal to the Third World: "We would wish that other States, especially the developing countries . . . would not be placed in a position where they would have to adopt, without criticism or comment, whatever is handed to them." Also supporting the Soviet and United Arab Republic position were Carvalho Silos of Brazil, Krishna Rao of India and the Mexican representative.

The Outer Space Treaty was unanimously adopted on December 19, 1966, without the Egyptian clause or any reference to direct broadcasting. At the same time, the United Arab Republic, Chile and Mexico proposed a resolution asking that the Committee on the Peaceful Uses of Outer Space study space communication. By 1967 the issue had been defined and was being discussed, especially by Third World countries.

Any narrative of a single idea, such as the story of the fear of cultural intrusion by direct-television broadcasts is inevitably misleading. It selects out of a noisy background a few relevant occurrences creating the impression of high attention and deep concern. The truth is quite different. Among the various comments on satellites that do occur, only a portion are expressions of fear of violation of sovereignty. The positive statements hailing great new prospects are more frequent and often exaggerated in portraying the educational and cultural improvements that satellites can bring, especially to the developing nations.

The UNESCO "Declaration of Guiding Principles On the Use of Space Broadcasting for the Free Flow of Information, the Spread of Education and Greater Cultural Exchange" illustrates positive themes balanced by negative themes in its paired clauses in Article VII:

> 1. The objective of satellite broadcasting for the promotion of cultural exchange is to foster greater contact and mutual understanding between peoples by permitting audiences to enjoy, on an unprecedented scale,

programmes on each other's social and cultural life including artistic performances and sporting and other events.
2. Cultural programmes, while promoting the enrichment of all cultures, should respect the distinctive character, the value and the dignity of each, and the right of all countries and peoples to preserve their cultures as part of the common heritage of mankind.

Indian and Brazilian plans for educational satellites stirred much enthusiasm for the potential of satellites. Since the distinction between broadcasting to unaugmented home receivers and broadcasting to modified receivers with dish antennas is seldom understood in lay discussion, the favorable attitude towards these development plans spread its aura to direct broadcasting, as a potential boon to mankind.

The main debate on direct satellite broadcasting has taken place since 1969. On November 15, 1972, the seventeenth General Conference of UNESCO adopted a "Declaration of Guiding Principles on the Use of Space Broadcasting for the Free Flow of Information, the Spread of Education and Greater Cultural Exchange." The philosophy of the declaration is strongly restrictive, stressing sovereignty; the requirement that news broadcasts be accurate; the right of each country to decide the contents of educational programs broadcast to it; the need for broadcasters to respect cultural distinctiveness and varied laws and the requirement for prior consent, especially regarding advertising. The declaration was adopted by a vote of 55 to 7 with 22 absentions. The United States was in the minority.

The French position was particularly influential. Pompidou had picked up the satellite-broadcast issue in a speech at UNESCO's Twenty-fifth Anniversary. The French motivation was, in part, their concern to maintain a communications relationship with the Francophone states especially in Africa, and not to permit the American lead in space activities to give the United States a wedge into that relationship. This stimulated what became a strong, solid and emotional African support for adoption of the declaration. Egyptian influence was also of some importance.

India also pressed for action. The Indian delegate, the minister of broadcasting, took a strong stand not well-attuned to the fact that the Indo-Pakistan border is one of the few places where signal spillover problems may be genuinely important.

The role of the Soviet Union was somewhat enigmatic. Earlier, at the Meeting of Experts, the Soviet participant had tried to introduce into the draft language about the right to destroy offending satellites, to eliminate references to the Declaration of Human Rights and to strengthen the language on prior consulation. However, in the UN September, 1972, discussion of the UNESCO declaration, they took a neutral stance. In the Paris preplenary discussions at UNESCO, they supported the declaration, only to abstain on the final plenary session vote. Clearly, UNESCO's adoption of the declaration despite Soviet ambivalence and American opposition, was one expression of the intensity of views on the subject by African, Asian and Latin American countries and of neutralist and anti-superpower sentiments there and in Europe.

In the UN, major discussions of satellite television began in 1969 with the formation of the Working Group on Direct-Broadcast Satellites. Under the Committee on Peaceful Uses of Outer Space (CPUOS), the CPUOS family of committees have certain traditions unique in the UN system. They proceed by consensus, never taking a vote. The United States and other states supporting the minority position in favor of free flow of information are thus protected from being overruled in either the CPUOS or in its working group, which has the same membership.

The first session of the working group was in February, 1969. Working papers submitted to the session included a joint one by Canada and Sweden. In the first fifty pages, it bases the argument entirely on technical considerations, such as broadcast interference. A few pages later political considerations are gingerly introduced.

Colossus of the South

In that respect, the document is typical of Canadian statements throughout the past few years. Fundamental to Canada's concern about unregulated direct broadcasting has been worry about the colossus of the South undermining the regulated Canadian system of broadcasting by advertently or inadvertently pouring United States broadcasts over the border. While they are concerned, the Canadians, who have a strong democratic tradition, have not been prepared to advocate a rigid censorship system. Also, the strong tradition of civilized relationships between these English-speaking neighbors, plus a degree of dependence of Canada on the United States space program for its own space activities, have inhibited Canada from the kind of sharp rhetoric that some other countries have adopted. Thus, the Canadian statements have systematically and, as a matter of formal policy, avoided using arguments about "propaganda" in their reasoning as to the importance of regulation and prior consent. Canadian spokesmen have tried to base their reasoning always on more specific and pragmatic considerations less offensive to the Anglo-Saxon tradition of media freedom.

The Canadian-Swedish paper moved from physical considerations of spectrum management, to the issue of maintaining regulatory systems intact, which is Canada's own deeply felt concern. From there it considered the problem of stability in the developing countries. Next the argument moved to problems of libel and advertising in countries with diverse laws and to considerations of social and cultural autonomy.

In its second session, held in Geneva in the summer of 1969, the working group received working papers from Canada and Sweden, France, Argentina, Australia, Czechoslovakia, Mexico, the United Kingdom and UNESCO. All of them raised the spectre of abuses by direct-television broadcasts and proposed steps toward regulation.

In the French paper, the rationale offered for taking such action is the inequality of capability between the space powers that will have the satellites and other nations that will not.

> This inequality will further increase the possibility of interference in the internal affairs of foreign States: television broadcasting can be a peculiarly effective medium for political propaganda or for advertising. Similarly, false reports can easily be propagated on an immense scale so as to confuse public opinion throughout entire regions. Lastly, national cultures, civilizations, and social systems will be presented with a further means of imposing themselves on others, through the suggestive power of television.

Most themes that have come up in the direct-broadcast controversy and are likely to come up again may be illustrated from the debate in the first committee in October, 1972.

> Diaz-Casanueva (Chile): . . . None of us believed that men would be walking on the moon as soon as they did . . . a great Power . . . employing subterfuge and fallacy and appealing to a false conception of what is known as "freedom of information" seeks to consolidate its domination over the passive masses of the dependent or underdeveloped nations.
> Diaz-Casanueva (Chile): . . . In the dependent countries our libraries are poorly stocked with books, our publishing houses are financially poor, and we have millions upon millions of illiterates and semi-illiterates. Into this world there enters television, which fascinates and hypnotizes both the literate and the illiterate masses; television, to a large extent commercialized, rarley subject to the influence of universities or the State; television which feeds on the worst, on the most vulgar, on the dregs of mass culture—violence, pornography, triviality and mediocrity. Commercialized television, with the rivalry among the channels and the necessity of satisfying the tastes of a public that has had no opportunity to raise its cultural standards, constitutes a source of concern for our educators, sociologists and statisticians and and for all of us who participate in a cultural policy that seeks to ennoble rather than to degrade our peoples.

The steam behind the feelings about sovereignty was the genuine imbalance of power between the countries with space satellite capabilities and those without. The fear overtly and frequently expressed was of "cultural imperialism" as a force tending to destroy indigenous traditions and values. From this fear stemmed the demand to be protected from broadcasts entering from abroad, unless they received government consent.

There was also a more positive form of reaction besides the impulse to ban unwanted broadcasts. Some delegations raised the demand that all countries should have access to satellites for broadcasting. The Soviet draft contained an allusion to the desire of nonspace powers to access. Article 1 says:

> All States shall have an equal right to carry out direct television broadcasting by means of artificial earth satellites. . . . All States shall have an equal right to enjoy the benefits arising from direct television broadcasting by means of artificial earth satellites, without discrimination of any kind.

What this right implies is not clear. Some countries have tried to make the right of access more specific. A number of countries raised that issue and a few have suggested that the UN or regional international organizations provide broadcasting facilities to less developed countries.

While protection of sovereignty was the main impetus to support of the Soviet draft declaration, there was also another significant impetus—dislike of the kind of material emanating from radio and television. This was illustrated in attacks on political propaganda, pornography, violence and commercialism.

Source of Attacks

Attacks on direct-satellite broadcasting and other assertions in defense of national culture may come from any political direction and may serve as a means to anyone of a large number of inconsistent political aims. The slogan of protection of national culture may be used to protect a local communications industry from stronger foreign competitors, such as protecting the Canadian Broadcasting Corporation (CBC) in Canada against the United States networks. It may serve to restrict advertising so as to protect local businessmen from competition by large foreign firms. It could also provide grounds for oppressing a minority culture that can be portrayed as antinational, especially if the minority has colleagues across the border (Asians in East Africa or Kurds in the Middle East). The slogan can also be used to combat the spread of a youth counterculture, as well as to repress radical or participatory political ideas. For example, some of the support for the Soviet draft convention on direct-broadcast satellites came from Third World countries whose conservative governments were more concerned about checking Communists than about American propaganda. They saw the Soviet-sponsored convention as ironically becoming a protection against Soviet broadcasting.

Often, what is described as protection of the national culture is rather protection of the existing government. The Indo-Pakistan frontier is one of the few places in the world where cross-the-border television penetration may become significant. India may acquire a television satellite which could be received by a Pakistani who makes an investment of only several hundred dollars. The terrestrial transmitters that India is also establishing are located in a pattern that makes it hard not to conclude that there is an Indian intention to reach a Pakistani audience. Yet, the Indian purpose is certainly not cultural evangelism. It seems more plausible that they want to use their cross-border capability to carry on psychological warfare in the event of renewed hostilities.

The most successful example of the effectiveness of international broadcasting is the broadcasting of Voice of America (VOA), Radio Free Europe and Radio Liberty to the Soviet Union and Eastern Europe. The information about world attitudes and trends provided by these broadcasts have made the evolution and persistence of the dissident movement for liberalization in those countries feasible. Youth learn about jazz, East Europeans learn what has been tried and permitted by the Soviets in other Warsaw Pact countries, intellectuals learn about current world debates and Soviet citizens learn the real facts of the news through those broadcasts. As a result, about one-sixth of the Soviet population (according to other research by this author) listens to foreign stations on an average day.

In contrast only about 2 percent of the American public listens to shortwave broadcasts at all. Rightly or wrongly, they are convinced that they are getting the essential facts via their own media. Very few families even have shortwave sets, compared to half of the families in the Soviet Union who do.

Foreign and Domestic Media

The main determinant of attention to foreign media is the responsiveness of domestic media to the desires and interests of the public. The marketplace for ideas is not one in which imports flow easily. Other things being equal, consumers pick local products. The latter have many advantages over imports: (1) They are protected by barriers of language. People would rather see a film made in their own idiom than one with subtitles or even one that is dubbed; (2) They are protected by barriers of social support. Much of the enjoyment of media is in discussing them with one's friends. Reading this year's best seller is a social experience. Top television shows or movies provide grist for conversation the next day and that is much of their drawing power and (3) Local products are protected by barriers of culture. Domestic products portray characters eating foods the people eat, wearing the clothes they wear, celebrating the events they celebrate and gossiping about the celebrities they follow. Allusion is a large part of art. Foreign works of art have jokes that are harder to get, stereotypes that do not ring a bell and situations that do not come from daily life.

In general, culture does not need protection. People are already attached to culture. If the culture is satisfactory, if it is not already in process of decomposition and if local media are doing their job of providing products which fit the culture, the audience will not look abroad.

Television in Vietnam in the latter half of the 1960s provided an almost experimental example. The government of Vietnam and its American allies decided that television could make a significant contribution to the conduct of the war. It could help the American troops feel at home, improve the quality of life and relieve the rural boredom for the population on the government side. A two-channel television system was set up. One channel provided standard United States programming in English for the American troops. The other channel, programmed and produced by the Vietnamese in Vietnamese, featured traditional opera and similar indigenous material. In the villages, people watched the Vietnamese channel. At those hours when the Vietnamese channel went off the air, but the American channel stayed on, instead of continuing to watch, *faut de mieux*, the audience would melt away from the village set. Not so in the cities where there were foreigners by the thousands. English signs and English-speaking customers, cars, bars, canned food, newspapers and salaried jobs had already smashed Vietnamese culture. Millions of Vietnamese turned by preference to the better produced, slicker American programs. Football games were popular. Batman won the rating race and became a popular folk hero. The urban population had acquired a new culture and new needs. Traditionalists deplored the fact and preferred not to admit it, but the Vietnamese television channel—aimed deliberately at the rural population—was not serving the modernized Vietnamese as well as the United States channel.

The situation of urban Vietnamese is the kind that those who argue for defense of culture against cultural imperialism have in mind. They point out that the indigenous society with its limited capabilities cannot compete with attractive but artistically degraded products imported from abroad. The situation is far more complex than that. Those members of the audience who were capable of understanding the United States channel turned to it, rather than to the crude, coarse stereotyped local programming because, poor as it was, the American programs were better. Any opposition to that foreign programming material could hardly be described as defense of national culture; it would be a nostalgic effort to reassert a culture long since gone from the cities. The American programs attracted more or less educated, middle-class and modern sector employees because those programs related better to their culture than did the other channel. What one can legitimately criticize is that the alternatives were not rich enough. Had there been a third channel of indigenous but modernized urban-oriented material, it would certainly have drawn much of the audience away from the foreign product.

Thus, there is a case to be made, not so much for defense of national cultures by protectionist barriers to foreign materials, but for positive fostering of production capabilities to meet otherwise unmet needs. The building of studios, establishment of training programs and subsidization of arts makes sense, but protectionism is generally a way of stifling development and reducing the prospects of meeting consumers' needs. People who like and want the kind of material available from abroad are barred from getting it. That does not create an incentive to producing equivalent, but more locally relevant, material at home. On the contrary, it eliminates the need to compete for the local audience. An open market for foreign imports is likely to demonstrate the existence of an unmet demand, to offer models and a learning experience for domestic producers and thus to result in a growth of local cultural expressions.

This can be illustrated by an American example. Hollywood has never been able to provide the American intellectual market (the 20 or 30 million of them) with sophisticated thoughtful film or television programs. It has not provided films for art theaters of programs like "The Forsythe Saga" and "Masterpiece Theatre" for television. The economics of the American film industry, with its featherbedding union contracts, residuals and weak noncommercial stations makes that sort of production very difficult to finance. Foreign films for the art theaters and the British Broadcasting Corporation (BBC) for public television have filled the gap. Their success has demonstrated that there is a market for such quality programs. Their success has also led to American imitation. The domestic product has a long way to go, but an increasing number of art films and the appearance of programs like Joseph Papp's "Much Ado About Nothing" on regular television, are signs of a trend.

Production Barriers

The example of quality drama on public broadcasting is instructive. It shows that the barriers to indigenous production do not beset only developing countries. Large developing countries or groups of them are quite capable of producing the film and videotape they need. Filmmaking is a labor intensive, not a capital intensive activity. It is expensive in the United States of America only because artificial monopoly structures, such as enormous rewards to talent, have been built into the industry. Noncommercial filmmakers, such as Richard Leacock, have demonstrated that high quality film can be produced cheaply. American commercial filmmakers are increasingly coproducing films abroad, often in developing countries, to avoid monopoly charges. India has proved that a poor country can build a major movie industry; Egypt has shown that a poor country can make a major broadcast effort and China has demonstrated that a poor country can build a low-cost system to communicate to the millions.

It is impossible for a small country (and most less developed countries are small) to produce enough programs to fill the airwaves with a dozen or more hours a day of new, original television material 365 days a year. But that is just as true for Norway or Belgium as it is for Zanzibar or Honduras. The fact that it takes a market area of hundreds of millions to support the enormous appetite of a television system for new programs is a severe limitation on television's ability to reflect a single national culture. It can do that only within the less than ten giant nations with populations of 100 million or more. Elsewhere, television production will have to be a cooperative regional or other group activity with procedures for exchange between countries. Television will be better if all countries engage in free exchange of the best products from wherever they are made—East or West, rich or poor. Nothing in the economics of development or of video production predestines which countries will succeed best in the competition to produce widely desired and successful artistic material.

The United States has succeeded so preeminently until now for several reasons. It was first into the business. Hollywood movies captured the market initially and only later did other countries cut back the United States share. American television covered its market first and only later did Japan and some Western European countries achieve over 90 percent coverage. The very large domestic market with four networks serving 200 million people provided the base for producing vast quantities of program material, from among which some is suitable for foreign syndication. Most important, the American system, being predominantly commercial, is geared to producing what the public wants.

What the American public wants is not so very different from what other publics want. Americans today are able to appreciate Aristophanes, the Ramayana, I Ching and the Bible. The rock music that appeals to our youth appeals to youth in many countries. "Batman," "Star Trek," "I Love Lucy" or "Donald Duck" are popular in other countries. The American video and movie production system gives unusual priority to finding out what strikes popular chords. All producing countries compromise in various ways between the criterion of the market and criteria of what civil servants or other salaried intellectuals believe should be produced. The philosophical issue between their selection criteria is a profound one and every country compromises in some way. Even in China, producers worry about keeping the interest of their audience, though telling the people what they should be told certainly has priority. In the United States, some production is funded by foundations and by public broadcasting, thus allowing selected professionals to do their thing, but this plays a smaller part in the balance than elsewhere.

It should be no surprise that in the country where producers try hardest to produce what the public wants, they succeed. The Americanization of world culture so often commented on and deplored might be better described as the discovery of what world cultural tastes actually are and adoption of those into American media. If American pop culture is successful around the world—and it is—it is by a circular process. American commerce seeks to reflect world cultural tastes; the product in turn feeds back into the system and reinforces that which was already found popular.

To say that the export of mass media is giving the world public what it wants is not to deny the severity of the resulting problems, which are those of transition. National culture changes slowly. Mass media and popular culture are objects of fads in constant and rapid flux. That mismatch is much of the problem.

National cultures, when lauded by their eulogists, are generally described as age-old traditions. To some degree, that is true. Every culture is the end product of thousands of years of history. To a very large degree, the claims to a hoary past are mythology. Each generation sees its culture as that with which it grew up. Its hallowed values and traditions are those learned in childhood. Many elements valued as native culture were controversial foreign imports a generation or two before.

There are no isolated cultures in the world. Each is an accretion of imports and borrowings. When we look at the history of symbols of cultural identity, we find that at some point they were a foreign intrusion. Peasant pottery is often symbolic of the quaint and unchanging ways of a preindustrial people. In Machiko, Japan, and in Atitlan, Mexico, there are beautiful folk arts of this kind. Yet, in each case, it was a foreigner engaged in technical assistance some generations ago who brought the art to the country to help the peasants modernize by acquiring a cottage craft for the cash market. The demand for cultural purity is but a demand to freeze this process of diffusion at some arbitrary present, which happens to be the advocate's youth.

Mass media messages march to a different drummer. Their tempo is that of our technology, in which change occurs with exponential acceleration. The time span of mass media fads grows shorter. The drum beat of new fads, new ideas and new styles brought forward every year by the mass media is in inevitable disharmony with the concept of a national culture and its slow rate of change. Believers in free discourse cannot accept a policy for the mass media that subjects them to censorship designed to prevent violation of norms of culture, but neither should humane people disregard the pain that rapid change imposes on those whose life cycle is no different than it was millenia ago.

Policy Alternatives

America faces a dilemma. We have a historical national commitment to the free flow of information. For both political and economic reasons, America favors openness of traffic among peoples. We also sympathize with the desire of developing countries for autonomy and the right to live in their own style. Direct-satellite broadcasting is not a matter of much importance to us, and we would like not to pick fights with friendly countries on such minor issues, but the principles and precedents at stake in this debate are important ones in other situations. We would much prefer that the issue of human rights be fought out on such important matters as emigration from the Union of Soviet Socialist Republics, where the reactionary character of closing a society is more obvious. But we are being compelled to debate the issue in a situation where the votes are not with us, where there are, as of now, few vested interests on the side of freedom, nor even any deep commitment on our part to the fight and no reality testing available. The dangers cited by our critics are fantasies, but there is no hard data to provide in refutation. In the debate, there are three basic postures available to this country. The first may be called the posture of accommodation, which essentially adopts the views of defenders of the integrity of national cultures. The argument is as follows:

(1) The issue is of no importance to us anyhow.
(2) The First Amendment is a domestic matter; we do not try to impose our free speech standards on others.
(3) The votes are on the other side; we cannot afford to be isolated in a small minority.
(4) The opponents of cultural imperialism are right in wanting to protect their people from the commercialism, sex and violence of our mass media.
(5) Developing countries are very different from us; they need to use their scarce resources for serious development purposes and cannot afford

the luxury of our consumerism and entertainment expenditure. Nor can they afford the instability of free speech.
(6) No country will stand for alien propaganda; we do not like it either.
(7) The balance of flow of information is so one-sided that we must help redress it; it is not free flow if some peoples have much more access to the media than others.
(8) People's concern about preserving their cultures is sincere. We cannot disregard such genuine feelings. We must learn to listen.

Against that view, the clearest counterposture is the firm libertarian principle expressed in Article 19 of the Universal Declaration of Human Rights.

> Everyone has the right to freedom of opinion and expression; this right includes freedom to hold opinions without interference and to seek, receive and impart information and ideas through any media and regardless of frontiers.

This approach refuses to concede to other governments our cooperation in trying to shackle what their peoples can see and hear. Such an approach is not only consonant with our traditions, it is also a realistic one for the United States to take, given its lead in satellite technology. International agreements in the present world system ratify established relations and practices; they lack the power to overturn them. While we would lose many votes, there is no realistic prospect of the nations of the world compelling us, the satellite-launching nation, to enforce a convention we decline to sign.

Thus, the second possible position could be called toughing it out. We can decide on the convergent basis of both our moral principles and power politics to refuse assistance to any censorship proposals. If we do that, since the issue of direct-satellite broadcasting will continue to be a hypothetical one, it will be in no one's urgent interest to press for actual action. Sooner or later, if forcefully and confidently presented, the arguments for free flow of ideas may get to many independent intellectuals. Governments in the past have rarely understood the arguments for freedom and presumably rarely will.

The arguments against that approach, like all arguments against heavy-handed use of power, point to the price one pays for failing to respect the deep and genuine feelings of other parties. One therefore hopes that there might be a third or mixed position that can respond to the genuine national sensitivities aroused by satellite broadcasting, while at the same time not compromising our position against censorship of international broadcasts.

One would also wish to find a posture that would support continued development of satellite communication. Such a posture would be one in which the United States takes a vigorous lead in making two-way satellite communication available to other countries and to international organizations for their own use.

Most, if not all, satellite-television transmission will be by redistribution rather than direct broadcasting, and most of that (in the absence of planned action) will be the same one-way flow from the United States and a few other advanced countries as is now seen in the export of tapes and films. That is the true offense to national sensibilities which, if not acted upon, will result in irrelevant obstructions to satellite development.

INTELSAT (International Telecommunications Satellite Consortium) is a commercial common carrier, hopefully blind to the content of what it carries. It is not its business to remedy the situation, but it would be very much in the United States government's interest to subsidize a flow of communication by satellite from the developing countries to the rest of the world and also of communication by the UN. The Agency for International Development (AID) should increasingly fund placement of ground stations in poor countries and help with the creation of cooperative exchange activities for television programs. The United States could propose that the UN establish a worldwide television network that would distribute programs originated all over the world. There are many variants to this basic idea of helping develop the two-way flow of television material by satellite.

Packet Data Transmission

Such cooperative measures need not be limited to television communication. Since direct-satellite broadcasting is not the real issue, but only a surrogate for a series of complaints about the unfair balance of power in world communications, some of the useful reform measures may use satellites to distribute signals other than video. A group at the Massachusetts Institute of Technology is working on an idea for a world packet data transmission system.

The idea of the packet data system is to narrow the gap in information resources between the industrialized and less developed countries. A chasm separates the research situation in the West with such facilities as the Library of Congress, Weidner, the New York Public Library, the British Museum and the Moscow State Library from that in less developed countries which create universities and research centers with libraries that would not satisfy a small college in this country. In the West, there is also extensive publishing of data series, newsletters, reference bulletins and periodicals which can be accessed directly or through libraries. It would take decades for less developed countries to catch up. Because of the computer, the gap will actually widen. Increasingly, data moves from hard copy form to machine-readable data bases. In twenty years, systems such as MEDLARS (Medical Literature Analysis and Retrieval System) or the New York Times on-line information system will be widely used in this country. Given the sophisticated technology required for time-shared data networks with remote access, the developing countries will fall increasingly behind.

With satellite communications, there is a solution. A worldwide packet data system could make access to all these data bases available from anywhere in the world at a communications cost of less than a nickel per 100 words. Overnight, developing countries could close the information gap. A researcher in a university or planning office in any country could pick up his telephone and retrieve a fact from whatever data base he wishes anywhere in the world for the cost of a domestic telephone call. The world's great retrieval systems would become worldwide resources.

The first packet data network is the ARPA (Advanced Research Project Agency) net which is now functioning and connecting about fifty university and Department of Defense computers across the United States and in England. Using low-cost small computers called TIPS and IMPS as interfaces, users at any of the places on the net can, via special phone lines, use any of the computers on the net. The data packet transmission procedure that makes the system possible is now being adopted by several commercial companies. They are proposing to establish networks covering the United States and Europe, wherever the volume of business is adequate to pay for the equipment and service.

No commercial company would now find it worthwhile to extend its net to cover the developing countries of the world. The technology for doing that exists, thanks to INTELSAT and the ARPA net. The cost of the system would be in the low tens of millions, if installed on a worldwide systematic plan. Like communication systems generally, such a system would easily pay for itself once it reached comprehensive coverage scale. If installed on a small scale, in the way that commercial investors are now willing to try to do on their own, it would pay only in a few heavy traffic locations that are in already industrialized places.

There are a number of difficult problems involved, but they are not in satellite communications technology. The difficulties are language barriers, political resistances, agreement on data formats and similar human factors. These could be worked on cooperatively if the United States proposed to less developed countries to try to establish such a system and offered to underwrite development effort and part of the cost. That kind of progressive proposal for the use of satellites will help the countries of the world see the value to themselves of satellite development.

To help ease the pain of social change, we must enable those who are alarmed to participate in the process in a way that will help them gain some of the values of respect and welfare that they seek. For progress in satellite communication, we must pay a small price to see to it that satellites are useful to people in all countries, not just to Americans. We must make satellites into channels for them to express their views to us, not just channels by which they receive. A world television network and a worldwide packet data communication system would help achieve that goal.

24

Free Press for a Free People

Eric Sevareid

I was not present at the creation of electronic journalism, but almost. What CBS's first real managing editor, Paul White, called the fine, careless rapture of the early radio days is gone. The miracles of communication have become commonplace. The gaudy process is now more routinized, institutionalized—but much better: more responsible, better educated, as well as more efficient. This has been the first truly new form of journalism ever, and I have no regrets of having been part of the agony and the ecstasy almost from the start.

We began with no form sheet, no precedents, no comforting tradition like that of the printed press, no proved techniques, no standards. We had to invent them as we went along; like politicians and children, we were educated at the public's expense.

Broadcasting News

Broadcasting as an industry began in its own special way. Most newspapers were started by men who wanted an outlet for their views, usually political. Most broadcasting stations were started by men who wanted an advertising medium, a business. They found themselves, in time, cotrustees of the First Amendment, a positive challenge to some, a discomfiture to others. But that goes with the job, with the right and the privilege. Station or network owners and managers unwilling to fight for full constitutional freedoms ought not be in the business.

I am not a spokesman for broadcasting as an industry. I have never paid much attention to its technical, managerial, or financial problems. My bosses do not tell me what to say on the air, and I do not tell them how to run the network's business. I do not quite know whether I am in the news end of the broadcasting business or in the broadcasting end of the news business.

But I do represent news, the hasty, often improvised and unstructured, often agonizing attempt to give the world a little glimpse of itself every day. It is not a profession in any strict sense, not exactly a business or a trade. It is a calling. We have to try to live at the growing points of human society, at the cutting edges of history. Wits and resourcefulness play a bigger role than learning or intellectual disciplines. We are pinch hitters every other inning. All one can hope for is a respectable batting average. What saves us is that the news business, broadcast or print, is a self-correcting institution.

Seeking Truth

Public officials, private cause groups, many lawyers, and quantifying sociologists who work by slide rule may not approve, but the fact is that the theory of the free press never was that the full truth of anything would be revealed in any one account or commentary. The theory is that with free reporting and free discussion, the truth will *emerge*. It is a process and must be followed, day by day, by readers and listeners as well as by writers and speakers.

There is, of course, the Sevareid Solution. I have offered it before; there were no takers. That is, news every other day. No newspapers or news broadcasts, except to warn of nuclear attack or bubonic plague, on Monday, Wednesdays, Fridays. We would do a better job; the public's nerve ends would be rested. Short of that, we are obliged to wing it. Our condition is no different from that of the printed press a hundred years ago.

But *that's the way it is*, as my colleague would say. I have been at this calling some thirty-eight years now, and I am perfectly sure that the grave, built-in fault of the press is not really bias. It is *haste*, and—particularly in broadcasting—the severe compression of the material required.

A central point about the free press is not that it be fair, though it must try to be; not that it be accurate, though it must try to be that; but that it be *free*. I do not even want it to be too respectable. I would rather it be at least a little irresponsible than overcautious and timid. It is the press that makes the community weather and sounds the notes of the day. Slide rules can provide only poor measurement of its performance.

Journalists and Lawyers

The city of Washington is the greatest single center of world news since ancient Rome. I incline to the notion that it contains, at present, too many of two kinds of people: lawyers and press people. The lawyers complicate and paralyze everything. The press chews everything to bits, or tries to—every reputation, new idea, policy line—before they have much chance to mature. Whenever lawyers and journalists come together, sometimes even when they are on the same side of an issue, they tend to reach a separating point. The lawyers are obliged to keep their eyes on the rules of the game; the journalists must keep their eyes on the game.

I have tried to do that over many years of reading and hearing the arguments about broadcasting and the First Amendment. The notions that occurred to my unscientific, nonlegal mind early on are still my notions, for whatever they are worth. They seem to be mostly negatives.

I have never understood the basic, legally governing concept of "the people's airways." So far as I know, there is only the atmosphere and space. There can be no airway in any practical sense, until somebody accumulates the capital, know-how, and enterprise to put a signal into the atmosphere and space. I have never understood why government should be empowered to affect the content of the newspapers carried in the newspaper truck on the people's streets. I thought that the traffic laws, in both cases, were enough.

I have never understood the concept of "the people's right to know"; they have the right to find out, but that depends upon the publishers' right to publish. Publishers, print or electronic, have no constitutional right to be read or to be listened to. That they have to earn, as the people have to earn knowledge.

I could never understand why so basic a right as the First Amendment could be diluted or abridged simply because of technological change in dissemination and reception of information and ideas, particularly when the new technologies are becoming, almost everywhere, the most pervasive technologies—though not necessarily the most persuasive.

I could never understand the court's argument that the Fairness Doctrine for broadcasting enhances the First Amendment. The First Amendment is a prohibition. How do you enhance a negative? No means no.

I have never understood the reasoning of those critics who seem to be saying that broadcasting will enjoy full rights under the First Amendment, when it is worthy of them. Who could be the timekeeper? In any case, constitutional rights do not have to be earned; we were all born with them.

I can understand those who say that three big commercial networks plus public broadcasting and smaller groupings are not enough, though I suspect they would say the same were there four. Four, or even five, would be all right with me and all right with most broadcast journalists, assuming they would be economically viable; and if they could provide the marvelously superior and different kinds of program fare that is supposed to be out there, somewhere, then everybody would be happy indeed.

Because there are only three, we are told their content must be monitored, guided by government at various points. Their alleged power is too concentrated, we are told. Suppose there were only three daily newspapers which everyone read. No doubt there would be official and officious types who would feel the need to lay hands upon them. But the great majority of people would insist that their very scarcity made even more imperative their absolute freedom from the power of government, if this is to remain a free society, as the First Amendment commands.

Censorious Instinct

I have never quite grasped the worry about the power of the press. It has influence, surely, and influence is a kind of power—but diffuse, hard to measure. The press, after all, speaks with a thousand voices, in constant dissonance. It has no power to arrest you, draft you, tax you, or even make you fill out a form, except a subscription form if you are agreeable. It is the power of government, especially the federal government and more particularly its executive arm, that has increased in my time. Many politicians have come to power in many countries and put press people in jail. I cannot think of any place where the reverse has occurred.

The censorious instinct is always present, and it shifts its operating base from time to time. The federal government, under Nixon, tries prior restraint, which not even the Alien and Sedition Acts permitted. The federal government went through a spasm of subpoenas against news people, but has since tried to restrain itself. Courts have increased their gag rules on journalists' disclosure, sometimes just to make their own work easier.

I can think of innumerable cases where the press has led authority to situations of crime and corruption. I cannot think of any case where sins of commission or omission by the press have resulted in gross injustice, at least in the sense of innocent people going to jail. History and experience have their claims, too; on the whole, the freer relationship has worked well.

Now we have entered a period where the censorious instinct concentrates on another nebulous concept called the right to privacy. As one leading communications lawyer has said, "in five short years the Supreme Court has taken a number of confused steps backwards, leaving journalists, broadcasters, and publishers at the mercy of unclear laws, inconsistent judges, and subjective juries." One result of all this nervous confusion is clear: it will increase another nefarious form of censorship—self-censorship.

Viewers Elect

Thomas Jefferson said that for his time the biggest threat of oppression would come from the legislature, but that the time would arrive when it would come from the executive. I do not believe he thought of the judiciary, which has had far too much responsibility thrown upon it and has asserted far too much in the compulsory arrangements of our daily lives.

Most judges are un-elected. That, said Spiro Agnew some eight years ago, is the trouble with those presumptuous characters, the network reporters and commentators. Literal election, of course, would mean that the majority would hear only commentary and see news reports agreeable to it. That is not quite the idea of the free press. But, in a sense, we are the most elected people around. Every time a listener turns his dial to the right number, he elects me; every time he turns it to the wrong number, he un-elects me.

Still, this is not good enough, Many years ago a psychologist said that the Achilles heel of television would prove to be the fact that people cannot talk back to the little box. They can, but not enough. Here the networks are found wanting, more than most local stations. I have argued this for years, at some risk perhaps of arguing myself out of a job or into a diminished job. It has not been a policy problem, but a problem of program rigidities. I want to see network air time opened up a good deal more to listeners' rebuttal and to differing persuasions. That would be one advantage inherent in expanding the network evening news programs to an hour. There must be ways to do it, not, certainly, under legal compulsion but by the free decision of broadcasting's managers.

Privileged Position

It has been in considerable part because of this imbalance between speaker and listener—as well as because my own temperament is what it is—that I have tried, all these years, to use this privileged position with restraint. I have been much criticized for my approach, especially by the zealots of so-called "advocacy journalism." I have my evangelical moments at times, but on the whole I have tried to illuminate more than to advocate, to teach more than to preach.

I have tried to remain objective, always aware, however, that objectivity and neutrality are not the same thing. Objectivity is a *way* of thinking *about* an issue, not the summation of the thought. Such an approach will not often excite the multitude or bring rave reviews. But it has seemed to me the best way, for all the seasons, for the long haul. And my haul has been a long one.

Broadcasting steadily evolves and changes—for the better. It must do so on its own, with the help of private citizens and their groups, with the help of the printed press, tainted with self-interest though it often is—not with the help of government and its powers.

The wonder of television is not that it is as bad as it is, but that it is as good as it is. It will get still better, in news and in entertainment, if we have enough confidence in ourselves. We must not just *react*, particularly to the printed press. We have to keep in mind that we are the only business that has its chief competitor as its chief critic. That set of dice is permanently loaded against us.

Honest Reporting

It is a long time since the night when I was sitting at a United Press desk in Paris and Edward R. Murrow called me from London, and asked me to throw in my lot with him. He said, in effect, that I would never be pressured to produce scoops or drama (though those things transpired), never expected to inflate the news beyond its honest dimensions. He said, "I have an idea people might like that."

So, in my unimaginative way, I did so and do so now. I conclude that by and large people *have* liked it. If they had not, it would not have taken the Stanton retirement rule at CBS to envelop me in the blessing of silence, come the year's end.

25

Screening Nuclear War and Vietnam

Marvin Maurer

Two major public affairs programs about the United States and contemporary warfare have been shown to vast television audiences. An ABC docudrama, "The Day After," directed by Nicholas Meyer and written by David Humi, drew record audiences for a television movie. An ambitious thirteen-part documentary from WGHB in Boston, "Vietnam: A Television History," was shown on public broadcasting stations across the nation. The production team included Richard Ellison, producer; Stanley Karnow, chief correspondent; and Lawrence Lichty, director of media research. The docudrama, utilizing a fictional format, stages a full-scale nuclear war on a city in Kansas; the documentary reports and reviews events of the Vietnam War and draws on assorted witnesses and commentators to supplement the historical materials.

Both programs would ordinarily be relegated to the film archives, but the producers are marketing them to reach wider audiences, with students among the prime targets. To the credit of both producers, their efforts are compared favorably with other television documentaries and news pieces dealing with the war in Indochina (marking the tenth anniversary of the fall of Saigon) and nuclear weaponry and star wars technologies (generally related to the Geneva disarmament discussions). Television's best reviewers and critics rely on the two earlier films as central references for their current evaluations. It is important to understand what messages these efforts are sending forth. While one film is future oriented and deals with the total destruction of an American city, the other probes the painful past of a limited war in Asia. Both raise doubts about the purposes and morality of America's defense and foreign policies.

The Day After

The first showing of "The Day After" coincided with a major effort by peace groups to halt the deployment of new U.S. missiles in Europe. The film is a scare piece, and its message about the horror of nuclear war cannot be dismissed. By implication the program criticizes and challenges current thinking; by implication it suggests alternative courses of action—some quite constructive. After the bomb is dropped, for example, audiences see that the local hospital and medical facilities are hopelessly swamped; the message is that American medical facilities should be prepared for the effects of a nuclear war. This, however, is a minor concern of the film. "The Day After" challenges America's containment and defense policies and questions other American values. The graphic scenes of the aftermath of a nuclear blast leveling a city in America's once secure heartland make it difficult to defend past assumptions about nuclear weapon defenses.

Prior to the attack, Kansans are shown pursuing their normal lives, but intermittent newscasts reveal a major international crisis in the making. East Berlin, audiences learn, is the scene of an uprising. The Soviet Union reacts swiftly. West Berlin is blockaded; West Germany is invaded; and Soviet air power attacks U.S. naval craft in the Persian Gulf. The implied message is that since nuclear war culminated from an apparent anti-Communist uprising, encouraging people to rid themselves of Communist rule may not be wise. After the initial Soviet reaction, the Soviet ambassador is summoned to the White House to be told of America's determination to stand by its allies. Apparently both powers refuse to back down; threats escalate—culminating in a dreaded exchange of intercontinental ballistic missiles (ICBMs), suggesting that the safeguards utilized to hold nuclear arsenals in check had failed.

State-of-the-art pyrotechnics produce frightening visual effects. Kansans are incinerated on the spot, survivors are bathed in lethal radiation, and surrounding farmland is poisoned. This scenario makes difficult a defense of America's policy of deterrence or its containment policies that assure protection of Western Europe. Americans are warned tacitly not to cooperate with the government. Film clips showing U.S. ICBMs being launched from Kansan farms suggest that cooperation with the Department of Defense merely makes one a target. This approximates the warning by peace groups that any community aiding the U.S. government to store its nuclear weapons invites disaster.

Frightening scenes question other values. Amid the carnage and ruins, for example, are damaged war memorials found in typical American cities. Their inscriptions are still visible. They read "In Memory of Our World War Dead," and "In Honor of Those Who Died in Defense of Liberty." This suggests that the heroic sacrifices of young men in the past may be understandable, but such valor is pointless in the nuclear age. Heroes cannot prevent homes and villages from being incinerated.

The immediate effects of the bomb are frightening, but the aftermath is even worse. Middle-class life is wiped out. Radiation poisoned Kansans grope about helplessly. Jason Robards, playing a dying medical doctor, stumbles to the ruins of his home. At first he reacts possessively by chasing a pathetic band of squatters from his property; but when a decrepit old man embraces him he realizes that defense of his possessions is futile, implying that defense of our way of life is fraught with danger. A punishment appears to have been visited on this city, just as other television disasters, such as airplane crashes and hotel fires, are implied punishments for sinfulness and selfishness. Middle-class values (home, possessions, patriotism) are legitimized and defended by the nation. The film raises the question of whether it is worth invoking the power of the nation-state to defend these values. Is life not worth more than our personal holdings?

After the attack, a composite president addresses the nation. This fictional president typifies many of our real ones in inadequately expressing the concerns facing the nation. His remarks are irrelevant to the survivors. He attempts to assure these hapless victims that the damage inflicted by the nuclear weapons was confined to military targets; he assures them there will be "no surrender, no retreat from principles for which the nation stands." This president is out of touch with the harsh realities; he cannot help. The film suggests that the people must act on their own to thwart the government's defense policies. This burden does not give people a sense that they have power or that they control their destiny. It encourages helplessness and fear. If constitutionally elected leaders fail, how can the people take action? Do they take to the streets and join peace groups? Would these acts influence the Russians? Given the expansionist nature of a militarized Soviet Union, the only alternative to a strong defense is some form of capitulation; nevertheless, the film suggests that strong public antidefense outcries are in order.

For its first showing of "The Day After," ABC invited an impressive array of experts to comment. Critics argued that deterrence has worked and that dramatic alternatives are not possible for the foreseeable future. Nuclear arms limitation treaties have their merits, but they cannot place the nuclear bomb back in Pandora's box. In order to assure balanced future showings, the producers should include these critical postscripts. The producers might reply. As the film implies, the theme is universal, and even the Soviet people would react with concern. This hope is part of the problem inasmuch as the U.S.S.R. does not permit such challenges to its military policies, nor do its people have institutional means to register their differences with Soviet policy.

Vietnam Syndrome

The producers of "Vietnam: A Television History" claim their thirteen-part effort is evenhanded and balanced in order to encourage viewers to make their own assessments. The film supplements its pictorial history with extensive narrational interpretations and comments plus accounts and evaluations of assorted actors from both sides of the struggle.

To maintain this evenhanded posture, the program attempts to show that both sides have moral claims and a plausible basis for their actions. Both protagonists are reported to have clearly set out goals: the Communists seek to unify Vietnam while their opponents attempt to prevent a Communist takeover. Suppose that an alternative perception was presented so that victory for one side, for example, results in totalitarian rule and interminable war for the people of Indochina. The producers would no longer be evenhanded, and the film history would take on a different coloring and emit a different message to audiences. In order to avoid a sharp distinction between the antagonists, the film softens and dilutes the case against the Communist side while overcriticizing the Americans and the South Vietnamese. Some of this reflects political bias by the producers, and other distortions can be attributed to structural biases; for example, limitations imposed by the television format or problems related to camera access to events.

The program lends support to the goals of Ho Chi Minh, which are to unify Vietnam and provide freedom and social justice for its people. Many of the film's accounts support this bias. The film mentions Communist repression and brutality, but in a matter-of-fact fashion rather than linking abuses to the Marxist-Leninist ethos of waging a national war of liberation or establishing rule over those they have liberated. The film fails to hold the Communists accountable for what occurred during and after the war. The thrust of the presentation is to chart the hurdles they had to overcome in order to unify the nation.

Another theme pervades this production—one that approximates what many call "the Vietnam Syndrome." The United States is seen as opposing the revolutionary aspirations of Third World people and lending aid to corrupt dictatorships. In particular, the film shows how the United States and its allies seek to thwart the national liberation movement of Vietnam.

Political biases might be offset, but structural ones pose more difficult problems for television. To assure balance, both sides are given an opportunity to present their positions. The American and South Vietnamese views are not as well presented as those of the Vietnamese Communists or their supporters. The latter are more effective and believable speakers. The producers do little to offset this imbalance. Viewers learn about the Communist goal of seeking national unity and freedom but are not given much of a chance to learn about Marxist-Leninist tactics and practices. For television, personality and bearing are more important than the message, and they even have a greater impact because of the more complex nature of the issues and ideas involved in the Vietnam War. Another aspect of the problem is that witnesses living under Communist control cannot be open, while Americans, and to a lesser extent South Vietnamese, are freer to criticize and comment openly.

One episode exemplifies the situation. As soon as a GI emptied his round into a Vietnamese village a television news crew was on hand to secure his reactions. They were understandably emotional rather than reflective and analytical. The soldier claims Americans attacked the village because villagers, including children, fired at U.S. forces. This was contradicted by an innocent-appearing Vietnamese woman who was interviewed at a later date. She insisted that only unarmed women, children, and the aged were in the village. A grubby, rough-looking GI is no visual match for a tearful woman. The narrator fails to resolve the testimonies by informing viewers that while American antiinsurgency operations were brutal, Communists hid in and among villages to wage war. Had the narrator been more diligent he could have linked this issue up to an earlier episode in which a North Vietnamese proudly relates how all people, including children, took part in fighting the aggressor.

Guilt-ridden and/or inarticulate Americans appear opposite self-assured Vietnamese Communists. A former American prisoner-of-war and a Vietnamese woman active with the Viet Cong describe their respective reactions to being tortured. The former said he broke down because his pride as "an American military man failed him." The woman claimed she refused to break under torture because of concern for her country. This weighted example might have been offset had the narrator explained that others had different reactions to this gruesome aspect of the war and told just how extensive torture was and to what degree the protagonists resorted to it.

Placing an avuncular Ho Chi Minh next to an ideologically inept and politically tainted Richard Nixon or Spiro Agnew hardly enhanced the American position. The producers might have modified the impact of these interviews by heeding *New York Times* columnist Tom Wicker's observation that American leaders are noted for failing to express themselves in "clear and forceful, memorable terms."

Ho Chi Minh is the film's hero. He is repeatedly described as first and foremost a nationalist and then a Marxist. Audiences are told how he admired the Declaration of Independence and that he believed nothing is more important than individual freedom; that after "victory and independence," Vietnam will be "ten times more beautiful." After reporting his death, the film indicates that his dreams had been realized as the end of the war resulted in "independence, peace and freedom and unification of . . . the land." The film fails to hold him accountable for the slaughter of tens of thousands of North Vietnamese during the collectivization drive of the mid-1950s. Bernard Fall, the late, highly respected journalist reported that many thousands of North Vietnamese were executed after having been selected from lists. Contrary to Communist claims, Fall wrote in the *New York Times Magazine*, "those men and women were not 'reactionary landlords' and many had a good record of anti-French fighting."

These mass killings, which the film tallies as 15,000, are mentioned briefly. They are attributed to the overzealous pursuit of policies—errors the North Vietnamese acknowledged. Joseph Buttinger, author of scholarly books on Vietnamese history, points out in *Dissent*, "nothing in the history of Communist persecutions can equal the scheme contrived in North Vietnam to get rid of as many peasants as possible."

In his perceptive *Wall Street Journal* review of this program, Stephen J. Morris, a researcher at the University of California at Berkeley, points out that several episodes dealing with the earlier years of the Vietnamese struggle are "straight Vietnamese Party line history." Contrary to these episodes idealizing Ho Chi Minh's role in Vietnamese history, Morris suggests that Ho was not primarily a nationalist but a hard-line Communist who connived with the French colonial government to exterminate the more popular, non-Communist Vietnamese nationalists in the 1940s. The film overemphasizes and dramatizes Ho Chi Minh's formal statements while barely mentioning the side of his record and beliefs that places him in the tradition of Joseph Stalin or Mao Tse-tung.

The television documentary presents Hanoi as representing the national aspirations of the Vietnamese people and fails to qualify this with some important evidence. In the mid-1950s, about one million Vietnamese Catholics fled North Vietnam; the film fails to mention their anti-French, anticolonial perspectives as well as their fear of the Communist regime. Another significant issue not pursued is: Why were there not population or large-scale refugee movements fleeing to the Communist side? Bernard Fall noted in *Foreign Affairs* in 1966 that whenever given the opportunity to defect to the Communists, even when abused and repressed by the Saigon government, South Vietnamese failed to do so. A full episode is devoted to the 1968 Tet offensive in which several important themes are explored; significantly one is omitted (save for a brief remark by South Vietnamese President Nguyen Van Thieu)—that the South Vietnamese did not rise up to support the Communists as liberators. Audiences do not learn that the flight of the boat people after the Communist takeover of South Vietnam in 1975 was the first time in the modern history of that nation that so many left it. Even under the harsh Japanese occupation there was no equivalent flight from Vietnam. To have focused on and stressed that there are other expressions of Vietnamese nationalism would have undermined the program's thesis that the Communists engaged in a singular struggle to fulfill the nationalist aspirations of the Vietnamese people.

The film finds few redeeming qualities in the South Vietnamese regime or political system. Startling pictures are shown, such as the pistol execution of a Communist prisoner by Saigon's police chief. There are no pictures of the Viet Cong systematically assassinating thousands of Vietnamese officials and village heads, resulting in what Douglas Pike, director of the Indochina archives at the University of California at Berkeley, describes in his book *Viet Cong* as wiping out a "human resource of incalculable value" which "amounted to genocide." In a perfunctory and brief statement, an American officer mentions the assault on village chiefs.

True, the film history relies heavily on films taken during the war, and the Communists did not let the major networks amble about freely to photograph the disembowelment of a village chief or the execution of a schoolteacher. Most of the vivid scenes shown came from American-controlled areas so that the gory details and repelling sights of the war reflect against the United States and its allies. This film history does little to offset what former *New York Times* columnist Harrison Salisbury calls the problem of "automatic bias," i.e., when a correspondent is unable to freely report events in a totalitarian country.

An important and fascinating aspect of the struggle for Indochina concerns whose ideological view prevailed. In this regard the Americans and the South Vietnamese were no match for the Communists. The producers did little to offset the impressive presentation by various Communist spokesmen. While there is a brief mention of a Soviet style Marxist-Leninist dictatorship, which is defined as a form of central planning, the terms *tyranny, barbaric methods, repression,* etc., are directed at the Saigon regime—not at the Communist side.

President Nguyen Van Thieu and his government are accused of rigging elections and repressing their critics. This is true, but it is not the whole picture, for there was evidence of growing pluralism in Saigon. Ironically this evidence was used by critics of South Vietnam. While arguing for American withdrawal from Vietnam, the Quakers, ardent foes of the U.S. effort to prop up the Saigon government, confront the matter of widespread political activity in South Vietnam. This is revealed in their New York publication, *Relay-Inform*. The Friends were optimistic that once the United States departed from Vietnam the Communists would engage in direct "discussion with all religious entities in South Vietnam." They refer to:

> the prominent Saigon editor and National Assembly member Ngo Cong Duc, who called for the termination of U.S. support and the withdrawal of

the U.S. military. His proposals have received widespread support from many sectors of the political system including . . . the Unified Buddhist Church, members of the National Assembly, the South Vietnamese Student Union . . . [and four political parties].

The Quakers conclude that "to most of us it seems incredible that thousands can still march in the streets of Saigon" and exhibit "a strength which makes vocal opposition possible to the repressive policies of the Thieu government." (The film shows protestors marching in Saigon.) The Quakers fail to go one step further and see this as proof that a pluralistic political system was already functioning.

Labor columnist Victor Reisel describes in the Baton Rouge *Morning Advocate* how the American labor movement fostered the Vietnamese Federation of Labor which had the right to strike and did strike. In contrast, he points out that any remnant of free trade unionism in North Vietnam was eliminated and its leaders executed. Aside from quoting President Thieu's hollow words on behalf of democracy, viewers do not learn that even though South Vietnam was at war it was becoming more democratic; it was already far more so than the Communist regime that replaced it in 1975.

While repeatedly revealing the failings of South Vietnam, the program fails to provide a clear picture of the victorious Hanoi regime. To suggest that Ho's forty years of struggle produced a totally repressive, poverty-stricken, warring, totalitarian state would undermine the legitimacy of his efforts and would lend support to those who supported the American intervention. It would also drastically modify the basic theme of this television history.

The narrator provides glimpses of Communist brutality. He mentions the executions that took place in North Vietnam in 1954, the 1968 massacres in Hue, the boat people, and the genocide in Cambodia. These significant events are presented as matter-of-fact occurrences or news events; they are not presented as events intrinsic to the Vietnamese (and Cambodian) Communist systems. The film's approach is similar to those that separate national socialism from the concentration camps of Nazi Germany.

The narrator repeats the assertion that a bloodbath did not take place in South Vietnam after the liberation. He mentions that South Vietnamese were sent to reeducation camps and new economic zones. Conditions were harsh and inmates were mistreated. Even the "tiger cages," in which prisoners were forced into crippling postures, were in use. He notes that economic conditions were so bad that South Vietnamese fled to other countries as boat people. No such migration took place under the Saigon regime. By failing to explain the purpose of these dreaded camps and zones, which are like concentration camps, where untold thousands perished, viewers do not learn that they function to dispose of unwanted population. They enable the Communists to exercise total control over the hapless South Vietnamese. These massive, brutal assaults are a variant of a bloodbath and, more significantly, they are attributable directly to the Communist government. The film fails to make this connection.

During the 1968 Tet offensive, the Communists temporarily occupied the City of Hue. After the city was retaken some 3500 residents were found executed and another thousand were abducted. Some 1200 were found tightly bound in mass graves. The film mentions this but dilutes the significance. Photographs of Communist brutalities are not shown, and the dramatic action scenes are at the expense of the American and the South Vietnamese. Equal time was given to witnesses from both sides to explain why selected citizens of Hue were systematically murdered. A Vietnamese woman explains how her father was abused and murdered; a North Vietnamese official asserts that the citizens of Hue so despised their oppressors they pounced on them as they would snakes. He claims the Communists do not commit such acts; their aim is to reeducate.

The gravity of the massacres at Hue are further diluted as the program presents them as part of the overall bloody and destructive struggle for the city rather than as a Communist policy to eliminate bourgeois enemies. A similar technique is used to prevent a direct linkage between the decimation of one to three million Cambodians by the Communist Khmer Rouge who waged war against class enemies. To link the massacres at Hue and the autogenocide in Cambodia to willful actions by the Communists would undermine the film's theme that their goal was to liberate and unify. To emphasize such a direct causal connection would challenge the legitimacy of the Communist movement in Indochina.

"Vietnam: A Television History" challenges the legitimacy of the Americans and South Vietnamese by its comparison of armed forces. GIs are described as trained killers (Aren't all soldiers?), lacking an understanding of why they are fighting, destroying Vietnam, and turning the land into a cesspool of drugs, corruption, and prostitution. South Vietnamese troops are shown as bloodthirsty and cowardly. At best these vivid charges are offset by clichés from President Thieu and others. This portrait of American forces is one-sided for they were among the best educated and best behaved in United States history. Viewers do not learn that many soldiers attended classes, went to local churches, and aided Vietnamese when off duty. An extensive contribution was made, for example, by the Marines Civic Action Program. Marines helped rebuild or restore schools, churches, roads, and public facilities. Others helped plant and harvest rice; they set up and aided orphanages and medical clinics.

The heavy casualties taken by North Vietnamese forces were mentioned in the context of sacrifices made to unify Vietnam. Unlike the exposé of South Vietnamese forces no mention is made of looting, corruption, desertion, or other illegal behavior by Communists. Repeatedly the film challenges American and South Vietnamese credibility and purposes, while either not challenging North Vietnam, in most instances, or doing so ineffectively.

The thirteenth and final episode, entitled "Legacies," attempts to draw lessons from the war. The United States is accused of repeating similar blunders in Central America by opposing the revolutionary yearnings of the masses. Absent are warnings that Third World revolutions can end up in a quagmire of mass brutality and repression should Marxist-Leninists prevail. This epilogue criticizes the United States for its aggressive actions but fails to mention that the Soviet Union enabled the war to continue. It does not challenge those who gave their assurances that once the United States left, Indochina would enter into a new era of peace, freedom, prosperity, and the right of national self-determination—even for the people of South Vietnam.

Television news reporting and public affairs programming constitute the main source of information and are the shaper of political reality for most Americans. Both "The Day After" and "Vietnam: A Television History" must be credited for tackling two difficult issues that will plague Americans for years to come. Unlike the Vietnam film, *The Day After* does not claim to be evenhanded; it is made to shock and to frighten. Since the options to change the nuclear reality are at best minimal, the film adds to the already widespread feeling of panic and helplessness.

In these programs the United States experiences a fictional disaster and an actual defeat. Both films challenge American policies based on military strength. America's bellicosity and its reliance on military power is seen as the instigating impulse for many of the world's problems. The U.S.S.R. and its clients are seen as the reactive powers responding to some misguided provocation from the United States. It is an anti-Communist revolt in Berlin that arouses the Russians or it is the bombing and invasion of Cambodia that sets the stage for the Khmer Rouge's rise to power and their subsequent atrocities. Both films succeed in blaming the United States and diverting blame from the Soviet Union and the North Vietnamese. While acknowledging the Soviet Union's role in waging nuclear war, it is the American government's misplaced values that are exposed. Mention is made of the atrocities and mass repression inflicted by the North Vietnamese, but these are separated from the ideological roots of Marxism-Leninism which rationalizes such means to achieve an alleged idealistic goal. Imagine if such interpretation were used to soften the image of the

Nazis before World War II. National socialism would be viewed as a reactive phenomenon rather than one fueled by Adolph Hitler's demoniac worldview. While it is important to critically access American policies, these programs do not alert audiences to the expansionist threat of the Soviet Union and its allies.

The effects of the political and structural biases found in both films are not favorable to America's image as a defender of democratic values or generally as a positive force on the world scene. Although his words were intended for the Vietnam War, CBS News chief William Small's insights apply to both films. Quoted by Edward Jay Epstein in *News from Nowhere*, he concludes that coverage of war "showed a terrible truth of war in a manner new to mass audiences. A case can be made . . . that this was cardinal to the disillusionment of Americans with the war, the cynicism of many young people toward America."

Coming to Terms with Television: A Selected and Annotated Bibliography

Robert Schmuhl

Several years ago, George Will remarked: "Disparagement of television is second only to watching television as an American pastime." Although a common exercise among the highbrow, the lowbrow, and all of the other brows in between, disparaging discourse is by no means the only response to the medium and its messages. In fact, writing about television has become a new growth industry in our country. During the past two decades, book shelves (in the libraries that Marshall McLuhan predicted would become obsolete) have begun to bend under the weight of volumes attempting to come to terms with the various aspects of TV.

What follows is an extensive yet selective list of books about American television: its history, structure, types of programming, role in society, and impact. The majority of the titles are academic studies; however, several notable popular or journalistic treatments receive consideration.

Adams, William, and Fay Schreibman, eds. *Television Network News: Issues in Content Research.* Washington, D.C.: George Washington University, 1978. Ten articles by such scholars as George Gerbner, George Comstock, and Michael J. Robinson probing different aspects of content research. This interdisciplinary collection explores what is being done and what could be done.

Adler, Richard, ed. *All in the Family: A Critical Appraisal.* New York: Praeger Publishers, 1979. A mixture of printed scripts, critical statements, and journalistic accounts about Norman Lear's successful and influential series. Several perspectives of "All in the Family," which were written at various times during the show's popularity.

———. *Understanding Television: Essays on Television as a Social and Cultural Force.* New York: Praeger Publishers, 1981. A humanistic and interdisciplinary introduction to television that argues for sustained academic attention to the medium and its messages. Contributors of the twenty-four essays include Michael Novack, Paul Weaver, and Michael J. Robinson.

Altheide, David L. *Creating Reality: How TV News Distorts Reality.* Beverly Hills, Calif., Sage Publications, 1976. A participant-observation study of a network affiliate's newsroom that leads to several telling conclusions about local coverage and television news in general.

Arlen, Michael, J. *The Camera Age: Essays on Television.* New York: Farrar, Straus, Giroux, 1981. A collection of essays focusing on "the experience of watching television in America." Stimulating statements about the paradoxes of TV.

——— . *Living-Room War.* New York: The Viking Press, 1969. The first collection of commentary by the television critic of *The New Yorker.* Arlen's work is consistently intelligent and perceptive. Several essays deal with TV's coverage of Vietnam.

——— . *Thirty Seconds.* New York: Farrar, Straus, Giroux, 1980. First-rate reportage that chronicles the making of one television commercial. The author never comments on what's happening, but the words and actions of the advertising people are revealing about TV and its values.

——— . *The View from Highway 1: Essays on Television.* New York: Farrar, Straus, and Giroux, 1976. Essays that "speak of television as if it mattered." The introduction, "Some Notes on Television Criticism," addresses the role of TV in society and the relationship of the critic to the medium.

Barcus, F. Earle. *Images of Life on Children's Television: Sex Roles, Minorities, and Families.* New York: Praeger Publishers, 1983. Study conducted in 1981 focusing on fifty hours of TV and how life is portrayed in cartoons and other programs. What television teaches the young.

Barnouw, Erik. *The Sponsor: Notes on a Modern Potentate.* New York: Oxford University Press, 1978. The development, role, and impact of commercial sponsorship on television. Treatment of the effects on content and on the audience.

——— . *Tube of Plenty: The Evolution of American Television.* New York: Oxford University Press, 1975. A condensation and updating of the author's definitive three-volume *History of Broadcasting in the United States.* Methodical marshalling of historical facts as well as cogent assessment of the way television has become "the environment and context of our lives."

Batscha, Robert M. *Foreign Affairs News and the Broadcast Journalist.* New York: Praeger Publishers, 1975. An examination of the behavior of television news people as they cover international affairs. Emphasis on "how that message is composed."

Bedell, Sally. *Up the Tube: Prime-Time TV and the Silverman Years.* New York: The Viking Press, 1981. Journalistic account of what Fred Silverman wrought during his years as an executive at CBS, ABC, and NBC. By focusing on Silverman and his career, the author effectively draws several conclusions about commercial TV.

Berger, Arthur Asa. *The TV-Guided American.* New York: Walker, 1976. The cultural implications of television through acute analysis of specific genres, programs, and series. What TV reveals about the American character, expressed in vigorous prose.

Bluem, A. William. *Documentary in American Television: Form, Function, Method.* New York: Hastings House, 1965. Historical treatment of the television documentary, with analysis of the different types produced in the 1950s and early 1960s.

Bogart, Leo. *The Age of Television: A Study of Viewing Habits and the Impact of Television on American Life.* 3rd ed. New York: Frederick Ungar Publishing Co., 1972. Pertinent facts and figures about watching television until the early 1970s. Some 120 tables and charts help present the data.

Brown, Les. *Televi$ion: The Business Behind the Box.* New York: Harcourt Brace Jovanovich, 1971. Fascinating reportage about how the American television system operates from the perspective of one typical season's ratings battle. The programs discussed have passed on to their rerun rewards—the book focuses on 1970—but the principles remain valuable.

Brown, Les, and Savannah Waring Walker, eds. *Fast Forward: The New Television and American Society.* Kansas City: Andrews and McMeel, 1983. A collection of 25 essays (by, among others, Robert Coles, Christopher Lasch, and Edwin Newman) analyzing contemporary programming and the impact of the new technology. The articles originally appeared in *Channels of Communication.*

Cantor, Muriel G. *Prime-Time Television: Content and Control.* Beverly Hills, Calif.: Sage Publications, 1980. Sociological study of the influence of different milieus—legal, political, organizational, and occupational—on the content of programming and how that content is produced.

Cassata, Mary, and Thomas Skill. *Life on Daytime Television: Tuning-In American Serial Drama.* Norwood, N.J.: Ablex Publishing Corporation, 1983. Humanistic and empirical studies of soap operas, emphasizing the people in the serials, their problems, and their environments.

Cater, Douglass, and Stephen Strickland. *TV Violence and the Child: The Evolution and Fate of the Surgeon General's Report.* New York: Russell Sage Foundation, 1975. Examination and critical assessment of the government study of the impact of televised violence. The authors suggest improvements in the process of doing research and forming public policy.

Cole, Barry, ed. *Television Today: A Close-Up View.* New York: Oxford University Press, 1981. A comprehensive anthology of contributions to *TV Guide.* More than sixty articles explore entertainment programming, news coverage, the role of the audience, the effects on society, and the future technology.

Comstock, George, Steven Chaffee, Natan Katzman, Maxwell McCombs, and Donald Roberts. *Television and Human Behavior.* New York: Columbia University Press, 1978. A thorough overview of the first twenty-five years of social and behavioral research about the influence of television on American life. Readable summary of effects as well as the implications of the findings on future research. An essential work.

Diamond, Edwin. *Good News, Bad News.* Cambridge, Mass.: The MIT Press, 1978. Criticism of contemporary journalism, with particular attention to the entertainment qualities of TV news and broadcasting's involvement in presidential campaigns. Seventeen essays dealing with events of the mid-1970s.

———. *Sign Off: The Last Days of Television.* Cambridge, Mass.: The MIT Press, 1982. A collection of articles and essays about current happenings in television and what a future of new technologies will bring. Close analysis (of "Disco News," "The Electronic Chruch," and other topics) that also includes larger statements.

———. *The Tin Kazoo: Television, Politics, and the News.* Cambridge, Mass.: The MIT Press, 1975. Rather than being a powerful political force, television is little more than a "kazoo," according to the studies in this book. The author questions claims that TV is terribly influential, proving his conclusions with relevant data.

Epstein, Edward Jay. *News from Nowhere: Television and the News.* New York: Random House, 1973. An examination of the internal operations and policies of the network news divisions, especially NBC. Organizational criteria frequently dictate the news, which is anything but a mirror of society. This remains a classic of media criticism.

Fowles, Jib. *Television Viewers vs. Media Snobs: What TV Does for People.* New York: Stein and Day, 1982. A counterpoint book that takes on television critics, professional and amateur. The thesis, that "television is good for people," is developed by emphasizing the positive and therapeutic qualities of the medium.

Frank, Robert S. *Message Dimensions of Television News.* Lexington, Mass.: Lexington Books, 1973. The theory and practice of systematic analysis of television messages for complete understanding of the medium's role in society.

Frank, Ronald E., and Marshall Greenberg. *The Public's Use of Television: Who Watches and Why.* Beverly Hills, Calif.: Sage Publications, 1980. An empirical study exploring the diverse reasons for people's use of television and explaining how television fits into their lives.

Friendly, Fred W. *Due to Circumstances Beyond Our Control. . . .* New York: Random House, 1967. A central figure in the history of broadcast journalism discusses his experiences as a producer and as president of CBS News. He also addresses the strengths and weaknesses of TV as a medium of information and entertainment. A combination of personal memoir and critical analysis.

Gates, Gary Paul. *Air Time: The Inside Story of CBS News.* New York: Harper and Row, 1978. A journalistic history of the news division that, over time, has received the most attention for its documentaries and news broadcasts.

Gilbert, Robert E. *Television and Presidential Politics.* North Quincy, Mass.: The Christopher Publishing House, 1972. A study, largely historical, of television's involvement in presidential campaigns through 1968. Emphasis on the nationalization of U.S. politics and the centralization of political life in the United States.

Gitlin, Todd. *Inside Prime Time.* New York: Pantheon Books, 1983. Based on more than 200 interviews and numerous visits to TV locations, this book explains how television operates and why we see what we do. Thorough reporting combined with shrewd sociological and cultural analysis. A work of considerable significance.

Goethals, Gregor T. *The TV Ritual: Worship at the Video Alter.* Boston: Beacon Press, 1981. Humanistic inquiry into the symbol-making power of television and what those symbols mean in our culture.

Goldsen, Rose K. *The Show and Tell Machine: How Television Works and Works You Over.* New York: The Dial Press, 1977. A sociologist with a crusading spirit assesses the effects of television and the television environment. Pointed discussions with illustrations of the dangers from a television "culturesphere."

Greenberg, Bradley S. *Life on Television: Content Analyses of the U.S. TV Drama.* Norwood, N.J.: Ablex Publishing Corporation, 1980. Thirteen studies of TV content about such subjects as the portrayal of minorities, the elderly, families, and the sexes.

Greenfield, Jeff. *Television: The First Fifty Years.* New York: Harry N. Abrams, Publishers, 1977. A coffee-table book that combines over 500 pictures with a perceptive explanation of TV's development, role, and cultural place. A stimulating blend of history and analysis complemented by well-chosen photographs.

Grote, David. *The End of Comedy: The Sit-Com and the Comedic Tradition.* Hamden, Conn.: Archon Books, 1983. Comparing comedy of the past to contemporary situation comedies on television leads to the conclusion that what we now have is "no laughing matter." A probing analysis that takes comedy and its implications seriously.

Hammond, Charles Montgomery, Jr. *The Image Decade: Television Documentary 1965-1975.* New York: Hastings House, 1981. Methodical analysis of the documentary form during a significant decade of it history. Coverage of the work done by ABC, CBS, and NBC.

Himmelstein, Hal. *On the Small Screen: New Approaches in Television and Video Criticism.* New York: Praeger Publishers, 1981. The theory and practice of television criticism. Five chapters focus on individual critics, including Horace Newcomb and John J. O'Connor.

———. *Television Myth and the American Mind.* New York: Praeger Publishers, 1984. The myth-making dimensions of television. The author explores advertising, comedies, melodramas, news, sports, religious programs, and talk shows. He argues that viewers "have come to believe in the psychic television landscapes of Mayfield, Mayberry, Minneapolis, and midtown Manhattan, while ignoring those of Saigon, Harlem, and Fernwood."

Hofstetter, C. Richard. *Bias in the News: Network Television Coverage of the 1972 Election Campaign.* Columbus: Ohio State University Press, 1976. In the wake of the Nixon-Agnew administration's charges of liberal slant, a systematic, social science inquiry through content analysis into questions of bias in TV news reporting. A principal conclusion: "Most coverage was neutral or ambiguous rather than favorable or unfavorable."

Intintoli, Michael James. *Taking Soaps Seriously: The World of Guiding Light.* New York: Praeger Publishers, 1984. A participant-observation study explaining the process of producing a soap opera series and examining how the series reflects society.

Johnson, Nicholas. *How to Talk Back to Your Television Set.* Boston: Little, Brown & Company, 1970. A prominent advocate of broadcasting reform offers a vigorously argued indictment of television and challenges the public to take action to improve the medium. Written while the author was a member of the Federal Communications Commission.

Johnston, Jerome, and James S. Ettema. *Positive Images: Breaking Stereotypes with Children's Television.* Beverly Hills, Calif.: Sage Publications, 1982. The evolution and development of the TV series *Freestyle* that was designed to alter, in a positive way, children's stereotypes about sex roles.

Lang, Gladys Engel, and Kurt Lang. *Politics and Television Re-Viewed.* Beverly Hills, Calif.: Sage Publications, 1984. An updated version of the Langs' classic work *Politics and Television* (1968). New chapters analyze Watergate coverage and the Carter-Ford debates, while there are references to the 1980 and 1984 campaigns in other places. A collection of related studies in political research.

Lesser, Gerald S. *Children and Television: Lessons from Sesame Street.* New York: Random House, 1974. An account tracing the development of *Sesame Street* from conception to production. Insights about children and television throughout.

Levinson, Richard, and William Link. *Stay Tuned: An Inside Look at the Making of Prime-Time Television.* New York: St. Martin's Press, 1981. A behind-the-scenes account of prime-time programming—its practices, problems, and potential. The authors (creators and producers of popular series and made-for-TV movies) explain their love-hate relationship with the medium.

Lichter, Linda S., and S. Robert Lichter. *Prime Time Crime: Criminals and Law Enforcers in TV Entertainment.* Washington, D.C.: The Media Institute,

1983. Content analysis of 263 programs during a six-week period in the 1980-81 season. The study reveals that TV entertainment sensationalizes crime while failing to portray the reality of criminal activity in the United States.

MacDonald, J. Fred. *Blacks and White TV: Afro-Americans in Television since 1948*. Chicago: Nelson-Hall Publishers, 1983. Historical study of the less-than-satisfactory relationship between television and Blacks since the medium became popular.

MacNeil, Robert. *The People Machine: The Influence of Television on American Politics*. New York: Harper and Row, 1968. A respected journalist explains—and criticizes—television's involvement in political and governmental affairs. He raises concerns that have taken on greater meaning since the book was published.

Mander, Jerry. *Four Arguments for the Elimination of Television*. New York: Morrow, 1978. One of the sharpest critical works about television. The author sees no hope for reform and several reasons that the world should be free of television.

Mankiewicz, Frank, and Joel Swerdlow. *Remote Control: Television and the Manipulation of American Life*. New York: Times Books, 1978. Journalistic treatment of television's diverse effects on American society. A critical but tempered account that concludes: "Television, in short, can be made more responsive to the public's needs, but television itself can never be made less powerful."

Marc, David. *Demographic Vistas: Television in American Culture*. Philadelphia: University of Pennsylvania Press, 1984. By focusing on various kinds of comedy programs, the author explains the centrality of television to contemporary culture in the United States. He considers the difference between "democratic" and "demographic" vistas, and discusses TV's role in understanding modern life. Sustained and stimulating analysis.

Matusow, Barbara. *The Evening Stars: The Making of the Network News Anchor*. Boston: Houghton Mifflin Company, 1983. An anecdotal yet valuable historical account of the evolution and standing of television news anchor people. The book emphasizes the events occurring off-camera.

Mayer, Martin. *About Television*. New York: Harper and Row, 1972. A solidly reported exposition of the television industry and its various kinds of programs. Informative, but now dated.

McGinnis, Joe. *The Selling of the President 1968*. New York: Trident Press, 1969. A classic of reporting that explains how the Nixon campaign used television to create a new image for a familiar face. Emphasizes the controlled communications environment the campaign maintained to project a specific impression.

Meehan, Diana M. *Ladies of the Evening: Women Characters of Prime-Time Television*. Metuchen, N.J.: The Scarecrow Press, 1983. A quantitative, interpretive study of the types of female characters on episodic television since the early 1950s. Studies focus on the imp, good wife, harpy, bitch, siren, courtesan, and witch.

Newcomb, Horace, ed. *Television: The Critical View*. 3rd ed. New York: Oxford University Press, 1976. Different viewpoints of various aspects of television by scholars, essayists, and creative writers. A collection of significant statements.

Newcomb, Horace. *TV: The Most Popular Art.* Garden City, N.Y.: Anchor Press/ Doubleday, 1974. One of the first works of humanistic criticism to take television programming seriously—as a "popular art" worth analysis. Intelligent analysis that concludes with a chapter, "Toward a Television Aesthetic," pointing the way to future inquiry.

Nimmo, Dan, and James E. Combs. *Nightly Horrors: Crisis Coverage by Television Network News.* Knoxville: The University of Tennessee Press, 1985. A combination of quantitative data and humanistic analysis concerning the three networks' coverage of six major crises by nightly news programs from 1978 to 1982. Topics include the People's Temple, Three Mile Island, the Iranian hostage-taking, and the Tylenol poisonings. The patterns of reporting reveal how TV network news portrays critical situations.

O'Connor, John, ed. *American History/American Television: Interpreting the Video Past.* New York: Frederick Ungar Publishing Co., 1983. Fourteen studies of series, programs, and individual figures and their significance in recent history. Topics include *See It Now, Marty, Roots,* Milton Berle, and Watergate coverage.

Patterson, Thomas E., and Robert D. McClure. *The Unseeing Eye: The Myth of Television Power in National Elections.* New York: G.P. Putnam's Sons, 1976. Empirical examination by political scientists of television's influence on voters and the public's understanding of issues during the 1972 presidential campaign. A study of both news coverage and advertising.

Pool, Ithiel de Sola. *Technologies of Freedom.* Cambridge, Mass.: Harvard University Press, 1983. The impact of the new broadcasting technology on freedom of expression. The author charts the way to retaining free speech in the electronic age.

Powers, Ron. *The Newscasters.* New York: St. Martin's Press, 1977. An exposé, with strong reporting and cogent analysis, of the impact consultants have on television news. How "happy talk" and other such phenomena trivialize the news.

———. *Supertube: The Rise of Television Sports.* New York: Coward, McCann & Geoghegan, 1984. An informal history of television's treatment of sports in the United States. Main concerns involve the transformation of sports by television and the influence of televised sports on American culture.

Ranney, Austin. *Channels of Power: The Impact of Television on American Politics.* New York: Basic Books, 1983. An introductory survey by a noted political scientist about TV's meaning to American political life. Treatment of such topics as the effects of TV on politicians, on our political culture, and on the process of governing.

Rowland, Willard D., and Bruce Watkins, eds. *Interpreting Television: Current Research Perspectives.* Beverly Hills, Calif.: Sage Publications, 1984. Eleven essays offer speculative and theoretical approaches to the study of television in society and culture. The book shows the range and depth of contemporary television studies research.

Rowland, Willard D. *The Politics of TV Violence: Policy Uses of Communication Research.* Beverly Hills, Calif.: Sage Publications, 1983. An historical and analytical account of research about the effects of violence, with probing questions about the uses of such research and its ultimate value.

Saldich, Anne Rawley. *Electronic Democracy: Television's Impact on the American Political Process.* New York: Praeger Publishers, 1979. A provocative and disturbing series of related essays about television and democracy. The author, a political sociologist, is critical of the networks, yet she sees TV as potentially "a great democratizer."

Shanks, Bob. *The Cool Fire: How to Make It in Television.* New York: W.W. Norton and Company, 1976. A television veteran describes how television works and the values of the industry. A revealing guide, especially for the outsider.

Shayon, Robert Lewis. *Open to Criticism.* Boston: Beacon Press, 1971. A respected television critic articulates his techniques and principles before offering a selection of his own work from the 1950s and 1960s. Useful combination of theory and practice.

Singer, Jerome L., and Dorothy G. Singer. *Television, Imagination, and Aggression: A Study of Preschoolers.* Hillsdale, N.J.: Lawrence Erlbaum Associates, Publishers, 1981. The account by psychologists of a two-year study of the impact of television viewing on preschool children, particularly the effects on the imagination and overt behavior.

Sklar, Robert. *Prime-Time America: Life on and Behind the Television Screen.* Oxford: Oxford University Press, 1980. A collection of reviews, critical essays, and journalistic articles that "illuminate the cultural processes of American television." The author considers the last five years of the 1970s.

Stein, Ben, *The View from Sunset Boulevard: America as Brought to You By the People Who Make Television.* New York: Basic Books, 1979. Reportage and analysis exploring the concept of television as "alternate reality." The author explains that the world we see on TV and real life are very different, with television reflecting the view of a few hundred California dreamers.

Tuchman, Gaye, ed. *The TV Establishment: Programming for Power and Profit.* Englewood Cliffs, N.J.: Prentice-Hall, 1974. Ten articles explore television "hegemony" and how the medium legitimates the status quo.

Turow, Joseph. *Entertainment, Education, and the Hard Sell: Three Decades of Network Children's Television.* New York: Praeger Publishers, 1981. Statistical and interpretive study of the various trends in children's series programming from 1948 through 1978.

Westin, Av. *Newswatch: How TV Decides the News.* New York: Simon and Schuster, 1982. A veteran TV news executive offers a behind-the-scenes look at broadcast journalism—the problems it faces and how they're resolved. Revealing anecdotes throughout.

Wicklein, John. *Electronic Nightmare: The New Communications and Freedom.* New York: The Viking Press, 1981. A cautionary study about the new communications technologies and their potential for threatening the freedom of the public. The author warns that instruments of communication could become devices of control.

Williams, Raymond. *Television: Technology and Cultural Form.* New York: Schocken Book, 1975. The uses and possibilities of television that makes comparisons between British and U.S. practice. Illuminating example of "culture science," which explains and evaluates the institutions of broadcasting and their impact on society.

Winn, Marie. *The Plug-In Drug*, rev. ed. New York: The Viking Press, 1985. A journalistic assessment of the effects of television watching on children's development. The writer, a crusader for change, believes of television, "we can learn to control it so that it does not control us."

Withey, Stephen B., and Ronald P. Albeles, eds. *Television and Social Behavior: Beyond Violence and Children.* Hillsdale, N.J.: Lawrence Erlbaum Associates, Publishers, 1980. Several essays concerning TV's influence on adult behavior, especially such special audiences as the elderly and minority groups.

About the Contributors

John H. Barnsley is the author of *The Social Reality of Ethics* as well as numerous articles on social and environmental subjects.

Arthur Asa Berger is professor of Broadcast Communication Arts at San Francisco State University. He is Film and Television Review Editor for *Society*.

Bert Briller is executive editor of the Television Information Office of the National Association of Broadcasters. Previously, he was a vice president of the ABC television network.

Steven H. Chaffee is director of the Institute for Communication Research at Stanford University.

Daniel Dayan is on the faculty of the Annenberg School of Communication at the University of Southern California. He has taught at the Hebrew University of Jerusalem, the new Sorbonne's and the University of California's Interuniversity Center for Film and Cultural Studies, and Stanford University's Paris campus. He is the author of *Western Graffitti*.

L. Patrick Devlin is professor of speech communication at the University of Rhode Island. An archivist and analyst of presidential campaign commercials, he is author of *Contemporary Political Speaking* and many articles on political communication.

Fred Fejes is an instructor in the Communications and Theater Department of the University of Illinois, Chicago Circle campus.

George Gerbner is professor of communications at the University of Pennsylvania, and editor of the *Journal of Communication*. He has written extensively on mass communication research and recently edited *Mass Media in Changed Cultures*.

Larry Gross is professor of communications at The Annenberg School of Communications and coeditor of *Studies in Visual Communication.* His research is on the cultural determinants of symbolic behavior.

Beatrix A. Hamburg is professor of clinical psychiatry and pediatrics at the Mt. Sinai School of Medicine.

Roger L. Hofeldt is a writer/producer/director for The Media Works, Inc., a Chicago-based production company.

Elihu Katz is on the faculty of the Annenberg School of Communications at The University of Southern California. He is a professor of sociology and communications at the Hebrew University of Jerusalem and editor of *Mass Media and Social Change.* He is coauthor, with Paul Lazarsfeld, of *Personal Influence: The Part Played by People in the Flow of Mass Communication.*

Guy Lometti is manager of social research for the American Broadcasting Companies, Inc. Previously, he taught at West Virginia University.

Marvin Maurer is professor of political science at Monmouth College in New Jersey. His articles on the mass media have appeared in *Midstream* and *New America.*

Steven Miller is assistant editor of the Television Information Office of the National Association of Broadcasters.

Michael Morgan an assistant professor of communications at the University of Massachusetts. His research is on role socialization and academic achievement.

Susan B. Neuman is assistant professor and director of the reading clinic at Eastern Connecticut State University. Previously, she was a research associate at the Yale University Family Television Center. Her current research interests include communications research with emphasis on the book publishing industry.

David Pearl is Chief of the Behavioral Sciences Research Branch of the National Institute of Mental Health. He organized and directed the NIMH project assessing television's behavioral influences and edited its two volume report, *Television and Behavior: Ten Years of Scientific Progress and*

Implications for the Eighties. Volume 1 contains bibliographic references for all studies discussed in this article.

Chester M. Pierce is professor of psychiatry at the Harvard Medical School.

David Paul Rebovich is assistant professor of political science at Rider College and vice-president of the Northeastern Political Science Association. His recent research is on contemporary Catholic social and political thought and its implications for public policy.

Eli A. Rubinstein is adjunct research professor in mass communications at the University of North Carolina.

Robert Schmuhl teaches in the Department of American Studies at the University of Notre Dame.

John A. Schneider is president of the CBS/Broadcast Group. He was assisted in the preparation of this material by the staff of the Office of Social Research of CBS, Inc., CBS Economics and Research, and David M. Blank.

Michael Schudson teaches at The University of California, San Diego. He is author of *Discovering the News: A Social History of American Newspapers* and *Advertising: The Uneasy Persuasion*.

Eric Sevareid, who first gained prominence as a European correspondent during World War II, was a regular commentator on the CBS Evening News. His article was adapted from a talk delivered before the National Association of Broadcasters on March 28, 1977. He is the author of *Not So Wild a Dream*.

Alberta E. Siegel is professor of psychology at the Stanford University School of Medicine.

Nancy Signorielli is research administrator at the Annenberg School of Communications. Her research is on television images and their effects upon people's conceptions.

Jerome L. Singer is professor of psychology at Yale University.

Rita J. Simon is professor of sociology, communications research, and law, and director of the graduate college program in law and society at the

University of Illinois. She is editor of *The American Sociological Review* and author of numerous articles, books, and monographs on law and society as well as public opinion.

Ben Stein is a columnist on TV and other forms of popular culture for *The Wall Street Journal*.

Gaye Tuchman is associate professor of sociology at Queens College, City University of New York, and vice-president of Sociologists for Women in Society. She has authored numerous articles on the sociology of news and on culture and sex roles.

Lilya Wagner is a freelance writer and consultant in hospital public relations. Previoulsy, she taught in the Division of Humanities at Union College in Nebraska, where she was director of the writing program. Her publications include several articles and four books.

Alan Wurtzel is vice president of broadcast standards and practices, East Coast, for the American Broadcasting Companies, Inc. Previously, he taught at the University of Georgia and the City University of New York.